SOVIET MONGOLIA

SOVIET MONGOLIA

A STUDY OF THE
OLDEST POLITICAL SATELLITE

BY

George G. S. Murphy

UNIVERSITY OF CALIFORNIA PRESS
BERKELEY AND LOS ANGELES
1966

University of California Press
Berkeley and Los Angeles
California
Cambridge University Press
London, England

Designed by John B. Goetz
Printed in the United States of America

To
MR. AND MRS. A. J. DOWDING
AND
MRS. M. A. MURPHY

Preface

In this study I analyze the relationship between Outer Mongolia and the Soviet Union during the significant period 1921–1960, with regard to both the objective costs and benefits to the Republic and the human burden imposed on the Mongolian people. Outer Mongolia is a very small country in terms of population, gross national product, military power, and political influence. Nevertheless, the study of even one small Soviet satellite does yield lessons of broad scope as well as knowledge that illuminates the dominant country–satellite relationship as opposed to the imperial-colonial one. In addition, the Mongolian People's Republic, although not strictly the first Soviet satellite (some previous satellites having been absorbed into the USSR), is the oldest surviving one, and its history enables us to evaluate satellite status over a period of more than four decades.

The basic source materials for this study are largely Russian. Needless to say, had I commanded the broad linguistic skills necessary to consult original Mongolian, Japanese, and Chinese materials, I would have preferred to do so. To compensate for this lack, I have made every possible use of comments by responsible Outer Mongolian politicians and historians which are available in Russian translation. One obvious weakness of this substitution for primary sources is that we may possibly gain a reinterpretation of the Russian (both tsarist and Soviet) view of Outer Mongolia's history, rather than learning how the Mongolian people themselves view their past. This flaw, however, is balanced by one advantage. The comparative use of Russian sources makes it possible to point out the inconsistencies, at times glaring, in the Soviet treatment of Outer Mongolia's history. In addition, even the facts documented by the Soviet Union herself lend themselves to telling a story that differs markedly from the Soviet truth about Outer Mongolia.

Two reasons prompted me not to bring this study up to the past year or two: first, I felt the need for the perspective gained from a lapse in time; and, second, I think that no fundamental change has occurred either in the Soviet-Mongolian relationship or in Outer Mongolian society during the past few years. Readers interested in very recent events will find a reliable guide in R. A. Rupen, *Mongols of the Twentieth Century* (Bloomington, Ind., 1964). Unfortunately, as Professor Rupen's book, which covers the same period as mine does, was published after I had sent my manuscript to the University of California Press, I have not been able to benefit from his work in the preparation of this volume. I do not believe, however, that the opportunity to consult his book would have substantially altered my conclusions.

The name Mongolian People's Republic and its Russian version, Mongol'skaia Narodnaia Respublika, occurs very frequently in the titles of articles and books referred to in footnotes. These names have therefore been abbreviated to MPR and MNR, respectively. Similarly, the names Mongolian People's Revolutionary Party and its Russian equivalent have been abbreviated to MPRP and MNRP, respectively. The system used to transliterate Russian titles is that used by the Library of Congress, except that no distinction is made between the hard sign and the soft sign and that diacritical marks are omitted. In order to suggest how much source material is available in Mongolian and in Russian sources, the bibliography is divided into three sections: Mongolian Sources, Soviet Sources, and Other Sources. Listing in a given section in the bibliography should not be construed as implying a particular bias on the part of the author. Books have been classified in the last two categories solely on the basis of place and date of publication. I have tried to indicate in the text when persons have spoken in an authoritative or official capacity.

The present study is an outgrowth of my doctoral dissertation, "The Economic Development of Outer Mongolia in Recent Times" (University of Washington, 1957). Chapter 7 is based on an article published in the *Journal of Asian Studies* (Feb., 1957). A small part of chapter 2 appeared in *Comparative Studies in Society and History* (July, 1961). Chapter 8 is based on a paper I read at the meetings of both the Association for Asian Studies in New York in March, 1960, and the 25th Congress of Orientalists in Moscow in 1960; it is published in the *Proceedings* of the congress (Moscow, 1963).

In doing the research for and in writing this volume I was the fortunate recipient of financial and other assistance from numerous agencies: the Inner Asia Colloquium and the Mongolian Project, University of Washington; the Inter-University Committee on Travel Grants, which sponsored two journeys of mine, the first to the USSR in 1958 to enable me to meet Soviet specialists on the Outer Mongolian People's Republic, and the second in 1960 to both the USSR and Outer Mongolia; the University of California, which awarded me a summer Faculty Fellowship in 1963 for the purpose of writing this book; and the Russian and East European Center at the University of California, Los Angeles. I also benefited from the courteous and competent assistance of the staffs of the Library of the Hoover Institution, Stanford University, and the Library of Congress in consulting their special collections.

My major personal debts in writing this study are to Professors Robert A. Rupen, Franklyn D. Holzman, and Hellmut Wilhelm, who have read many drafts of all or of parts of this study as it progressed from dissertation to book manuscript, and to Professors William B. Ballis and George F. Taylor, who first made it possible for me to engage in a study of Outer Mongolia. The very capable editors of the University of California Press, Miss Ruth Mueller and Mrs. Grace H. Stimson, did much to improve the style and form of the manuscript. Naturally, I remain fully responsible for any error of fact or interpretation. Finally, I owe a considerable debt to my wife, Joanne, for her sensible criticisms and encouragement.

Those who have had contacts with the Mongols have rarely failed to be charmed by them as a people. I count myself among this group. My personal hope is that this volume will in some small way promote a better understanding of the true facts of their recent history and their contemporary situation.

G. G. S. M.

Contents

1

SOVIET INVASION AND HEGEMONY,
1921 TO 1924

On June 28, 1921, a committee of Russian Bolsheviks met in the small town of Kiakhta on the Russian-Chinese border in Siberia. The following persons were present: Mulin, chief of both the Politburo and the War Soviet of Siberia; Kosich, military commissar of the Fifth Red Army; Liubimov, chief of staff of the Fifth Red Army; and Iudin, representative of the Commissariat of Foreign Affairs of the RSFSR.[1] The committee, after deliberating the matter, ordered Red Army troops to invade Outer Mongolia and to strike southward to capture Urga, its major city.

On July 3, 1921, the 103d and 104th Infantry Brigades, the 1st Sretensky Cavalry Brigade, and a small detachment commanded by the Siberian guerrilla, Shchetinkin, all troops of the Fifth Red Army, crossed the border in the neighborhood of Kiakhta. With them was a small force of Mongolian irregulars.[2] Neiman, commander of the troops, detached the 103d Brigade and dispatched it to Van-Kuren, a monastic town to the northwest of Urga.[3] By this

[1] The composition of the committee is given by V. I. Iudin, "U istokov mongol'skoi narodnoi revoliutsii," in A. T. Iakimov (ed.), *Mongol'skii sbornik, ekonomika, istoriia, arkheologiia*, Akademiia Nauk SSSR, Institut vostokovedeniia (Moscow, 1959), p. 121. Mongols were present at this meeting, but, as becomes clear later in this chapter, they did not participate in the decision to invade. Because modern Soviet sources omit the names of purged persons, we cannot be sure that this was the full composition of the committee.

[2] *Ibid.* Another important eyewitness, Khorloin Choibalsan, gives a slightly different description of the invading force. Inasmuch as Iudin was at this time playing the more important part in the events both men eyewitnessed, I consider his the more useful account of the two. For Choibalsan's version see *Kratkii ocherk istorii mongol'skoi narodnoi revoliutsii* (Moscow, 1952), pp. 67–68.

[3] According to Iudin, p. 121, Neiman was the commander, and I infer that the decision to detach the troops was his.

action he was able to forestall any threat to his main line of advance and to protect his communications. The remainder of the battle group made a forced march to Urga, reaching it on July 6, and occupied the city. On July 9 a government of men favorable to, and manipulable by, the invaders was installed in Urga.

The leaders of the Soviet Union thus were able to establish influence over what was to become their first permanent satellite.[4] It is important to note the phrase "leaders of the Soviet Union," for, while the committee in Kiakhta gave the orders to march, its right to do so had been predetermined by the government in Moscow.[5] It was a decision that certainly paid off.

FACTORS CONDUCIVE TO SATELLITE STATUS

Soviet Military Power

Military force made possible the establishment of the first enduring political satellite of the Soviet Union. Years later, modern Soviet historians would invent a "revolutionary situation" in the Mongolia of 1921; they would manufacture "revolutionary heroes"; they would minimize the role played by Soviet troops and agents, and would portray the events of 1921 as a genuine national uprising. The modern Mongols, in turn, accepted these fictions, for they fostered Mongol pride.[6] But the facts were otherwise. Admittedly, in the invasion of July 3 about 400 Mongolian troops and a score of

---

[4] For a more detailed definition of what I mean by "satelliteship," see George G. S. Murphy, "On Satelliteship," *Journal of Economic History*, XXI (1961).

[5] In a letter to me dated July 4, 1963, Academician I. M. Maiskii writes:

"You ask me what were the considerations, and who were the chief decision-makers, in the decision to commit Soviet troops to enter Outer Mongolia in July 1921 to destroy baron Ungern-Sternberg?

"My reply to this question is as follows:

"The chief decision-makers were the Soviet Government of the day headed by V. I. Lenin;

"The main consideration for taking such a decision consisted in the necessity to destroy baron Ungern-Sternberg, an arch enemy of the Soviet Russia [sic], who tried by force of arms to defeat the Soviet Government or at least to make for it as much harm as he could. The Soviet Government had every right to defend itself. The question of the Chinese sovereignity [sic] hardly arose because (a) Outer Mongolia at that time de-facto did not recognise it, (b) as the then Chinese Government made no move to disarme [sic] Ungern-Sternberg it played indeed a role of an accomplice of the baron in his fight against Soviet Russia and (c) the Chinese Government of that time did not wish to recognise the Soviet Government."

[6] The authoritative Soviet account is the collectively written history, *Istoriia MNR*, published by the Academy of Sciences, USSR (Moscow, 1954). A Mongolian edition of this work has also been published, and both editions are sponsored by the Committee of Sciences of the MPR. There are many other authoritative accounts: Choibalsan's is one; a Mongol work, translated into Russian, B. Shirendyb, *Narodnaia revoliutsiia v Mongolii i obrazovanie MNR* (Moscow, 1956), is another. I use the term "authoritative" to describe accounts that have received the highest official recognition.

members of the Mongolian National Party (MNP) moved with the
Soviet forces.[7] Also, in the government set up for Outer Mongolia
on July 9, members of the MNP occupied most of the positions of
manifest power. Nonetheless, the Red Army, its commissars, and
representatives of both the Commissariat of Foreign Affairs of the
RSFSR and the Comintern remained in Urga; it was they who
really controlled the new government. Indeed, in the days to come
the members of the small Mongolian party were to be used
ruthlessly, like an expendable resource, to bring about the extension of Soviet power.

The Mongols who arrived in Urga were not "Lenins" arriving to
control a "national revolution"; they did not head an organized
party engaged in promoting discontent in a seething countryside.
Mongolia was passive and quiet in 1921. When members of the
MNP reached Urga, they were met by two or three of their fellows,
the only other members of their party in the country. The Mongols
who had joined the MNP were simply naïve puppets, acting as a
screen for the desire of the Soviet Union to move into this part of
Central Asia. In fact, the move into Outer Mongolia was a tactic
similar to that used in Bukhara and Azerbaijan during this period:
direct Soviet military intervention under the pretext of a request
from a small revolutionary group.[8]

How could Soviet troops move into Chinese territory? What prize
did they expect for their efforts? To answer such questions is not an
easy task. Until the 1950's, Outer Mongolia was a region hidden
even from most Soviet citizens. Soviet control over Outer Mongolia's press, intellectual life, public opinion, and libraries and
archives—in fact, all the sources for unbiased historical writing—
was complete. Rather successfully, the bitterness of power politics
could thus be disguised with the sugar of propaganda. Consequently, Mongol accounts of their "revolution" read like a fairy tale.
Nevertheless, we are able to find out a great deal about Outer
Mongolia, even if we will not know the whole story until the
archives of the Soviet Union and her satellite are opened. The
purpose of this book is, given known facts, to analyze the reasons
for the success of the invasion of 1921 not only in the immediate
sense of military success, but in the broader sense of continuing
satellite status for Outer Mongolia. How can men be led to accept

---

[7] Choibalsan, p. 44, puts the number of Mongol troops, prior to the attack, at
about 400. According to Shirendyb, p. 65, the MNP members arrived in Urga on
July 8.

[8] See Xenia Joukoff Eudin and Robert C. North, *Soviet Russia and the East,
1920–1927: A Documentary Survey* (Stanford, 1957), p. 125.

satellite status? What are the gains they seem to see behind their acceptance, and what are the costs? How were the costs justified to the actors in those events? What, in fact, do more than forty years of this satellite's history have to tell us?

Outer Mongolia's Political History

To discover the reasons that permitted Soviet troops to march into Outer Mongolia, we must briefly review the major developments in the country's political history. From the late seventeenth century onward, Outer Mongolia was almost a province of China. "Province" is, however, not quite the right word; the region was administered in a fashion different from that used in regions where Chinese-born populations predominated. For the moment, suffice it to say that Chinese governors enforced the writ of Peking in the area, with no central Mongolian regional authority to contest their decisions. In 1911, after the Chinese revolution of that year, the Urga Khutukhtu, head of the Lamaist church in Mongolia, became head of an autonomous government, an action resulting almost entirely from the promptings of tsarist diplomatic agents in the area. Furthermore, the autonomous government accepted the protectorship of Russia. Tsarist Russia had been attempting to gain a toehold in the area since the mid-nineteenth century, and the internal weakness of China in 1911 favored tsarist Russian intentions. The Chinese had to accept the *fait accompli* of autonomy, if most unwillingly, for they were militarily unable to reverse it. The Soviet foreign minister, Chicherin, told Louis Fischer that tsarist archives show such recognition to have been the price the Chinese government paid the tsar for recognition of their republic.[9]

Whether this is true or not, after the year 1911 Mongol autonomy under Chinese sovereignty was accepted by the Chinese in agreements with the Russian government. Naturally, Chinese sovereignty was merely a face-saving myth. After 1911, despite the presence of Chinese representatives in Outer Mongolia, the area was run with tsarist Russian advice. In the aftermath of the Russian Revolution of 1917, however, the Russian government was increasingly less able to hold on to Outer Mongolia; for that matter, it had difficulty in holding on to the Russian Far East. The Chinese were not hesitant to seize their chance: they began to strengthen their consular guard in Urga and to intrigue to restore their full control.

---

[9] Louis Fischer, *The Soviets in World Affairs* (New York, 1960), p. 390.

In 1919 a Chinese warlord, Hsu Shu-Ch'eng, gifted with more energy and capacity for action than diplomatic skill, forced the Mongols by threat of arms to return to the status they had held in 1911. His troops, which enabled him to enforce his threat, earned the hatred of the Mongolian populace, thanks to their brutality, pillage, and plunder. If Hsu Shu-Ch'eng had not proceeded with such arrogance, and if his troops had been better disciplined, it is likely that the Mongols would gradually have gravitated back toward Chinese influence. They were highly dependent economically on the Chinese, and the Russians were unable to take the place of the Chinese in this respect. Circumstances might have remained that way, fating Outer Mongolia eventually to become absorbed into a Communist China, as Inner Mongolia had been.

But the effects of the Russian Revolution had not yet played themselves out. On October 2, 1920, Baron Ungern-Sternberg, a White officer, rode southward into the eastern part of Outer Mongolia. He brought with him a motley band of troops, about a thousand in all, of whom two hundred were White Russians and the remainder were Bashkirs, Buriats, Mongols, and Tartars. The baron even had a company of former Japanese troops of the Manchurian command under a Captain Suzuki.[10]

Ungern-Sternberg and his troops were survivors of Kolchak's forces, which had been defeated early in 1920 by the Bolsheviks after an offensive starting in the summer of 1919. All along the Mongol border scattered remnants of White troops moved southward to seek refuge during the latter part of 1920, the year of total defeat for the White forces in the Far East. This maneuver was easy for them, as the Chinese garrisoned only the major towns and cities of Outer Mongolia.

Ungern-Sternberg moved southwest, approached Urga, and shelled the city on October 26, 1920. Unfortunately for him, he did not have sufficient forces at his disposal to overcome the Chinese garrison and therefore had to call off his attack and withdraw. He returned to mount another attack on the city on January 24, 1921, which lasted until February 4 and ended with his victorious occupation of Urga. The length of the second attack was evidence of the weakness of Ungern-Sternberg's forces. Yet, despite this weakness, once in occupation of the city he began planning to attack Russia by striking northward to Irkutsk to separate Russia proper from its trans-Baikal regions then under the control of the satellite Far Eastern Republic.

---

[10] Michel N. Pavlovsky, *Chinese-Russian Relations,* trans. Ruth Krader (New York, 1949), p. 171.

SOVIET PRETEXTS FOR INTERVENTION

The Baron's plans and their implementation presented a unique opportunity to the Soviet government. One bitter and disillusioned White soldier's comment was that Ungern-Sternberg's "historic mission consisted in killing the White movement in Russia and in adding to the Soviet empire the new territory of Outer Mongolia." [11] Although this comment imputes too much importance to Ungern-Sternberg, his plans did indeed present a perfect excuse for a Soviet invasion of Outer Mongolia.

Ungern-Sternberg's plans were clearly those of a disturbed man, and, in fact, his ruthless and demented activities in Urga clearly indicate his state of mind. He was driven by the fanaticism of a man who had suffered severe personal losses. He tortured and killed those he hated—Jews, Bolsheviks, Chinese, even his own men—in the most brutal fashion. He dreamed of an Asiatic empire based on levies of Mongol troops, with himself as emperor. Because he believed he had a historic mission to destroy Bolshevism, Ungern-Sternberg planned a northward strike against Russia and the Bolsheviks he hated. No fully rational man soberly assessing his forces and the means at his disposal would have made such plans. By 1921, the Red Army in the Far East heavily outweighed the White survivors. The Mongols around Ungern-Sternberg were not of the same warlike temperament as those who in earlier centuries had filled the ranks of Genghis Khan's armies; hence, Ungern-Sternberg could hardly expect much from them. However, the Russian Civil War in the Far East warped many men in its ferocious battles; only the most desperate and ruthless survived to lead,[12] and, of the Whites, only the irrational.

The Bolsheviks were quick to seize the opportunity presented them by Ungern-Sternberg's threat to Siberia. They manufactured a "revolutionary movement" of Mongols. They located its "government" directly on the line of Ungern-Sternberg's attack. When his skirmishers came into contact with these Mongols in the early summer of 1921, as they had to in order to realize the Baron's plans to strike northward, a pretext for Red intervention existed. The Soviet government had the excuse of the plea of a so-called friendly

---

[11] Dimitri Alioshin, *Asian Odyssey* (New York, 1940), p. 230.

[12] For a striking pen picture of Ungern-Sternberg, see Roland Strasser, *The Mongolian Horde* (London, 1930), pp. 98–106. Strasser claims that Ungern-Sternberg's wife and children were killed during the Russian Revolution. Quotations from Ungern-Sternberg's letters which include his plans for world domination are available. There is no question about the state of mind of this military adventurer.

revolutionary government for military assistance. In addition, they had the justification of threatened self-interest. These pretexts were used to gamble for two prizes: (1) destruction of the surviving White troops and (2) extension of Soviet Russian influence. Russian troops thus were ordered into Outer Mongolia.

Threatened Self-Interest

It is clear that the two pretexts for the invasion of July 3 were transparently thin. Certainly, only an exceptionally ill-informed command, or one in a state of panic, could have appraised the military threat offered by Ungern-Sternberg as serious. Although it is true that the pace of events in the Far East was rapid and their nature complex, it nevertheless seems reasonable to conclude that the Soviet authorities there were not ill informed. Furthermore, they were at the end of a victorious struggle, and both their morale and their confidence were high.

It is important to realize the extent of the Soviet Far Eastern command's information about Outer Mongolia, for it is pertinent to a correct appraisal of the element of long-term planning in the invasion of 1921. Admittedly, we are not privy to the archives of either the Soviet government, the Far Eastern authorities, or the military forces, and hence we must form a correct understanding of events indirectly. Nonetheless, it seems clear that the Soviet authorities in the Far East and interested parties in the Moscow government had extremely reliable intelligence.[13] They must have had accurate knowledge of the size of Ungern-Sternberg's forces, and they must have known that the Mongols were well disposed toward the Russians and were in any event notoriously passive, without modern military training, and armed only with obsolete hunting pieces. In addition, the Red command must have known that the Mongol military force of battalion strength, formed by tsarist agents in Mongolia, had been disbanded. The Soviet authorities must have known this partly because some of the so-called Mongolian revolutionaries were disaffected ex-members of that force. But the Soviet Union had a more important source of information: Iudin writes that Comintern representatives had visited Mongolia as early as the spring of 1920, and it seems likely that the Comintern had links with Urga as early as the autumn of 1919. If such were the case, this would be early indeed, considering the state of the battle against the Whites in 1919. From mid-1920

---

[13] The Russians were surely better informed about, and were making more realistic appraisals of, the Outer Mongolia of 1921 than the Chinese in Peking.

onward, Comintern offices in Irkutsk had links with an "information bureau" organized by Soviet citizens in Urga. Iudin comments
that these links ensured the "correct direction of the unfolding of
the national liberation movement in Mongolia." Moreover, the
information bureau ensured a flow of intelligence back to Irkutsk
and, hence, to Moscow.[14] It seems likely, in addition, that such
underground visits to Urga may not have been the only source of
information open to the Bolshevik leaders.

In 1919 the economist Ivan Maiskii, a former member of the
Menshevik Central Committee and later Soviet ambassador to
Great Britain, led an expedition to Outer Mongolia. His task on
behalf of the Russian consumer cooperative Tsentrosoiuz was to
evaluate Outer Mongolia as a potential market. This visit took place
while the Chinese were still occupying Urga. Subsequent to Maiskii's visit, the Chinese had misgivings about Tsentrosoiuz; they
viewed it as an agency of the Red Army and confiscated its property
in Urga. Moscow considered this action by China as so important
that it was the subject of a sharp passage in a note to Peking on
January 15, 1921,[15] from Foreign Minister Karakhan himself.

That Maiskii should have been in Mongolia at all, on behalf of a
Soviet trade agency, when the Bolsheviks were fighting for their
lives far to the west of Outer Mongolia on their native soil (the
White forces were holding Omsk at the time), is highly surprising.
It is certain that Maiskii's expedition was no ordinary trade
mission. In addition, it ran risks no ordinary trade mission normally undergoes; one of his four companions later was captured
and executed by Ungern-Sternberg.

While in Outer Mongolia, Maiskii visited Urga and also the
western towns of the country, that is, precisely those areas that
later were involved in the events we are to describe. D. P. Pershin, a
reputable eyewitness and at that time a director of the Mongolian
National Bank, had no doubt that Maiskii masterminded the events
that led to the invasion of 1921.[16] Perhaps we should not neglect
other members of Maiskii's expedition, for they were to play
important roles in Soviet Mongolia. There was the Mongol, Erdeni
Batukhan, who was later to be minister of education, and the

[14] Iudin, p. 107 ff. It is not quite clear from Iudin's treatment when the Urga
links with the Far Eastern Secretariat of the Comintern were established.
[15] For details see Allen S. Whiting, *Soviet Policies in China, 1917–1924* (New
York, 1954), p. 160.
[16] D. P. Pershin, "Baron Ungern, Urga and Altan-Bulak: An Eyewitness' Account
of the Troubled Times in Outer (Khalkha) Mongolia during the First Third of the
Twentieth Century" (MS in Library of the Hoover Institution, Stanford, Calif.), p.
31.

Russian, Anatolii Kallinikov, who was an authoritative commentator on political affairs in Mongolia.[17] However, we do not know definitely whether Maiskii's mission was confined to examining the possibility of trade in Mongolia for Tsentrosoiuz, or had the wider purpose of arranging entry of Soviet forces into Outer Mongolia.

If it is true that Maiskii opened up Comintern links with Outer Mongolia, it would indicate a very early concern on the part of the Soviet government to reestablish traditional Russian interests in that area. But whether or not Maiskii played a key role in the events we are to describe, no doubt can remain that the information he garnered about Outer Mongolia went unused. In 1920 he returned to Irkutsk, and subsequently, in 1921, his book *Sovremennaia Mongoliia* was published there. It surveys the economic, social, political, and religious conditions in Outer Mongolia and includes the results of the census conducted under tsarist auspices, the first reliable one in Outer Mongolia's history. Maiskii's work also reviews the available literature on Outer Mongolia's history and recent affairs and blends the data thus gleaned into a shrewd assessment of the country's social state. He called unambiguously for the expansion of Soviet influence over Outer Mongolia. But one thing he did not do: he raised no fear of Mongolian levies as the basis of another invasion of Russia. Quite the reverse, for he continually noted the conservatism and passivity of the Mongols:

The most important trait in the spiritual character of the Mongol, the foundation of his entire psychic being, is undoubtedly his deep passiveness. . . . This passiveness—strange, and difficult to understand from the European point of view—at every step manifests itself even at the present time. Whether you take state administration, political life, religious beliefs, character, or customs—everywhere, absolutely everywhere, you shall find obvious marks of a decay-fostering spirit of resignation and indifference.[18]

Later Maiskii remarked:

The Mongol has forgotten his past, and does not have the slightest idea about the history of his people. . . . He is illiterate. . . . He rarely leaves the limits of his native community. Urga seems to him to be something like a fairy tale situated "far, far away," and as for the world existing beyond the borders of Mongolia, he simply does not even dream about it.[19]

It is impossible to believe that Maiskii's information, whether official or not, was ignored in the Irkutsk of 1920, any more than

---

[17] I. M. Maiskii, *Mongoliia nakanune revoliutsii* (Moscow, 1959), p. 7 ff., reports Kallinikov's death in 1940, at a comparatively early age. Kallinikov was a productive writer until the mid-thirties.

[18] I. M. Maiskii, *Sovremennaia Mongoliia* (Irkutsk, 1921), p. 31.

[19] *Ibid.*, p. 36.

were his reports from Harbin to the Comintern in 1922.[20] Yet, no command or government given such a report as his would consider for a single moment the possibility of a major Mongol threat to the Soviet Union.

If the Mongols presented no danger, the Red command must have appraised the threat to themselves as largely that of the forces of Ungern-Sternberg, with perhaps a few Mongolian irregulars accompanying them. Yet, it is almost absurd to talk of Ungern-Sternberg's "forces." Of the mixture of nationalities in the original force he took with him to Outer Mongolia, only a small core were disciplined White troops. Furthermore, the White remnants in Outer Mongolia actually consisted of a number of small private armies under White officers—Kazagrandi, Rezukhin, Kazantsev, Kaigorodov, and Bakich—which had moved southward into Mongolia at several points, widely scattered along the border. They lived in this vast countryside as small but desperate bands surviving on pillage, not as a unified, disciplined command. There may have been telegraphic communication among these groups, but it seems unlikely. By horseback they were several days, if not weeks, apart.

When he eventually attacked his homeland, Ungern-Sternberg was in direct command of only 5,000 troops, supported by a mere twenty machine guns and twelve artillery pieces;[21] troops so few and scattered were obvious targets for mopping-up operations. Certainly, the forces the Fifth Red Army deployed to conquer Ungern-Sternberg were also small in number, but only a man with Ungern-Sternberg's psychotic personality would have seen his troops as the future praetorian guard of an empire. We may be sure that the competent Red generals of the Far East, like Vasilii Blücher, did not share such delusions when they allocated forces to the destruction of this tatterdemalion band. The most striking piece of evidence, however, for the belief that the threat of Ungern-Sternberg's troops was not the real reason for Red intervention in Mongolia was that they had in fact already been destroyed before the decision to invade Outer Mongolia was taken.

The Mongolian Desire for Nonrevolutionary Change

If the pretext of a serious threat to Soviet Siberia was transparently thin, so were the calls for assistance from a so-called Outer

---

[20] Whiting, p. 89 ff. In *ibid.*, p. 115, he describes Maiskii as a "Comintern writer."

[21] Choibalsan, p. 60. Choibalsan (*ibid.*, p. 60 ff.) attributes to Ungern-Sternberg's command in the attack only 3,500 men, and to Rezukhin, 2,000.

Mongolian revolutionary government. To show this we must go back to 1911. In that year tsarist Russian advisers had come to Outer Mongolia as friends, helping the Mongols to engage in political activity that might influence the course of their lives, and bringing Western ideas and techniques to the country. Tsarist Russia before 1917 was, after all, well in advance of China in both social and economic development. Furthermore, the Chinese had attempted, as a conscious policy, to preserve the Mongols in their ancient customs and ways. Nevertheless, the official impact of Russia on Mongolia was small, and was largely confined to the capital city, Urga. But the wind of change, however light its breeze, is irreversible in its effect. The restoration of Chinese control in 1919 and the resultant loss of autonomy were not to the taste of some of the Mongols who lived and worked in Urga and had benefited from the changes after 1911.

The Urga Khutukhtu himself accepted the loss of autonomy only under pressure. He commenced, through various channels, to put out feelers for protectorship under Russia, Japan, and, surprisingly enough, even the United States. Owen Lattimore has commented that it was not in the thinking of Mongolian politicians, if they deserve that appellation, to think in any terms except patronage under a foreign government.[22] Later, after a description of the basic social institutions of Outer Mongolia before 1921, it will become clear that this was a highly realistic position for the country's leaders to take. Although there was always a pro-Chinese group among the Outer Mongolian religious and secular leaders, anti-Chinese sentiments prevailed. Granted a suitable patron, even the Urga Khutukhtu would have preferred a non-Chinese protectorship, although he could hardly have viewed an accord with the Soviet Union without misgivings.

Others who had been affected by the tsarist Russian presence in Outer Mongolia were the princes and the lamas, who had been ministers or officials in the autonomous government and now found themselves without office, particularly the minor officials. Mongolian princes and higher-ranking lamas naturally retained some position of authority, however circumscribed by the Chinese. In addition, there were those, some of them also lamas, who had come under the influence of liberal-minded Russians during the

---

[22] Owen Lattimore, *Nationalism and Revolution in Mongolia* (New York, 1955), p. 35. This work contains not only Lattimore's own reflections on events in Mongolia, but also a translation of a life of Sukhe Bator written by Sh. Nachukdorji and information from the Dilowa Khutukhtu. In citing these three sources, I use Lattimore, *Nationalism and Revolution,* to refer to his contribution; Nachukdorji to refer to the life of Sukhe Bator; and Dilowa to refer to the Dilowa Khutukhtu.

period of autonomy. Many of these lamas actually had held jobs with the Russians which they now lost: teachers at the Russian school of interpreters, clerks at the Russian consulate, laborers in the Russian consular employ, and workers in the printshop that published the tsarist-sponsored newspaper. Some Outer Mongolians had come under the influence of an outstanding Buriat-Mongol intellectual, Tsyben Zhamtsarano, who ran a newspaper and a school during the period of autonomy. Khorloin Choibalsan, best-known Mongolian premier, was briefly a student under Zhamtsa-rano.[23] Finally there were those who lost posts as soldiers in the small Mongolian army raised by tsarist advisers. Some of these men came under the influence of Soviet Bolsheviks, laborers in the printshop, or workers in the Russian consular compound about half a mile outside Urga.

Thus, although the bulk of the population of Urga were lamas steeped in the conservatism of their religious institutions who had, as a matter of fact, been astounded and indignant at some of the small changes the tsarist agents had brought with them, there was a handful of men who dreamed of positions of responsibility for themselves or, more altruistically, looked forward to an independent Outer Mongolia, perhaps even a Pan-Mongol state consisting of Buriat Mongolia, Manchuria, and Inner Mongolia—a Pan-Mongol state that would attain some measure of progress in its social life. Others, animated only by a deep dislike of the Chinese, considered anything better than Chinese rule. It is, however, necessary to stress, if we are to depict the general state of mind of the malcontents as exactly as possible, that they had no precise image of the future of their country to use as a program for action, no parties, no platforms, but only a general feeling that Outer Mongolia as it was in 1919 had to be changed.

JOINT MONGOL-SOVIET SUBVERSION

In late 1919, as a consequence of the arbitrary actions of Hsu Shu-Ch'eng, a small group of ex-soldiers formed around a young noncommissioned officer, Sukhe Bator. Although he was then comparatively young, twenty-six, he had already distinguished himself for personal bravery as a soldier. Another young man of twenty-four, Choibalsan (already mentioned), formed a conspiratorial group. Choibalsan's parents had sent him at an early age to a monastery, from which he ran away to spend a brief time in

---

[23] Robert A. Rupen, "Cyben Zamcaranociv Zamcarano," *Harvard Journal of Asiatic Studies*, XIX (1956), 131.

Zhamtsarano's school. Later, under tsarist sponsorship, he attended school in Irkutsk. At least part of his time in Irkutsk he spent under the guidance of Pershin, whose eyewitness account we have already found valuable.[24] Choibalsan's group seems to have sprung up at the Russian consular compound under the influence of some Bolsheviks, notably Gembarzhevskii, clerk in the Russian town hall, and Kucherenko, a typesetter in the consular plant. Both Gembarzhevskii and Kucherenko were later to be executed by Ungern-Sternberg. In November, 1919, the two groups, after establishing contact, were contemplating joint action, such as capturing arms in the arsenal of the Mongolian Army, a plan that did not succeed.[25] In addition, they opened up channels to disaffected former officials and lamas, some of the Urga Khutukhtu's court, notably Danzan, Dindub, Doksom, and Galsang.[26]

Choibalsan himself speaks of the formation of a true political party and its program, of which he gives some details.[27] Its full nature has, however, been disclosed only recently; the account of it may be part of the retroactive history writing that complicates any attempt to understand the events we are dealing with. Pershin himself had no doubt that the small revolutionary circle was formed by Maiskii, and Maiskii was too much of the Soviet politician not to have thought in terms of a program. It is therefore possible that Choibalsan is correct. In any event, it is known that the revolutionary group was aware that Soviet Russia had offered friendship and support to former colonial peoples.[28]

In February, 1920, Sukhe Bator tried to cross into Russia, an attempt that understandably proved unsuccessful. In that month, after fighting between Reds and Whites, Troitskosavsk (later Kiakhta) was occupied, and Verkhneudinsk (later Ulan Ude) was occupied on March 2. In some way or other, the Bolsheviks learned of Bator's plan and in April, 1920, dispatched Sorokovikov, a Comintern agent, to Urga,[29] where he arrived in May. Sorokovikov then returned to the Russian Far East and S. S. Borisov, another Comintern agent, was ordered to Urga, with a group of Soviet Russians, to advise the Mongols. Borisov was to play a continuous role in the events that were to follow in 1920 and 1921. Under his

---

[24] Choibalsan, *passim;* Pershin, *passim.*

[25] Choibalsan, p. 20; Pershin, p. 20.

[26] Nachukdorji, p. 124.

[27] Choibalsan, p. 21. The program, though only vaguely revolutionary, places considerable emphasis on party discipline.

[28] *Ibid.*, p. 20. The authors of *Istoriia MNR*, p. 239, specifically assert that these men knew of the August, 1919, proclamation to the Mongols (see p. 19 and nn. 48 and 49 of this chapter).

[29] Iudin, p. 109.

promptings, a delegation was formed to go to the Soviet Union to ask aid for the Mongols. The leader of the delegation, according to modern accounts, was Sukhe Bator. But N. N. Poppe asserts that the leader was in fact a lama, Bodo, who later was to be the first prime minister of the puppet government installed in Urga in July, 1921.[30]

In June and July, 1920, three separate groups moved northward to Russia. The first to arrive in Troitskosavsk, by his own account, was Khorloin Choibalsan, who further claims he then telegraphed back to Urga that it was essential that the parties to follow carry a letter requesting assistance which bore the seal of the Urga Khutukhtu.[31] Of the two other groups crossing the border, one arrived at Verkhneudinsk on August 8, carrying with it a letter with the Urga Khutukhtu's seal, as requested. Whether Sukhe Bator carried this letter, as modern sources assert, or Bodo, as seems more likely, is a moot question.[32]

The letter itself had been procured through Puntsuk Dorji, a high religious official and former minister of the interior during the period of autonomy. Dorji was the most important member to join the revolutionary group and, perhaps as a reward for his help, later was appointed minister of the interior in the first puppet government.[33] In mid-August the group moved to Irkutsk, where its presence was known personally to Boris Shumiatskii, prime minister of the Far Eastern Republic and one of the most prominent Bolsheviks in the Far East. Significantly, he then held among his many appointments that of plenipotentiary of the People's Commissariat of Foreign Affairs for Siberia and Mongolia.[34]

Earlier sources assert that Rinchino, a Buriat-Mongol politician, was responsible for the introduction of the Mongols to Shumiatskii and for attempting to interest other prominent Bolsheviks, such as Ianson,[35] who was then foreign minister of the Far Eastern

---

[30] N. N. Poppe, "MNR," *Vestnik institut po izucheniiu istorri i kul'tury SSSR*, no. 4(11) (1954), p. 9.

[31] Choibalsan, p. 25.

[32] Iudin, p. 111, claims that Sukhe Bator carried the letter and that the group comprised Choibalsan, Dembril, Doksom, and Losol, but not Bodo.

[33] Choibalsan, p. 25. The revolutionary group met Sorokovikov in Verkhneudinsk (Nachukdorji, p. 139).

[34] See Eudin and North, p. 462, for details of his appointments. Iudin, p. 111, reports that Shumiatskii informed him of the group's presence.

[35] The point at issue is not whether Rinchino was involved in the matter but whether he planned it (see I. I. Genkin, "Dva s'ezda MNP," *Novyi Vostok*, no. 12 [1926], p. 202). Genkin also asserts ("Konets Ungerna i nachalo novoi Mongolii," *Severnaia Aziia*, no. 2 [1928], p. 81) that Ianson set up machinery in 1920 to promote revolutionary work among the Mongols, under the supervision of the Siberian Regional Bureau of the Russian Communist Party.

Republic, in the small group of Mongols. But more recent sources are probably more reliable. Rinchino was a Comintern agent; but, unless he was the person responsible for dispatching Sorokovikov and Borisov, which seems unlikely, the Bolsheviks needed no one to introduce the group to them. In any event, Rinchino immediately translated the Urga Khutuktu's letter.[36] An official modern Mongol account of Sukhe Bator's life tells of a most revealing incident that took place in a meeting with Kupun, head of the department dealing with Far Eastern affairs. Kupun is reputed to have said: "You delegates have brought a document with the Bogdo's (Urga Khutukhtu's) seal. It is something that will be in the record for you in the future. But in this matter it is important that you delegates should submit a document which makes clear your own desires and carries the seal of your own party."[37]

Although this was indeed a moment of importance, it is likely that few of the Mongols present realized its full significance. The Bolsheviks were asking those who came as representatives of the Urga Khutukhtu for help in establishing under him an autonomous government, to transform themselves instead into a revolutionary party. If it is factually true that Sukhe Bator and Choibalsan already were members of such a party, this Soviet ploy would have come as no surprise to them. We do know, however, that Bodo, Danzan, and Doksom hotly opposed that scheme and have been branded for their recalcitrance in modern Soviet histories.[38] Later, when we go into more detail about these men, we shall see that Danzan and Doksom, former officials of the autonomous government, were loyal to their religious monarch. Had they been more experienced, they might have withdrawn at that point, their loyalty to the idea of an autonomous Outer Mongolia and their hatred of the Chinese notwithstanding. But they must have thought their protests were heard, or else they were won over with promises of positions of authority, or possibly they thought that they could use the Bolsheviks to their own ends. Whatever their motives, they were subsequently to pay dearly for their naïveté. Again, modern sources assert that a party program was now submitted to the Bolsheviks (August 28, 1920). However, copies of the program, which are available in Russian translation but are not mentioned in earlier accounts, have a rather false ring to them. Whether this is due to the translation of older documents into contemporary officialese,

---

[36] Iudin, p. 111.
[37] Nachukdorji, p. 139 ff.
[38] *Istoriia MNR*, p. 224, names Danzan and Bodo; Nachukdorji, p. 140, names Danzan and Doksom.

which alters their flavor, or whether they were manufactured is as yet impossible to tell.[39]

Be that as it may, events started to move at a rapid pace. The group of Mongols first visited the Revolutionary War Council of the Fifth Red Army at Omsk.[40] Next, a delegation from that group was sent to Moscow on November 16, 1920, for interviews and a briefing by the Bolshevik leaders; the delegates were Danzan, Losol, and Chakdorjab. Bodo and Doksom returned to Urga to watch matters there. Sukhe Bator and Choibalsan were detached for training with the Red Army. Puntsuk Dorji and Dalai were sent to Kiakhta, where another young Mongol, a telegraphist named Damba Dorji, maintained communications with Urga through a man named Sereiter.[41] Iudin may have accompanied them, for, from October, 1920, he was detailed as representative of the RSFSR Commissariat of Foreign Affairs in the border zone.[42] The group that went to Moscow was escorted by Rinchino and had as its interpreter another Buriat Mongol, Zhambalon. When the Mongols arrived in Moscow, Shumiatskii took them to meet the Soviet officials, and later they attended a Politburo meeting in which Lenin, Stalin, and Bukharin took part.[43] Danzan, a man of considerable personal courage, drew Lenin's fire at the meeting. Inspired by anti-Chinese feelings, he wanted merely an autonomous Mongolia free of the Chinese. But this idea did not please Lenin, who, though viewing the Chinese warlords as enemies, considered the Chinese people suitable for conversion to the revolutionary cause.[44]

Leninist Ideological Considerations

By reviewing the opinions of Bolshevik leaders, we can see how the Mongols and their problems must have appeared to the top policy makers at the time. Few Bolsheviks had paid much attention to the Far East, largely because orthodox Marxist theory focused their expectations for revolutionary developments on more economically developed countries. Eventually, however, historic events demanded attention: both the Boxer Uprising (1900) and the Chinese Revolution (1911) called for analysis. In July, 1912, Lenin himself laid out his views on the strategy for Communist

[39] See Choibalsan, p. 25; Iudin, p. 113.
[40] Genkin, "Konets Ungerna," pp. 79–81.
[41] Anatolii D. Kallinikov, "U istokov mongol'skoi revoliutsii," *Khoziaistvo Mongolii*, no. 3(10) (1928), p. 62.
[42] Iudin, p. 111.
[43] Genkin, "Dva s'ezda," p. 203.
[44] *Istoriia MNR*, p. 246; Genkin, "Dva s'ezda," p. 203; B. Shumiatskii, "Na zare osvobozhdeniia Mongolii," *Pravda*, July 12, 1936, p. 5.

parties in dealing with revolutions in predominantly agricultural countries. His exposition, provoked by Sun Yat-sen's views with which Lenin partly agreed, essentially came down to supporting reformist bourgeois and nationalist parties, developing agrarian movements, speeding the transition to capitalism, and building up the proletariat. Such formulations left huge areas of disagreement over specific tactics, as subsequent Comintern debates on China have shown. Which movement to support, when to abandon it, and when to attack—questions such as these provoked the hottest debates. By 1916 Lenin had also formulated in bare outline what is tantamount to the modern Soviet theory of imperialism, what we might call the doctrine of the extension of the power of the victorious proletariat. The victorious proletariat was to use its strength in underdeveloped countries to nourish and support revolutionary movements, even bourgeois, democratic movements. Lenin said:

We Great Russian workers must demand that our governments should get out of Mongolia, Turkestan, and Persia. . . . But does that mean that *we* proletarians *want* to be separated . . . from the Mongolian, or Turkestan, or Indian worker or peasant? Does it mean that *we* advise the masses of the toilers of the colonies to "separate" from the class-conscious European proletariat? Nothing of the kind. . . . We shall exert every effort to become friendly and to amalgamate with the Mongolians. . . . We shall strive to give the nations, which are more backward and more oppressed than we are, "unselfish cultural aid," to use the happy expression of the Polish Social-Democrats, i.e., we . . . shall help them on towards democracy and socialism.[45]

The doctrine concerning the role of the victorious proletariat was laid out much more clearly when Lenin reported to the Second Congress of the Comintern (1920) on the work of the Commission on National and Colonial Questions: "The Communist International must outline and theoretically explain the thesis that, with the help of the proletariat of more advanced countries, backward countries can proceed to a soviet regime, by definite stages of development, to communism, bypassing the capitalist stage of development." [46] If we translate these broad phrases into concrete political realities, the mechanism for extending the power of the victorious proletariat was, at least in Outer Mongolia, the troops of the Red Army, an example that has been followed in most of the Soviet Union's satellites. But this implied idea is not the only one in

---

[45] Cited in Whiting, p. 22. Whiting's discussion of the whole issue of Bolshevik revolutionary strategy in the Far East is lucid.

[46] V. I. Lenin, "Doklad Komissii po nationalnomu i kolonialnomu voprosam," *Sochineniia*, XXV, 351 ff.

the paragraph which is an important revision of Marx. The idea that countries can leap the capitalist stage is so revisionary as to gut the body of Marxist doctrine. *Das Kapital* itself is concerned almost entirely with the dynamics of capitalist society in motion, and Marx concentrated on that stage of social development because, to him, it was the most critical in the development of communism. Marx would have been frankly unbelieving that historical processes in any country could leave out the capitalist stage. It is truly astonishing that today's Communists can repeat the shibboleth, "proceeding to communism, bypassing the capitalist stage," and still think themselves Marxists. This amounts to as critical a revision as, for example, a Catholic's denial of the doctrine of divine existence.

In any event, the Mongols who arrived in Moscow were introduced to men who saw the possibility of immediately creating socialist states in underdeveloped countries, without waiting for long historical processes to take their inevitable course. Furthermore, the Comintern debates of 1920 show that such men were prepared to tolerate nationalist movements, although not broader ones like the Pan-Muslim and Pan-Asiatic movements. In line with such ideas, the Buriat Mongols had already been granted a measure of autonomy a few weeks earlier, on October 14, 1920.

Danzan, Losol, and Chakdorjab clearly wanted autonomy for their country. Rinchino, who was with them and was attempting to mold them to his own ends, wanted to promote Buriat independence concomitantly with Pan-Mongolism. He was not discouraged from this goal, because the Comintern had placed no specific prohibition on the nature of Pan-Mongolism. The delegation's aspirations thus could be supported by the Comintern so long as the delegates were prepared to promote socialist ventures rather than confine themselves to establishing the Urga Khutukhtu as a monarch of an autonomous region protected by the Soviet Union. The price the Mongols had to pay was to promote agrarian cooperation and peasant party organization; they had to act as though they wanted to promote revolution. These theoretical views were held at least by Lenin, although they were by no means accepted by the entire Bolshevik leadership.

Tactical Considerations

Apart from the ideological considerations that would animate Comintern agents in dealing with the Far East, purely tactical criteria would have to be considered in the decisions, proposals, and notes and counternotes of the Soviet Commissariat of Foreign Affairs and would have to be integrated with the broader strategy mapped out. By late 1920 there was a growing concreteness about Soviet foreign policy: it had already become less visionary, tougher, and more concerned with the maintenance of Soviet interests. This change in the flavor of policy was partly related to the march of events. As the Soviet Red Army pushed eastward, as the Far Eastern Republic became more viable, and as the Soviet state itself reached the end of its frantic battles for survival during the period of War Communism, there was less propaganda and more hard political maneuvering.[47]

The growing concreteness in Soviet policy manifested itself also vis-à-vis Outer Mongolia. Trotsky, as foreign minister, had originally repudiated tsarist agreements, published many of the secret ones, and called for a new, open diplomacy. Conforming to this pattern, the Soviet government addressed to the Mongols on August 3, 1919, the following proclamation:

> Mongolia is a free country. . . . All power and law in this country must belong to the Mongolian people. Not a single foreigner has the right to interfere in the internal affairs of Mongolia. By overthrowing the 1913 agreement, Mongolia, as an independent country, has the right to carry on direct relations with all countries, without any interference on the part of Peking or Petrograd. The Soviet Government, publicly announcing this to the Mongolian people, offers immediate entry into diplomatic relations with the Russian people, and asks her to meet the representatives of the Red Army.[48]

Official Soviet historians assert that the group of Mongol conspirators in Urga had knowledge of this visionary proclamation.[49] Assessed realistically, it was a propaganda device rather than a concrete program, for the Red Army had still not occupied the areas north of Urga.

When Danzan, Losol, and Chakdorjab were in Moscow, however, the possibility of action existed; inasmuch as the headquarters of the Far Eastern Republic had been moved westward to Chita, the road from Urga to Irkutsk was already open. In addition, Chicherin had been attempting to make use of Ungern-Sternberg's presence in Mongolia, even though the latter had not yet captured Urga. Two

---

[47] See Whiting, in particular his fascinating discussion of how the Karakhan Manifesto of 1919 was actually changed to accord with the march of Far Eastern events.

[48] Whiting, p. 140.

[49] *Istoriia MNR,* p. 239. Doksom (in I. Ia. Zlatkin, *MNR: strana novoi demokratii* [Moscow, 1950], p. 121) is cited to the effect that this appeal made a "tremendous impression" on the Mongols, a statement that is probably retroactive exaggeration of the proclamation's importance.

notes, one on November 11 and the second on November 27, 1920, suggesting joint action with the Chinese against Ungern-Sternberg, were dispatched to Peking. The first note was a direct offer; the other, more a résumé of the situation. The second note said that Chicherin had actually contemplated the dispatch of troops, but that Ungern-Sternberg's first repulse at the walls of Urga showed that the Chinese could handle the matter; the offer of aid, if needed, remained open.[50]

Any Mongolian adventure was clearly to be subordinated to general Far Eastern considerations, and the Soviet Union was interested in friendship with China. At the same time, the Soviet government also wanted to reestablish the position its tsarist predecessor had enoyed in this vast buffer zone. The two notes helped to probe Chinese intentions.

On December 31, 1920, while the Mongols were in Moscow, the Soviet leaders were apprised of the rejection of their second note through the Chinese representative in London. We do not know whether these two facts—the interest of a group of Mongols in Mongolian independence, and the Chinese rejection of Soviet assistance in the destruction of Ungern-Sternberg—combined to trigger the historic decision to invade Mongolia. It is not unlikely that the news of the Mongolian delegation had preceded them to Moscow and had, in fact, caused the two notes of November to prepare diplomatic grounds for the subsequent Mongolian adventure. Probably the answers will be known only when the archives are opened. But indirect evidence (to be discussed later) suggests that the Soviet leadership had finally decided to commit itself to the invasion of Mongolia before March, 1921, although even then it could have held back had it wished to do so.[51]

This, then, was the climate of opinion into which the Outer Mongolians moved. It must have been a heady experience for them. They had come to Soviet Russia as emissaries of the Urga Khutukhtu, and now they were being asked to return to Mongolia as "leaders" of a "revolution." We do not know what inducements were offered them, or which they accepted. Nevertheless, as we shall see later, the Mongols must have decided to accept Soviet help.

They returned to Irkutsk in the last week of February to find that

---

[50] Whiting, p. 158 ff., discusses the two notes. The first asserted that the Chinese authorities in Urga had requested help, a claim that the Chinese in Peking subsequently denied. See Eudin and North, p. 200, for the November 11 note in full; *Izvestiia*, January 5, 1921, gives the Chinese reply of December 31, 1920.

[51] The Bolsheviks manufactured the Mongolian revolutionary movement and kept it on hand for use until the political situation was ripe. Military planning demanded that a definite decision be made for troops to be massed. Even then, the whole business could have been called off.

the situation there had changed little. Sukhe Bator and Choibalsan had not undergone much military training, the duty allotted them in August, 1920, because Bator had fallen ill. Consequently, the transaction of business was moved to the hospital where Bator was a patient.[52] While there, the conspirators had learned that a price of 10,000 Mexican dollars had been put on their heads by the Chinese authorities in Urga, and Bator and Choibalsan also seem to have published a newspaper. On November 18, 1920, they decided to move to Kiakhta, but almost immediately changed their plan in the hope of finding supporters among the Mongols to the west of Kiakhta and on the Sino-Russian border.[53] Their success in this task was very limited. Apart from promises of future assistance, they managed to raise a band of only fifty supporters, with whom they reputedly engaged in minor actions against the Chinese.

FORMATION OF THE MONGOLIAN NATIONAL PARTY AND A PROVISIONAL NATIONAL GOVERNMENT

On February 27, now that the mission to Moscow was completed, seventeen of the conspirators met to review the situation. They discussed the results of the mission to Moscow as well as Comintern views on the future of Mongolia. Sukhe Bator was designated war minister, and delegates were sent out to agitate in Mongolia, particularly in its western towns.[54]

Iudin speaks of a later meeting of four members of the "party" with Borisov, in which it was decided that the latter was to be plenipotentiary of the Far Eastern branch of the Comintern in dealing with the conspirators. As a matter of fact, Borisov held this position until the occupation of Urga.[55]

On March 1, 1921, the delegates came together in Kiakhta, formed a party, and hammered out a program. Earlier accounts show the formation of this party, the Mongolian National Party (MNP), as the origin of formal political life in Outer Mongolia, whereas modern accounts attribute political beginnings to the party formed by Sukhe Bator in 1919. Twenty-six delegates attended the meeting, including the two Buriats, Rinchino and Zhamtsarano, and Borisov, the Russian. As this is a critical point in the development of our analysis of the Mongolian invasion and its subsequent

---

[52] Choibalsan, p. 27.

[53] *Ibid.*, p. 36. Iudin, p. 115, speaks of an issue of a *Mongol'skaia Pravda*, oddly enough on November 18, the day Sukhe Bator and Choibalsan left Irkutsk.

[54] Iudin, p. 117. According to Choibalsan, p. 41, the date of the meeting was February 28, and twenty-one conspirators were present.

[55] Iudin, p. 117.

effects, it is necessary to take careful stock of the persons who attended what is known as the First MNP Congress.

Party Leaders and Membership at the First Party Congress

There was, of course, the delegation returned from Moscow: Danzan, Chakdorjab, and Losol. Little is known of the latter two except that Chakdorjab, a close friend of Bodo's, was a lama and was known in court circles.[56] Yet they were important actors in the events because subsequently Chakdorjab was elected prime minister and Losol finance minister in the provisional government formed at the First Party Congress. If Bodo was still in Urga, as apparently he was, he may have wished his friend Chakdorjab to take care of matters for him. Danzan, an able man of lower-class origins, had been an official in the autonomous government's Ministry of Finance.[57] He was a person of much independence of character and intensely patriotic, and had considerable animus against the Chinese. Pershin comments that Danzan "loved his nation with his whole soul." [58] These three men were former officials in either the autonomous government or the church. Bodo and Doksom, also back in Urga, were men of similar backgrounds. Doksom had held high rank in the Mongolian ministries of war and finance and was a well-educated man.[59]

At least two representatives of the traditional nobility of Mongolia also were present at the First MNP Congress: Velik Sai-khan and Sumia Beise. The latter had already offered the support of the Mongols under him, although this did not amount to more than a hundred men. Puntsuk Dorji, also a noble, and the only man of any personal prominence, was still in Urga.

Finally there were the commoners at the congress: Choibalsan, Sukhe Bator, Tsyden Ishi, and Damba Dorji the telegrapher. Sukhe Bator at this time played a more significant role than Choibalsan, but neither had been important enough to be sent to Moscow. Sukhe Bator was later to be apotheosized into the Lenin of a Mongolian revolution; yet, from his personal history it is difficult to understand why he has enjoyed so much posthumous prestige. He has been described as an energetic, honest, and keen soldier, but naïve in matters outside his profession.[60] He seems to have had the limited perspective of an able noncommissioned officer; in the

---

56 Genkin, "Konets Ungerna," pp. 79–81.
57 Dilowa, p. 124.
58 Pershin, p. 22.
59 Dilowa, p. 124.
60 Pershin, p. 31. The official biography of Sukhe Bator was written by Sh. Nachukdorji.

period prior to the congress, when the conduct of military affairs had been left in his hands, he had tried to get help by talking to friendly Mongols of a rank similar to his own. He seems to have contributed nothing in the way of ideas, policies, and programs to the "revolution." Undoubtedly, the chief reason for his success was his death at an opportune time in 1923, which enabled the Mongols to see in him their Lenin, and this at a time when his actions had been largely concerned with warfare so that no subsequent shift of the party line could discredit his posthumous fame.

Choibalsan was to attain the premiership during the Stalin era. Pershin states that Choibalsan was the younger brother of the lama Bodo and, as Pershin knew both Choibalsan and Bodo, perhaps he is correct. He judged Choibalsan to be of limited ability and of good conduct, but noted for passivity and complete indifference to his environment. Choibalsan had, in Pershin's view, considerable ability to adapt himself to situations.[61] Transcripts of the earlier Mongolian party congresses show Choibalsan to have been an almost silent participant. It may have been his ability to keep silent, and at the same time to know to what winds to trim his sails, which preserved him at a time when Mongolian puppet leaders had a high mortality rate. Although probably the only dedicated Bolshevik among the group in Kiakhta, Choibalsan was not to attain the premiership until much later in the 1930's. This should be taken, however, as a reflection not so much on the speed of the Bolsheviks' rise to power, for this was accomplished earlier in Mongol affairs, as on Choibalsan's own lack of ability. One thing is certain: he was an able soldier. He prided himself on this characteristic, and during his premiership the building of a Mongolian army was probably his sole real achievement. Typically, his memoirs of the events of 1921 are most interesting when they deal with military matters.

The lama Bodo, who was installed as prime minister when the Red Army arrived in Urga, had been a clerk in the Russian consulate there. He had also taught Mongolian in the tsarist school for interpreters. To Pershin, Bodo was a naïve man who had come to believe Bolshevik propaganda but later had become disillusioned. (The latter comment is an understatement, as Bodo was soon to fall to a firing squad.) Pershin judged him a good man in the common sense of the word, and said he was respected by his fellows, although he was in no way suited to be a leader of a republic.[62] A phrase from another source—"the effusive lama Bodo,

---

[61] Pershin, p. 30. The official biography of Choibalsan is Iu. Tsedenbal, *O zhizni i deiatel'nosti Marshala Choibalsana* (Moscow, 1952).

[62] Pershin, p. 30.

somewhat influenced by European culture"[63]—captures the man better.

All the Mongols, with the exception of Puntsuk Dorji, the former minister of the interior, were men unfamiliar with the exercise of affairs. All were young men with limited experience, brought up in and familiar only with Urga, a small town in a deeply conservative and theocratic country. They were men almost without political sophistication; the Bolsheviks could manipulate them easily and did so ruthlessly. To liken any of them to a Lenin or a Stalin (or, for that matter, even a Castro) is to exaggerate their personal force and character.

The two Buriats in the group, Rinchino and Zhamtsarano, were of a different sort. Rinchino was to prove himself a man of determination and ruthlessness, for he later arranged the execution of some of the Mongols whom he had manipulated for the Comintern. He had played an important role in the Buriats' aspirations for autonomy and had been chairman of the National Committee of the Buriats. He was a Social Revolutionary and a Pan-Mongolist. Later he became a left-wing nonparty Communist. He was a man steeped in politics and had participated in the Social Revolutionary and the Siberian *oblastnichestvo* movements. He had mixed in Populist, Social Democratic, and Bolshevik circles.[64] By his own account, he was planning to deliver Outer Mongolia to the Soviet Union in return for both more favorable treatment of the Buriats and the advancement of Pan-Mongolism.[65]

Zhamtsarano, like Rinchino, had also been a chairman of the National Committee of the Buriats. He was a man of liberal views and much more to the center than Rinchino. Primarily, however, he was a scholar and educationist; his fascination was for Mongol culture and religion. He had hopes for a united Mongol nation, with its center at Urga, based on the tremendous religious prestige of the Urga Khutukhtu. One source asserts that Zhamtsarano actually hoped to stall off the Red Army invasion of Outer Mongolia.[66]

The MNP Program

Borisov was the representative of Shumiatskii, who had by this time returned to Irkutsk and had shifted his interest from the Far

[63] Genkin, "Konets Ungerna," p. 79.

[64] Robert A. Rupen, "The Buryat Intelligentsia," *Far Eastern Quarterly*, XV (1956), 388. This information comes largely from Genkin.

[65] "Buriat Mongoly Vostochnoi Sibiri," *Zhizn' Natsional'nostei*, May 28, June 11, 1921.

[66] Ladislaus Forbath, *The New Mongolia: As Related by Joseph Geleta*, trans. Lawrence Wolfe (London, 1936), p. 167.

Eastern Republic to Soviet politics. Borisov naturally pressed for a party program that would be pro-Russian and pro-Bolshevik. But Zhamtsarano moderated these demands, insisting that the Urga Khutukhtu be retained as head of state.[67] Borisov must have been forced to acquiesce, for the whole temper of the meeting was more in line with Zhamtsarano's views than either his own or Rinchino's.

The program they hammered out was frankly Pan-Mongol: it demanded independence for the Mongols, but within the framework of protection by another power; it made no assault on the traditional religion of the country. In all other respects the program was vague, making concessions to the Soviet Union only by expressing a desire for friendly contacts with other revolutionary organizations. Interestingly enough, it did not call for an outright break with China.[68]

Nonrepresentative Provisional Government

On March 13, 1921, a provisional government was set up. Velik Saikhan was minister of the interior. The other cabinet posts were held by Chakdorjab, Losol, and Sukhe Bator, as already mentioned. A proclamation issued to the Mongols called for the following measures: the elimination of slavery and feudalism in Outer Mongolia; a tax system bearing equally on all; and a constitutional government headed by the Urga Khutukhtu.[69]

The events that followed show that the Soviet leaders were already committed to a Mongol adventure. Kiakhta lay on the Sino-Russian border; the provisional government had been set up within Soviet territory. On the other side of the border, there was a Chinese trading settlement, Kiakhta Maimaicheng. Sukhe Bator issued an ultimatum to the Chinese garrison, declaring his intention to enter the city on March 15. Failing to receive a reply, he entered the city with his troops, now numbering perhaps 400, and took it by force. (Three days later Kiakhta Maimaicheng was renamed Altan Bulak.) Thus, force was used under Soviet protection against Chinese troops, and a government was installed on Mongol territory.

From this review of the pertinent facts it must be quite clear that the new government represented nothing but itself. The Buriat

---

[67] Pershin, p. 30.

[68] The platform of the MNP may be found in Kallinikov, pp. 62–63.

[69] Ma Ho-t'ien, *Chinese Agent in Mongolia*, trans. John de Francis (Baltimore, 1949), p. 99, gives the proclamation.

Mongols in it were meddling in the affairs of another country. If the Mongols themselves had any authority at all, it was as agents of the Urga Khutukhtu. They could not claim to represent a party that had been excluded from office despite a broad popular mandate. They had a program, it is true, but it was not one that Mongols generally desired. For that matter, the program had not grown out of the aspirations of the Mongols in the revolutionary group but out of Buriat aspirations. Therefore, we cannot take seriously any claim that the Soviet forces marched to Urga at the request of a responsible government with a broad mandate or, for that matter, with any mandate at all.

THE TRIUMPH OF SOVIET INTERVENTION

In all likelihood, the choice of Kiakhta as the center of the new government was neither accidental nor based merely on its proximity to Irkutsk. Once the Mongol government was installed on Mongol territory, it was essential to the Soviet Union that it come under attack by Ungern-Sternberg so as to justify intervention by the Red Army. Kiakhta lay astride the natural route to the north from Urga; it was logical that Ungern-Sternberg attack it. If intelligence failed, this would be a wise location from the Soviet point of view. But more likely than not, Soviet intelligence, usually good during this period, was aware of Ungern-Sternberg's plans. Ungern-Sternberg's broad strategy of attempting to separate the Soviet Far East from Russia proper was to be implemented as follows: one column under his command, with a vanguard of Mongols under Bayar Gun, was to strike at Altan Bulak. This town cleared, the main attack was destined for Verkhneudinsk. A second column under Rezukhin was to strike up through Van-Kuren and then swing over to assist the Verkhneudinsk attack. Far to the west, the small band of Kazagrandi was to make a diversionary attack to distract the Fifth Red Army.

Attack by Invitation

On April 10, 1921, prior to the attack, the provisional Mongolian government in Kiakhta called for Red Army assistance.[70] It is not surprising that subsequent to this call dispositions were made in advance of Ungern-Sternberg's attack. Sukhe Bator remained in Altan Bulak, Bayar Gun's objective, and was supported by Soviet

---

[70] Shirendyb, p. 60.

troops. Soviet forces and Mongol troops under Choibalsan were located on Rezukhin's line of advance. Ungern-Sternberg gave plenty of notice of his intentions. His offensive started on May 22, but Altan Bulak was not attacked until June 5. The attack, involving some 5,000 White troops, failed in its objective and was easily turned back by the Red troops. By the first week of June, Ungern-Sternberg's troops had fallen back, essentially a rabble, and with Ungern-Sternberg himself wounded.[71] On June 15, Chicherin dispatched a note to China informing her of these events and giving the reason why the Red troops had had to violate the Chinese border.[72] Thus, Ungern-Sternberg was defeated before the committee of June 28 made the decision to invade.[73]

Other Reasons for the Soviet Success

Comintern agents had given accurate intelligence about Ungern-Sternberg's intentions and movements, and the experienced troops of the Fifth Red Army had had no difficulty in defeating the Baron. The threat to Russia's border thus was removed. As the Civil War generally was nearing its end, the Red forces could easily have protected the Mongolian border against a further attack by Ungern-Sternberg. At the least, they could have waited to see if he could maintain himself as leader of the remnants of the White troops, given his defeat, his shortage of food and ammunition, and his lack of definite hope of outside support. Given Maiskii's reports, the Soviet leaders could hardly have believed in the likelihood of an Outer Mongolian revolution. Bodo was no fiery revolutionary, nor for that matter was that young but competent noncommissioned officer, Sukhe Bator. It is therefore impossible to accept the view that the Soviet leaders had deluded themselves with their own revolutionary fervor into really believing they had a Mongolian revolution on their hands. Yet the goal of Urga, and of acquisition of influence over the vast region of Outer Mongolia, seems to have been irresistible to the Soviet government.

In retrospect, the preparation for the invasion was neat and calculated. Yet, had China reacted differently, had Ungern-Sternberg followed other plans, in fact, had a number of different actions been taken by the most important parties in this account, the outcome might have been different. Plans that succeed have an

---

[71] Choibalsan, p. 62 ff., describes the battle.

[72] Whiting, p. 163, cites this note.

[73] The committee of Russian Bolsheviks was in Kiakhta from June 22 on (Iudin, p. 121).

air of inevitability, and to describe them fails to capture the problems of decision individuals must face in trying to implement plans in a changing world. The Bolsheviks *had* been brilliantly successful in Outer Mongolia and *had* obtained quickly what decades of tsarist Russian diplomacy had not succeeded in obtaining: a strong presence in Urga. Of the many adventures planned along the Central Asian and Far Eastern borders of the Soviet Union, this was the most successful.[74]

Some of the proximate reasons for this success should now be clear. Shumiatskii, Rinchino, Borisov, and Sorokovikov had served their masters well. The Moscow government had been quick to avail itself of the opportunity the Bolsheviks of the Far East had seized. Politicians, Comintern agents, and army authorities had collaborated swiftly and effectively. The "revolutionary" Mongols themselves had proved pliable instruments. The Chinese government had not been able to respond effectively to Soviet violation of China's border, nor had it been able to maintain adequate forces in the area. Finally, the Mongols had remained apathetic to the successive seizures of their capital city by competing forces. As we make the list of proximate reasons, there is one we clearly cannot include: a revolutionary situation in the Outer Mongolia of 1921. Whatever equation we use, 20 party members and 400 troops from a country of 750,000 population do not amount to a revolution. If any doubts remain on this score after this account of the manufacture of a Mongolian "revolutionary party," the next chapter should dispel them.

---

[74] A similar adventure in the west of Outer Mongolia led to the establishment of a "People's Revolutionary Government of Mongolia" (see Konstantin Noskov, *The Black Year* [Harbin, 1930], p. 56; Siren Shoizhelov, "Zapadnaia Mongoliia," *Novyi Vostok*, no. 4 [1923], and "Natsional'no-osvoboditel'noe dvizhenie v Mongolii," *ibid.*, no. 6 [1924]; and Ulan Otorchi, "Ozero Tolbi," *Khoziaistvo Mongolii*, nos. 1–4 [1928]).

2

SOCIAL, POLITICAL, AND
ECONOMIC CONDITIONS

The Outer Mongolia that Neiman's troops had entered presented immense tasks to the invaders, should they wish to change the country's social institutions. By no stretch of the imagination can one speak of a revolutionary state of affairs existing there at that time. The average Mongol was deeply conservative, showed little concern for "Mongolian" as contrasted with local politics, and was intensely loyal to his religion in a country as much under theocratic domination as Tibet. Although the economic system that supported the Mongol was underdeveloped, it nonetheless nurtured a stable society which was not rent by class antagonisms. If there was any divisive force in Mongolian society, it was the competition between the nomadic and the sedentary populations, which produced at the worst a mild Chinese-Mongol antagonism.

Having manufactured a "revolutionary party," the Soviet Union next had to engineer a revolution in a country possessing the characteristics just described. This chapter examines each of these features in order to dispel any doubt that a revolutionary climate of sorts did exist, a situation that made the invaders' task easier. The remaining chapters describe how the "revolution" was brought about, and how change was initiated in a country fundamentally so little desirous of change.

Mongol Social Conservatism under Chinese Imperialism

The Mongols' entrenched social conservatism was partly due to the lack of economic change in their history. Economic change usually has side effects, not the least important of which is a growing tolerance for novelty. The major cause of Mongol social conservatism, and, to a great extent, of the lack of economic change itself, was China's imperial policy. The Chinese had run Outer Mongolia as a great reservation, paralyzing the Mongols psychologically by preventing them from controlling their own lives and by shielding them from change.

The Power Structure

The Chinese had gained control of Outer Mongolia in 1691, when the princes of the Khalkha Mongols accepted vassalage from the Chinese emperors. Most Mongols, having lost their powerful position under Genghis Khan and his immediate descendants in internal wars, had come to accept Chinese suzerainty. The princes of Inner Mongolia had yielded earlier than the Khalkhas, and under somewhat different circumstances. As a result, the Khalkhas received what the Chinese must have considered more favorable treatment. (The Khalkha princes became the princes of Outer Mongolia, so known because it was farther from Peking than Inner Mongolia.) This difference in Chinese policy was to have a lasting effect on the subsequent history of the two Mongolias.[1]

For Russia, the seventeenth century was a period of vigorous territorial expansion. Among Russia's objectives was the acquisition of Outer Mongolia, but the government considered the realization of that goal by force as too costly and by diplomacy as unlikely. As a consequence, although the Mongolian border had been left undefined by the Treaty of Nerchinsk (1689), it was fixed by the Treaty of Kiakhta (1727), and Outer Mongolia was recognized as Chinese territory.

Outer Mongolia, like other areas of their empire where the Chinese were a minority, was controlled through the Li-fan Yuan, or Board of Administration of the Dependencies. The direct authority was the Chinese military governor of Uliasutai (in the western part of Outer Mongolia) who had two subordinates in the cities of Kobdo and Urga. Also subordinate to the governor were the Mongolian princes, each of whom had to be confirmed by the

---

[1] The Inner Mongolian princes had been conquered. In contrast, the nobles of Outer Mongolia gave personal allegiance to the Manchu after the conquest of China and hence could consider themselves vassals. In fact, after the overthrow of the Manchu dynasty in China in 1911, the Outer Mongolians used the fiction of vassalage to support their bid for independence. They asserted that they had not declared their vassalage to the Chinese emperors qua Chinese, but merely to a given family. Hence they considered their vassalage terminated by the revolution.

Chinese as military leader of the region he controlled. Emperor K'ang-hsi (1662–1722), under whom the Mongolian settlement began to take permanent form, created seventy-two new princes. In this way the likelihood of a single prince or khan emerging to unite the Mongols against the Chinese was diminished. The Mongolian princes, at first, were military leaders of troops raised from their respective regions, and were subject to call by the Chinese. Over time their appointments to command their regions became, in fact, civil and political appointments, although continuing to be military in form.

The emperor of China formulated and proclaimed his edicts, his governors relayed them, and the Mongolian princes enforced them. Despite some minor changes, this system remained in force until 1911. Separated as the princes were by vast distances and brought together for no common purpose, the possibility of a Mongolian politics growing up among them was slight. Moreover, the Chinese took care to win over the princes with honors, subsidies, and titles, and to ensure that no common grievance existed to unite them.

Chinese-Controlled Change

Outer Mongolia's status as a reservation.—A series of important edicts dealing with political and social life in Outer Mongolia had turned the country into a reservation. In 1716 Mongols were prohibited from leasing land to Chinese, a prohibition that, though not always in force, was generally maintained. In 1719 Chinese-Mongol marriages were prohibited. Chinese citizens, after 1808, were repeatedly ordered not to enter Mongolia to cultivate land. In general, the Chinese emperors wanted the Mongols to be untouched except by trade. Merchants were allowed to enter Mongolia upon being licensed, but they could not take their families with them or become permanent colonists.

The Chinese emperors also sought to nullify any threat of a Mongolian uprising against them. Not only did they create new princes, but in 1793 the emperor prohibited princes from becoming leaders in Mongolian religious life, thus preventing a merging of secular and religious politics. To remove sources of friction between tribal groups, the region each prince controlled was strictly defined, and his subjects were permitted freedom of movement only within that area. Battles between uncontrolled nomadic groups are endemic, especially over pasturage rights; the Chinese saw to it that conflicts of this nature did not arise. Owen Lattimore has suggested that early Chinese policy may have concerned itself with maintaining "reservoirs" of non-Sinified troops,[2] one important such reservoir being the regiments of the Mongols. In the long run, however, Chinese policy pacified the Mongols socially, rendering them useless as troops. In fact, Chinese policy rid Mongolian society of the necessity for social aggressiveness.

It is not possible to prohibit change completely. Two major sources of change persisted in Outer Mongolia and were, in fact, encouraged by the Chinese emperors: the growth of Lamaism, and the growth of Chinese trade with the dependent territory. Neither of these sources of change threatened the goal of preserving the Mongols as pacified nomads. In fact, quite the reverse was true.

The growth of Lamaism, trade, and nomadic stock raising.—The growth of Lamaism, by drawing a large share of the male population into the religious sector, helped in the process of pacific change. It did not do this in a direct way by changing the Mongols' values, but affected the people indirectly. As monasticism spread in the country, it offered advancement within its hierarchy to able persons. As with any broad-based monasticism, however, the ideals of the creed became blunted; thus, the religious vows professed by believers became formalities rather than realities. Lamaist monastic life, in other words, was corrupt in terms of its own ideals. The monasteries were subsidized, and most of the ranking positions in them were subject to Chinese approval. The search for the more important reincarnations, that of the Urga Khutukhtu for example, came under Chinese control. Ranks and pensions were awarded by the Chinese government to prominent religious leaders. Thus, this innately conservative religious institution tended to be favorable to the Chinese so long as the Chinese were politically strong themselves, for official Chinese policy helped it to grow, partially financed it, and, most important of all, controlled it.

The growth of trading relationships with the Chinese also worked to prevent trouble in Outer Mongolia. The nomads could come to depend on trading rather than raiding for goods they needed. There was another more subtle, and probably unintended, effect: since the Chinese were more skilled as artisans and agriculturalists, both the traditional craftsmen of Mongolia and the practice of agriculture by the nomads disappeared when trade was

---

[2] Owen Lattimore, *Manchuria: Cradle of Conflict* (rev. ed.; New York, 1935), pp. 38–41. Lattimore suggests in *Nationalism and Revolution in Mongolia* (New York, 1955), p. 15, that the reservoir policy was abandoned by the Chinese emperors when modern weapons eliminated the Mongol's value as a soldier. In the early part of the twentieth century the absence of inspection, of drills, and of exercises certainly points to a lack of concern with preservation of the Mongols as effective troops.

developed. Comparative advantage and the specialization that comes with it thus led the Mongols to concentrate almost exclusively on raising stock. In this dominant economic activity the Chinese could not help their dependents. Mongolian stock raising continued to use age-old techniques; it had nothing to learn from Chinese practices.

The nomadic way of life.—The concentration on stock raising implied more than the growth of an economic specialization; the whole style of life was shaped by the technique of nomadic herding. Mongols, brought up in a nomadic life, came to despise agriculturalists and, to some extent, traders, so that only the least able among them sought employment under the Chinese. Mongols with any entrepreneurial talent tended to be siphoned off by the religious institutions, for the wide scope of activities in the monasteries offered numerous opportunities for economic, and thus for social, advancement for those not of noble birth. Through this policy of selection, the nomadic sector of the population, heavily concentrated in stock raising, was robbed of its more able members. It was also protected against change, partly by Chinese policy, partly by high transport costs. Thus the Mongols were either lamas or nomads, neither posing a threat to the existing order.

Nomadic life is periodically subject to great natural catastrophes: murrain of cattle and drought. In Inner Asia, the intense winters compounded these inherent difficulties with severities of nature which took toll of the Mongol herds. Prohibited from political activity and deprived of able secular leaders, Mongolian nomads had no choice but to accept such disasters. Life in a religious sector favorable to the Chinese rulers or in a nomadic camp, where acceptance of natural misfortune was the rule, bred resignation, indifference, and passivity. And Mongolian Lamaism, partly Buddhist, partly shamanistic, reinforced these attitudes. The Mongols of the time of Genghis Khan had proven themselves capable men and superb organizers, ready to accept military innovations, open to new ideas, and, above all, energetic and decisive in action; a prior history of clan warfare had given them martial characteristics. The Mongols of the twentieth century, as described by Maiskii, were a far cry in temperament from their ancestors.

Nothing in Chinese society, in the period of Mongolian dependency, worked to change the settlement that had been largely laid down in the eighteenth century. The Chinese population explosion, which pushed agriculturalists into Inner Mongolia and Manchuria, spared Outer Mongolia. Little of its land was suitable to the Chinese style of agriculture, and the vast distance of the Gobi was a social and economic barrier to colonists. When Chinese settlers came to the north of Outer Mongolia they came under government colonizing schemes, not in individual search of opportunity. In addition, when they did come they brought with them little to change the Mongols' way of life; the gulf between nomads and agriculturalists was too broad to bridge. There was little technical diffusion from one group to the other, for, as we shall see later, the two were essentially noncompetitive both in labor markets and in production patterns.

Chinese dominance on the wane.—The Chinese policy toward Outer Mongolia broke down in the nineteenth century. The Russians of the mid-nineteenth century came to Outer Mongolia as explorers, traders, scholars, and diplomats. Although from a country relatively backward itself, they brought fresh ideas, a belief in change, Western medicine, and Western science. As traders, they were typical men of the Siberian frontier who could earn the respect of the Mongols with whom they came in contact. As scholars and diplomats they could, in part, find some rapport with the religious leaders of Outer Mongolia. Even so, their impact was slight and, more often than not, was frustrated by Mongolian conservatism.

That conservatism, engendered and deliberately fostered by Chinese policy, had a paradoxical result. The Chinese government lost no time in reacting to the abandonment of buffer status for Outer Mongolia. From the 1880's on China promoted colonization schemes in Outer Mongolia, and Chinese peasants began appearing in the river valleys to the north, close to Siberian Russia.[3] Military forces and border troops were increased in the area; they were very unpopular with the Mongols. The major effect of these Chinese moves was to antagonize the Mongols, who had come to prize their isolation, destructive to themselves though it may have been. The fear of the Mongolian religious and secular nobility that change would affect their status adversely was, however, the main reason for their acceptance of the tsarist Russian overtures in 1911.[4] In short, when the country accepted Russian guidance in 1911, it was not because of a desire for change. It is not surprising, then, that the effect of autonomy on the social fabric of the Mongols, like the effect of the preceding half-century of Russian contacts, was slight.

[3] According to Robert A. Rupen, "Outer Mongolian Nationalism, 1900–1919" (unpublished Ph.D. dissertation, University of Washington, 1954), p. 140, the peak number was 10,000 in 1912.

[4] Gerard M. Friters, *Outer Mongolia and Its International Position,* ed. Eleanor Lattimore, intro. by Owen Lattimore (London, 1951), p. 159 ff.

The Red troops and their commissars marched into a country that was still virtually a reservation in 1921, and wished to remain one. There still was no Mongolian demand for change. The traditional leaders of the country, the princes and the higher lamas, did not want it, and the broad mass of the people were politically indifferent.

Mongolian Autonomy

This much must have been known to Rinchino, to Borisov, to Iudin, and to all the unknown representatives of the Soviet Russian Commissariat of Foreign Affairs and of the Comintern who accompanied the Red troops to Urga. All must have been impressed by how few Mongolian troops had rallied to support Sukhe Bator. Perhaps they also knew that Outer Mongolia had been virtually without uprisings against the status quo—a tribute to the success of Chinese policy.[5] Actually, there was no such thing as Mongolian politics, formal or informal.

In 1921, it was still a flight of imagination to call Outer Mongolia a "nation" or a "state." In 1911, under the Chinese governors, it had been ruled by 111 regional princes (hoshun jasak's) and 4 religious princes (khutukhtus).[6] There were also four khans, governor-generals of subprovinces (aimak's), who were essentially without function, a vestige of the past power of the great khans of Mongolia. The Russian scholar Vladimirtsov likened the regional princes to the rulers of the feudal principalities of Europe.

The Urga Khutukhtu, however, possessed widespread lands and property, and controlled numerous religious serfs, especially in comparison with all other khutukhtus and princes. The operation of this vast religious domain required a considerable administrative apparatus. Hence it was natural that the Urga Khutukhtu became monarch during the period of autonomy, for of all the Mongol leaders he bore the greatest responsibility and had the broadest perspective. He was, furthermore, a man of some ability and

---

[5] For reasons that will become clear later, more peasant uprisings had occurred in Inner Mongolia (see S. K. Dylykov, Demokraticheskoe dvizhenie mongol'skogo naroda v Kitae, ocherk istorii [Moscow, 1953]). Marxist-Leninist writers who have looked diligently for such troubles in Outer Mongolia have been unsuccessful. Thus the Istoriia MNR (Moscow, 1954), p. 161 ff., restricts itself to the uprising of Amursan in 1755–1758.

[6] I. M. Maiskii, Sovremennaia Mongoliia (Irkutsk, 1921), p. 15. There were 13 khutukhtus in 1911, but the remaining 9 had subjects who lived within the territories of lay princes, and were subject to both authorities. These nine had no specific lands of their own. Khutukhtu was a Chinese title. A khutukhtu was a Chinese appointee, and was a khubilgan or reincarnation.

independence of character, though quite corrupt by the standards
of his religion.

Tsarist Influence and Assistance in Reform

Slight centralization.—We should be careful in considering the
extent of political innovations grafted onto the hoshun system,
which had prevailed prior to 1911. At tsarist suggestion, a bicam-
eral legislature, consisting of an upper house of princes and a lower
house of lesser dignitaries, was set up to advise the Urga Khutukhtu. The executive functions of government were planned to
flow through five ministries: those of the interior, war, foreign
affairs, finance, and justice, the ministers being appointed by the
Urga Khutukhtu. For the first time religious and political authority
were merged.

The Urga Khutukhtu did not make wide use of his powers,
however. Such changes as took place during the period of autonomy were largely the result of Russian initiative, particularly
changes in the ministries of finance and war. We can see the
nature of the executive when we consider the men who headed the
ministries. At the beginning of autonomy, the prime minister and
minister of the interior was Da-Lama Tseren Chimit who, as the
term "Da-Lama" indicates, was a high religious official. All other
appointees were nobles: minister of war, Dalai Wang; of foreign
affairs, Hangda Dorji; of finance, Tushetu Wang; and of justice,
Erdeni Wang. The title "wang" denoted a prince of the second
Chinese rank; Hangda Dorji was a prince of the first rank.
Significantly, the Mongols retained Chinese ranks. There were
some changes in appointments during the period of autonomy, but
essentially the high nobility held most of the positions throughout
those years.[7]

The politics of autonomy proceeded in a leisurely, bland fashion,
with not a little intrigue. For example, Prime Minister Sain Noion
Khan, who soon succeeded Da-Lama Tseren Chimit, thereby making the cabinet entirely secular in composition, was poisoned. The
conduct of day-to-day affairs consisted partly of the Mongol princes'
attempts to influence the Urga Khutukhtu in favor of either pro-
Russian or pro-Chinse policies, as their needs dictated, but mostly
of feathering their own nests. A few Mongols envisaged the
creation of a Pan-Mongol state composed of Outer Mongolia,
Tannu-Tuva, Barga, and Inner Mongolia. Inner Mongolian nobles

---

[7] The best study of the politics of autonomy is Rupen. See also Friters, p. 44 ff.

who gathered at the court of the Urga Khutukhtu also played a role in this scheme. Both Russia and China, however, worked to frustrate it. The Sino-Russian accord of 1913, and the Tripartite Agreement of 1915 among Russia, China, and Outer Mongolia, while recognizing the changed status of tsarist Russia relative to Outer Mongolia, confined the latter's jurisdiction to the territories of the Khalkha princes and to the Kobdo region in the west.

Improvements in finance.—Any impulse to change Outer Mongolia had to come from without. In 1914 the tsarist government persuaded the Mongols to accept a financial adviser, Kozin, as a condition for a 3-million-ruble loan to rehabilitate Mongolian finances, improve stock raising, and promote internal reform. The condition was made because previous Russian loans had been quickly dissipated by the Mongol princes with no result other than their personal gain. Now it would be possible to introduce a measure of reform in the Ministry of Finance. Kozin was, however, unable to accomplish much. He set up a budget financed by *likin* (internal tariff) duties, and organized expenditures along the lines stipulated in the loan agreement. But, if we analyze the budgetary expenditures given in table 1, we see that they were largely confined to operations of the central government, with comparatively little provision for regional (hoshun) administrations. The bulk of the budget was concerned with funding support of the Urga Khutukhtu, the clergy, and the princes, a necessity since Chinese subsidies to them had been cut off.

The Fund for Reform was the only real innovation in expendi-

TABLE 1

OUTER MONGOLIAN BUDGETARY EXPENDITURES, 1913–14 to 1917–18

(In thousands of gold rubles)

Purpose	1913–14	1914–15	1915–16	1916–17	1917–18
Maintenance of Urga government	280.5	280.5	305.3	387.0	367.6
Maintenance of subprovincial governments [a]	31.8	35.5	45.5	62.7	72.2
Office and household expenses	300.0	300.0	300.0	428.6	239.6
Army	351.9	351.9	354.0	456.0	530.6
Pensions for princes	125.5	125.5	125.5	179.3	173.9
Fund for Reform	175.5	373.7	500.2	623.3	716.5
Total	1,265.2	1,467.1 [b]	1,630.5 [b]	2,136.9	2,100.4

[a] The subprovinces, four in all, were subordinate to a khan. These administrative units had little authority and few responsibilities, as implied by their budgets.
[b] Maiskii's totals for cols. 2 and 3 read 1468.9 and 1730.4, respectively.
SOURCE. I. M. Maiskii, *Sovremennaia Mongoliia* (Irkutsk, 1921), p. 283.

ture besides the money spent on the small new Mongolian army. The percentage allocations of the fund in 1916 are given in the itemization that follows: [8]

Administrative expenses	40.0
Expeditions and investigations	9.0
Veterinary services	3.0
Telegraph and telephone	16.5
Urga power station	16.0
Public education	5.3
Brick factory, coal mine, and printing plant	4.3
Miscellaneous	6.0

These expenditures assume their proper perspective when given comparative assessment. The power station constructed in Urga was hardly powerful enough to operate a single American home with a full complement of consumer durables. Expenditure on education was less than 0.05 gold rubles per capita per year. The public enterprises the government embarked on were tiny: the Nalaikha coal mines near Urga, the largest venture, employed only forty workers who used the most primitive techniques, including hand labor, to extract coal.[9] Furthermore, the Fund for Reform was largely expended on projects in Urga.

Such changes, small though they were, outraged many of the Urga Mongols. Some tsarist innovations—for instance, Zhamtsarano's school and newspaper—did not have the approval of the autonomous government; Korostovets, the very able tsarist minister in Urga, had set them up on his own initiative.[10]

Creation of a Mongolian army.—Another change was the formation of a Mongolian army, a difficult task for the Russians.[11] Although the Mongols were good shots and superb horsemen, they disliked soldiering as regulars and were useless as infantry; disease was rife among them and had a deteriorating effect on their physique. Even more important, the princes objected to having their subjects become soldiers. Despite these obstacles, the Russians did train a force of about 1,000 men, armed with machine guns and a few light field pieces, and had some influence on them, if we remember the personal history of Sukhe Bator and his group.

These, then, were the major changes during the period of autonomy: slight centralization of government functions, and

---

[8] I. Ia. Zlatkin, *MNR: Strana novoi demokratii* (Moscow, 1950), p. 98.

[9] Maiskii, p. 220.

[10] Robert A. Rupen, "The Buryat Intelligentsia," *Far Eastern Quarterly,* XV (1956), 394.

[11] For a competent British account see H. G. C. Perry-Ayscough and R. B. Otter-Barry, *With the Russians in Mongolia* (London, 1914), p. 114.

some progress brought about by the ministries of finance and war. A truly centralized political life had yet to evolve. In substance, power still remained with the hoshun princes, who continued to exercise the real military, executive, judicial, and administrative responsibilities in a countryside untouched by reform. The average Mongol not was drawn into political life at all. If he had a grievance he took it to his prince, who arbitrated it according to the customary law of the Mongols.[12]

The Social, Economic, and Political Structure

Classless social stratification.—The conditions described thus far raise the critical question: Was the Mongol of 1921 generally discontented with his prince? Reports vary, but the Mongol princes, judged according to their limited perspective, seem to have ruled not unfairly, and even wisely, in their hoshuns.[13] They were benefited by the fact that, although in theory there was considerable social stratification in Outer Mongolia, the Mongols displayed little sense of class.[14] The ruling princes (*noyan's*) and the nonruling ones (*taiji's*) alike were so by birthright, and claimed to trace their descent from Genghis Khan.

The commoners fell into three groups. The first, comprising the bulk of Mongols, were the *albatu's*, those who paid *alba*, a series of taxes and levies on labor of four kinds. First, they were responsible for their region's horse-relay (*urton*) system and had to provide horses, labor, food, and hospitality to passengers.[15] Second, they were liable to military, police, and sentry duty and to service as

---

[12] On Mongol law see V. A. Riasanovsky, *Fundamental Principles of Mongol Law* (Tientsin, 1937), and *Customary Law of the Mongol Tribes* (Harbin, 1929).

[13] One picture, perhaps idyllic, of the relationship between the princes and their subjects is given by Frans August Larson, *Larson, Duke of Mongolia* (Boston, 1930). Lattimore, *Nationalism and Revolution*, p. 58, drawing on A. M. Pozdneev as his source, asserts that Mongols held deep bitterness against their princes. Pozdneev was in Outer Mongolia partly to educate himself so that he could train the young tsarist Russians who would eventually take over Mongolia. His sense of mission in this endeavor is obvious from his book, A. M. Pozdneev, *Mongoliia i Mongoli*, I–II (St. Petersburg, 1896–1898). He came to find discontent in Mongolia and he found it. The pages Lattimore refers to (I, 45–46) give an account of Pozdneev's conversation with one Mongol and the conclusions Pozdneev all too readily drew from it.

[14] Maiskii, p. 127. Modern Marxists have tried to juggle the facts. The revised edition of Maiskii's book *Sovremennaia Mongoliia*, which appeared with the new title *Mongoliia nakanune revoliutsii* (Moscow, 1959), presents statistics to show that class stratification existed in Outer Mongolia at the time of his visit. The first edition presents the converse judgment based on the same statistics.

[15] It has been estimated that, in 1915, 36 percent of all regional expenditures were devoted to the horse-relay service (see Zlatkin, p. 99; and also Ia. Ryzhik, "Khoziaistvennoe i kul'turnoe stroitel'stvo MNR," *Planovoe Khoziaistvo*, no. 6 [1936], p. 170). The horse-relay system was the major means of communication used by Chinese and Mongol authorities.

orderlies at regional and subprovincial offices. Third, they were liable for regional debts and had to provide the salaries of the ruling prince. Fourth, they were subject to levies for the support of the political system either at the subprovincial or the regional level. The albatus owned property and had full rights to it. The second group, the *khamjilga*'s (half as numerous as the albatus), owed personal service to the princes and nobles, could be called on to pay their masters' debts, and had to pay some form of alba, but they were not liable to military service. The khamjilga tended his prince's herds, receiving a portion of the stock's output in return. The prince had exclusive property rights, but the khamjilga had customary rights to both the herds and the lands that supported his nomadic life. The *darkhan*'s, the third group, were commoners who had been freed from tax and other duties in return for distinguished services to the community; their number was small.

As far as we know, tax levies on the commoner in Outer Mongolia do not seem to have been increased just before 1921—a point of importance because in Inner Mongolia they had. There the nobility had tried to tax their subjects more heavily in order to maintain a style of life increasingly affected by expanding contacts with the West. In addition, the Inner Mongolian nobility had rented land to agriculturalists to increase their own incomes, an action highly unpopular with the average Mongol. To sum up, the tax system operating in Outer Mongolia was an old and traditional one to which the individual Mongol was fully adjusted.

One other point needs stressing: natural disaster had a way of leveling distinctions between rulers and ruled. The major wealth, as well as source of income, of the Mongols was their stock. But, given their primitive techniques of caring for their herds and the severe natural hazards their country presented, today's wealthy stock owner could become tomorrow's pauper. It was not unusual for princes to share the suffering of their khamjilgas, and the nonruling princes had little chance to recoup their losses by exactions from the population at large. Thus, nature's capital levies blurred and distorted class boundaries and the sense of class membership. This was probably the reason that the Mongols did not fear their nobility and that ancient ways could be preserved among them. In Inner Mongolia, in contrast, the nobility had augmented their wealth by collecting land rents from Chinese immigrants, had grown rich, and had become alienated from their subjects by taking up a sedentary life.

The secular authority of the prince.—The basis of secular political life in Mongolia was still the court of a hoshun's ruling prince. There the Mongols found a justice that squared with their sense of custom and precedent. This state of political affairs had, of course, been of initial help to the invaders. The Outer Mongolian was loyal to his religion and to his prince; he had no notion of loyalty to a state. These circumstances explain how the rapid shifts in control of Outer Mongolia in barely more than a decade (1910–1921) could occur, with Chinese, tsarist Russians, White troops, and Red troops controlling Urga in succession. So long as any foreign power was careful to rule through the traditional nobility and through the Urga Khutukhtu and other religious dignitaries, the population was compliant. Thus the Outer Mongolia of 1921 gave little evidence of a revolutionary spirit. There were not even organizations offering a broad social mandate, nor was there a Mongolian "nationality" at all.

The religious authority of the lama.—Like the princes and the nomads, the leaders of Lamaism were not interested in change. We have already noted that Lamaism, as an organized church, generally was favorably inclined toward the Chinese. Its structure was more centralized than that of the secular polity, and it was an extremely wealthy institution.[16] Above all, a substantial segment of the Mongolian population willingly accorded it a customary loyalty.

Maiskii (table 2) gives the breakdown of the male population according to the 1918 census for Khalkha, that is, for the whole of Outer Mongolia with the exception of the western Kobdo region. Almost 50 percent of the male population of Khalkha came under

TABLE 2

The Class Structure of the Outer Mongolian Male Population in Khalkha, 1919–20

Class	Number	Percentage of total
Princes	205	0.1
Lesser nobility	13,274	5.6
Albatu's	62,048	26.1
Khamjilga's	39,389	16.6
Lamas and *shabi*'s	105,577	44.5 [a]
Classless	16,915	7.1

a If we estimate for the country as a whole from the internal evidence of the census information that Maiskii gives us, the percentage of lamas and shabis would be slightly reduced.

Source: I. M. Maiskii, *Sovremennaia Mongoliia* (Irkutsk, 1921), p. 29.

16 Maiskii, *Sovremennaia Mongoliia*, p. 127, shows that the church owned 17 percent of all livestock. Were we to include an estimate for immovable wealth, the percentage of all wealth owned by the church would be much higher.

religious authority, but not all these men were lamas; *shabi* status was essentially the same as either albatu or khamjilga status, except that the shabi owed loyalty or services to a religious rather than to a secular authority, and did not have to render military service.

In 1919, only 40,000 lamas actually lived in monasteries.[17] The remainder, the lay lamas, lived like the average Mongol, except for personal restrictions according to the number of Buddhist vows each had taken (vows they appear to have honored rarely). Like the secular commoner, the lay lama married, had children, and engaged in economic activity. Maiskii puts the population of Outer Mongolia in 1918 at 647,600, at worst an underestimate of about 100,000.[18] Of this population, 5,000 were Russians; 100,000, Chinese; and 542,600, Mongols.[19] Monastic lamas thus constituted some 7 percent of the population. The 115,000 lamas and shabis in the whole of Outer Mongolia constituted about 20 percent of the Mongol population. Since the shabis could be heads of households, perhaps upward of one-third of all Mongols came under religious rather than secular authority, the majority being of course subject to the Urga Khutukhtu.

The social pervasiveness of Lamaism.—Despite their status, the secular Mongols, the remaining two-thirds of the population, had deeper loyalties toward religious leaders than toward their princes. For one thing, the religious leaders were closer to him; many secular Mongols had lamas as relatives and might either be supporting them or be supported by them. For another, religion was an inseparable part of Mongolian life. Consequently, all important occasions and decisions would be referred either to the representatives of Lamaism or to its rules and precedents. Moreover, those subject to some form of religious control were taxed more lightly and treated more favorably, a factor that helps to explain the growth of the religious sector.

Life in the monasteries did not impose severe restraints on the individual lama, because of a general conformity to an intrinsically strict mode of life. The official attitude adopted toward lamas was even tolerant and permissive.[20] The monastery provided opportu-

---

[17] *Ibid.*, p. 107. Rupen, "Outer Mongolian Nationalism," p. 29, disputes Maiskii's overall figures for lamas and shabis as too high. There have been higher estimates, such as that of A. P. Boloban, cited by Maiskii, *Sovremennaia Mongoliia*, p. 28.

[18] Maiskii, *Sovremennaia Mongoliia*, p. 16. I have rounded Maiskii's figures, as his use of more exact figures gives a spurious indication of census accuracy.

[19] The total for Mongols is probably an underestimate.

[20] B. B. Baradin, "Buddiiskie monastyri," in M. N. Bogdanov (ed.), *Ocherki istorii Buriat-mongol'skogo naroda* (Verkhneudinsk, 1926), p. 126. Baradin discusses the typical school monastery of Buriat Mongolia. A brief but good treatment of monastic life in Outer Mongolia may be found in G. C. Binsteed, "Life in a Khalkha Steppe Lamasery," *Journal of the Royal Asiatic Society*, XXIII (1914), 847–900.

nities for advancement to posts of considerable status. A *tsant-sotba*, for example, performed civil duties in an area ruled by a khutukhtu and enjoyed a status and rights comparable to those of a regional prince. Higher posts in the religious sector were open to all in practice, although according to the rules members of the nobility were supposed to be excluded. The man who by birth was prohibited from exercising secular authority could, on the basis of his ability, do so in the service of a prominent khutukhtu.

Mongols who accepted their religion either from piety or because of custom and familial attachments—the loyal shabi, the contented and usually illiterate and ignorant lama as well as the able man who occupied a position of religious authority, or, in other words, the Mongol population at large—benefited from Lamaism and were steeped in its conservative attitude toward life.

MONGOL-CHINESE RELATIONS

So far the picture drawn of Outer Mongolia prior to 1921 has been one of a culture displaying great solidarity and cohesion. The Mongols' specialization in stock raising, however, made them highly dependent on the Chinese economy. The direct consequence of this situation was the buildup of a Chinese population in Outer Mongolia. It is pertinent, therefore, to investigate whether there was a strong antagonism or a conflict of interests between the Mongols and the Chinese.

Chinese Dominance in Trade and Finance

The bulk of the Chinese in Outer Mongolia in the period under discussion (some 75 percent, according to Maiskii's estimate [21]) were traders. They supplied about one-third of the Mongols' consumer needs,[22] largely with commodities manufactured abroad.[23]

[21] Maiskii, *Sovremennaia Mongoliia*, p. 108. The description of Chinese trading which follows rests on Maiskii unless otherwise indicated.

Of the 100,000 Chinese, 15,000 were artisans and 5,000 were agriculturalists. The latter figure indicates a decline in the number of agriculturalists from the 1912 peak, given by Rupen, "Outer Mongolian Nationalism." The number of artisans and traders may also have declined, so that the proportion of Chinese relative to Mongols in 1911 would have been higher than one-seventh. In addition to the occupational groups mentioned above, there were some domiciled bureaucrats in 1911.

[22] Maiskii, *Sovremennaia Mongoliia*, p. 157, estimated that 69.2 percent of consumption was out of home production. I. M. Morosov, cited by Zlatkin, p. 30, estimated it to have been 63.2 percent. These figures, arrived at by examination of household budgets, are really educated guesses. As Outer Mongolia was not foreign territory to China, there are no official import and export data for comparison with national output data.

[23] Maiskii, *Sovremennaia Mongoliia*, p. 189, estimated that 6 percent of Chinese trade goods were manufactured in Outer Mongolia.

The Chinese at the time were, and historically always had been, primarily concerned with exchanging consumption goods in return for the by-products of the nomads' stock-raising output. There are only two exceptions. First, some transit trade had taken place in Mongolia, but the opening of the Chinese seaports, the construction of the Suez Canal, and the construction of the Trans-Siberian and Chinese Eastern railways killed what had never amounted to a sizable economic activity.[24] Second, two of the large Chinese mercantile houses functioned primarily as banking houses: Ta Sheng Kuei and Tian I Deh. They financed the Urga Khutukhtu, the Mongol princes, the church, and the regional administrations. Ta Sheng Kuei, which had been in Mongolia for 300 years, had great prestige, for most of the regional administrations did business with it. While both banking houses handled trade goods, they did so largely in connection with the servicing and requital of their own loans.

The two mercantile houses apart, some twenty-five Chinese firms,[25] which Lattimore has likened as firms to the Hudson's Bay Company, dominated the Mongol trade. These firms sold the Mongol all the goods he needed for personal consumption and for raising his stock, and in return purchased the stock raisers' output. This general trading was a natural consequence of the limited Mongolian market, which could not support more specialized firms. Of course, none of the large firms was exclusively concerned with that market. The network of their trade and their agents extended to nomadic encampments, of which there were many thousands in Outer Mongolia. Hence, trading as an economic enterprise was a heavy user of labor and required few fixed facilities, except for warehouses in the major towns such as Urga, Uliasutai, and Kobdo.

In addition to the large firms, there was a host of small ones, dependent on the larger traders for supplies, capital, and their own market. These small firms were usually owned by men who had been salesmen in the larger firms but thought they could do better working for themselves. The larger firms permitted the smaller ones to exist because this arrangement cheapened the cost of procuring the Mongols' products and because the small traders constituted a remunerative source of return by paying interest on the working capital extended to them.[26]

---

[24] Rupen, "Outer Mongolian Nationalism," p. 167 ff.
[25] Owen Lattimore, *Inner Asian Frontiers of China* (2d ed.; New York, 1951), p. 92.
[26] A major cost in procuring goods was the salaries of salesmen. Permission to salesmen to work for themselves probably lowered the effective salaries they earned.

The presence of Chinese other than merchants in Outer Mongolia caused no political problem. There were some 15,000 Chinese artisans in the region who either kept small shops in Urga or wandered from nomadic encampment to encampment selling their skills. Chinese artisans do not seem to have been unpopular in Outer Mongolia, although they were despised as being "different." In 1921 there were also 5,000 Chinese agriculturalists in the area. This represents a decline from their peak number in 1912, which even then had not been large. There is no doubt that the agriculturalist was unpopular with the Mongol nomad, although perhaps not so unpopular as the squatter in the American West was with the rancher. In any event, the problem was small and was confined to a few regions in the north. Prior to 1911, quite a few Chinese bureaucrats had been domiciled in Outer Mongolia. They had been as unpopular there as their kind had been throughout the Chinese empire, and by 1921 most of them had left. If there was a "Chinese problem" in Outer Mongolia in 1921, it was tantamount to the problem of Chinese trading institutions.

A potentially irredentist minority may pose a problem to any regime, and may be thoroughly unpopular with the population at large. But the extent of the problem hinges upon the power of the minority, upon its political ambitions, and upon its relationship with the majority. The larger Chinese trading houses in 1921 still preserved good relations with the Outer Mongolian princes and religious leaders, despite the fact that there was no formal Chinese government in the region. Apart from their desire to maintain these friendly relationships with the secular and religious authorities, the Chinese had no political ambitions, influence, or power. The critical issue was their relationship with the people at large. Had this relationship proved to be an embittered one, the Mongols would have had reason to be strongly discontented with the state of their society in 1921.

The general opinion of both tsarist and Soviet explorers and scholars, and of those Westerners who visisted Outer Mongolia, was that the Chinese trader battened on the Mongol, exploited him ruthlessly, and consequently was hated. One tsarist source, for example, asserts that the large firms parceled out the market among themselves, acting in this collusion to maintain market control with the connivance of the Chinese bureaucrats.[27] Maiskii, representing Soviet thought, concurred with his tsarist predecessors in believing that the prevailing trade system was used to impover-

---

[27] W. Karamisheff, *Mongolia and Western China* (Tientsin, 1925), p. 288.

ish the Mongols. According to the Russian scholars, this result was partly due to the circumstance that individual trading houses constituted regional monopolies and monopsonies, and was also partly attributable to the fact that easily extended credit had gradually led the Mongols to mortgage not only their future output for immediate consumption but also their herds, which were the source of salable by-products. The latter interpretation, however, seems exaggerated.

Mongolian Economic Indebtedness

It was inevitable that the Mongols should resort to credit. Whereas they could sell their livestock and its by-products only from March to September, their need for goods such as tea, cereals, and cloth had to be met throughout the year. It was credit that enabled the Mongol to spread his purchases over the year and to buy in anticipation of his expected output. Should his planned stock-raising output fail, however, or should he be a spendthrift, the use of credit could lead him into irretrievable debt. As interest charges were high, it was not long before a debt approached the value of a man's personal wealth.

The Mongol was also subject to levies for public debts. When a regional administration became indebted, all Mongol households in that region were held collectively responsible for restitution. Princes thus could incur debts at will and tax their khamjilgas. In the Russian literature on Outer Mongolia this practice is called *krugovaia poruka* (mutual guarantee).[28] Burdened with these additional debts, the individual Mongol eventually stood to lose not only his personal equity in the livestock he tended but also faced heavy debt-service charges.

Nevertheless, the picture of heavy Mongol indebtedness to the Chinese which is conveyed by some Russian observers definitely seems overdrawn. Even Grumm-Grzhimailo, a usually reliable source, comments: "Little by little all the cattle mortgaged by the Mongols became the property of the Chinese traders, the Mongols playing the role of herders of another's herd, bearing nonetheless all the responsibility for the life of the livestock, for neither losses due to natural disaster nor losses caused by wolves were taken into account."[29] The evidence that is available to support Grumm-

---

[28] For a typical Western account of this practice, see Lattimore, *Inner Asian Frontiers*, pp. 94–95.

[29] G. E. Grumm-Grzhimailo, *Zapadnaia Mongoliia i Uriankhaiskii krai*, Vol. III, Pt. II (Leningrad, 1930), p. 496. Grumm-Grzhimailo did, however, think that much of Maiskii's account was based on fables propagated by Russian merchants in Outer Mongolia.

Grzhimailo's gloomy picture is neither convincing in itself nor supported by quantitative data. For one thing, the tsarist Russians who largely propagated such pessimistic views felt they had a mission in Outer Mongolia, and it is not at all unlikely that they collected evidence to suit their preconceived ideas. One such preconception was that Outer Mongolia felt oppressed by Chinese rule. There was, moreover, the general tendency among writers on Central Asia to view lending as an injurious practice, to consider any form of taxation of the population as bad policy, and to decry as harmful the growth of trade and specialization.

Maiskii, whose sympathies regarding territorial expansion in Outer Mongolia lay entirely with tsarist Russia, certainly seems to exaggerate on the topic of indebtedness. Whereas he mentions interest charges at an annual price of 80 to 100 percent of the principal, Pozdneev states that interest charges in the Chinese empire were 36 percent.[30] Furthermore, as soon as interest charges accrued to the size of the principal sum, the total debt was frozen. This, of course, would be onerous enough: in practice it meant that if one borrowed $100, for example, the maximum debt would grow to $200, with a service charge of $72 annually. In other words, the price of loans was high. The Mongols were, however, not forced to take loans at such interest; if they did, often it saved them from personal hardship, even starvation. Moreover, Grumm-Grzhimailo says that the Chinese charged the Mongols no explicit interest for the first six months of credit for the purchase of trade goods.[31] Normally, therefore, the effective price of short-term credit lay in the higher prices of goods, and so was levied in a way the Mongol could easily handle.

The laws and customs about interest tell us nothing about the effective rate of interest the Mongols paid. Neither do they inform us about the really important question: the volume and dispersion of indebtedness. According to Maiskii, the combined debts of the individual regional administrations or hoshuns amounted to 11 million liang, or 15 million gold rubles, in 1918.[32] To this total must be added the autonomous government's debt of 4 million rubles to the tsarist government. But the servicing of these nonpersonal debts, even at 36 percent interest, should not have been too onerous. Maiskii puts such obligations per household at 35 rubles per year, which at the legal interest rate would amount to an annual service charge of about 13 rubles. Against this we must set

<hr />

[30] Pozdneev, I, 41.
[31] Vol. III, Pt. II, p. 494.
[32] Maiskii, *Sovremennaia Mongoliia,* p. 286.

an average household income of 700 rubles and average personal wealth of 1,850 rubles. Another source puts the personal debts of the Mongol princes at 668,000 liang, or about 1 million gold rubles.[33] This would be a per capita debt of about 2 rubles, assuming that the princes did not meet the interest charges out of sales of their own herds of livestock, but levied them on the population at large. In short, although some Mongol households were heavily burdened and some regions were crippled with debt, the evidence we have does not point to general heavy indebtedness.

Outer Mongolia's Gain from Russo-Chinese Trade Rivalry

After 1860 the Russians gained a toehold in Outer Mongolia by diplomatic action, and until 1911 slowly expanded trade with the region. Thus commenced Russo-Chinese competition in that area. Prior to the revolution of 1917 Russian journals and periodicals concerned with Far Eastern questions had complained incessantly that the Russians were being driven from the Mongol market by Chinese competition,[34] a complaint that appears to contradict the facts. It is true that the buildup of a Russian population and of Russian traders in Outer Mongolia was slow (see table 3). Next, because Russian traders were largely concerned with procuring commodities from the Mongols rather than with supplying them with goods, Russia always had a sizable import surplus with Outer Mongolia. In addition, changing transportation routes had affected the profitability of vending some and of procuring other commodi-

TABLE 3

THE NUMBER OF RUSSIANS DOMICILED IN MAJOR TRADING TOWNS
IN OUTER MONGOLIA, AND IN THE COUNTRY AS A WHOLE,
IN SELECTED YEARS BETWEEN 1876 AND 1920

Year	Urga	Uliasutai	Kobdo	Whole country
1876	a	15–20	4–5	20 +
1892	100	15–20	15–20	130 +
1900	a	a	a	300–400
1910	600	40–50	40–50	680 +
1912	a	a	a	1,500
1919–20	3,000	100	300	5,000 b

a Data unavailable.
b Of the 1919–20 total, 4,000 were traders.
SOURCE: I. M. Maiskii, *Sovremennaia Mongoliia* (Irkutsk, 1921), p. 88.

---

[33] Dispatch no. 33, *Krasnyi Arkhiv*, XXXVII (1929), 29.
[34] For instance, many articles in issues of *Vestnik Azii* stress this theme.

ties in the Mongolian market. Despite these facts, trade statistics [35] do not seem to confirm a reversal of the total volume of Russian trade with the Mongols. We know the Chinese were perturbed by Russian trade penetration of their territory, and that the Russians in turn complained of Chinese countermeasures. We may conclude, therefore, that this rivalry placed the Mongols in a healthy competitive situation. As the Mongols lived by trading livestock by-products, they always had the choice of herding their stock to the best market. Thus, unless all Chinese and Russian firms agreed on what prices to offer and to pay, the charge of regional monopolization is hard to understand. The Russians would have had to collude with the Chinese to prevent competition from emerging at all.[36]

Initially, Russian traders in Outer Mongolia had been Siberian merchants who, compared with the Chinese, had been poorly financed and organized. By the turn of the twentieth century, however, larger and better Russian firms started to move into the Mongol market.[37] It should be noted, however, that the total circulation of Russian imports from, and exports to, Outer Mongolia, measured against the Chinese total, never reached a substantial proportion.[38]

Consequences of the Decline in China's Favored Position

After 1911 Russia's trade with Outer Mongolia naturally benefited to some extent, partly because the Mongols, both individually and officially, gave vent to anti-Chinese feeling. Quite a few Chinese had to flee the country, abandoning their stock and warehouses or selling them to the Russians at disaster prices. We have no exact idea of how many Chinese merchants were affected in this way, but the number was probably small.[39] More important, the Russo-

[35] Statistics are available in M. I. Bogolepov and M. N. Sobolev, *Ocherki russko-mongol'skoi torgovli*, I (Tomsk, 1911), 165. Most sources have accepted the Russian view (see Friters, p. 54 ff.; Rupen, "Outer Mongolian Nationalism," p. 182 ff.; Maiskii, *Sovremennaia Mongoliia*, p. 206; B. Gur'ev, "Russkaia torgovliia v Zapadnoi Mongolii," *Vestnik Azii*, no. 10 [1911], p. 93; Violet Conolly, *Soviet Economic Policy in the East: Turkey, Persia, Afghanistan, Mongolia and Tana Tuva, Sin Kiang* [London, 1933]).

[36] There had been new Chinese entrants even before the Russians entered the Mongolian markets (see Grumm-Grzhimailo, Vol. III, Pt. II, p. 486).

[37] The following firms entered the market: Stuken and Co. in 1904, Biderman in 1909, and Shvetsov in 1911.

[38] As Outer Mongolia was a region of China, no separate import and export data for Mongolian trade with Russia were recorded. But through one trade town, Kukukoto, Chinese trade with Mongolia in 1908 and 1909 was six times the Russian trade (see Bogolepov and Sobolev, I, 165).

[39] Maiskii had found 100,000 Chinese in Mongolia in 1919. Furthermore, the receipts of the budget during the period of autonomy show increasing returns from imposts on the Chinese. This could hardly be consistent with a striking decline in their number.

Mongol agreement of November, 1911, gave Russians the right of free trade with Outer Mongolia, the right to lease and own property, and the right to lease land for cultivation.[40] At the same time, however, Chinese imports were being subjected to a 5 percent tax. This tax in itself was not seriously discriminatory, but it became so in combination with the likin taxes which rested exclusively on the Chinese. Generally, however, the Russians were not in Outer Mongolia long enough after these changes for the market forces to have had a chance to work themselves out and for Russian traders to have moved into the Mongol market in significant numbers.

In the years directly after 1911, it is interesting to note, the dislocation of Chinese trade caused the Mongols much dissatisfaction. In 1913 Baranov heard many complaints from Mongols about Russian traders; he believed that the good feelings of 1911 toward Russians had been dissipated.[41] In September, 1913, the Urga Khutukhtu himself gave strict orders for the safe passage of a Chinese caravan from Kalgan to Urga to relieve shortages.[42] The Chinese also received Russian help in reentering the market by being permitted to use the names of Russian firms as forwarding addresses to circumvent both the 5 percent import tax and the likin duties.

Nonmarket forces also affected Russia's trade position. By 1914, Russian merchants in the Far East were complaining that mobilization was affecting them.[43] By 1916, Russian exports of goods to Outer Mongolia had practically ceased. And by the second half of 1917, the rapid inflation of the ruble dislocated Russian-Mongolian trade completely. By 1919 "nearly all the Russian firms were inactive, regional branches in many areas were closed, and the warehouses were empty of goods." [44] Although after 1911 other countries and their traders had become interested in Outer Mongolia as a market, they did little to cultivate it.[45]

This survey of the relevant information indicates that the experience of the years 1911–1914, years uncomplicated by war,

---

[40] Friters, p. 71.
[41] A. M. Baranov, *Khalkha-Aimak Tsetsen Khana* (Harbin, 1919), p. **4 ff.**
[42] G. C. Binsteed, in *China Year Book*, 1914, p. 628.
[43] *Vestnik Azii*, no. 35–36 (1915), p. 115.
[44] Maiskii, *Sovremennaia Mongoliia*, p. 209.
[45] Outer Mongolia is scarcely mentioned in G. C. Allen and Audrey G. Donnithorne, *Western Enterprise in Far Eastern Development: China and Japan* (London, 1954), pp. 37–38. Russian accounts that try to prove capitalistic and imperialistic exploitation of Outer Mongolia prior to 1921 have a hard time of it. See, for instance, the slender evidence presented in I. G. Iur'ev, "K voprosu ob inostrannom kapitale vo Vneshnei Mongolii do narodno-demokraticheskoi revoliutsii 1921 g. i v pervye ee gody," *Kratkie soobshcheniia instituta vostokovedeniia*, no. 6 (1952), p. 56.

established the dimensions of the task of ousting Chinese traders from Outer Mongolia. Chinese trading was highly important to the Outer Mongolian economy. Despite this fact, the Russo-Chinese trade rivalry gave the Mongols competitive opportunities in selling their products.

More generally, the problems of indebtedness and competition touch on the fundamental Mongol attitude toward the Chinese in the historic year 1921. The fact that the Chinese traders had stayed on, despite taxes, administrative harassment, and personal danger, leads us to suspect that they were in Outer Mongolia because the Mongol populace wanted them there as an important segment of the native economy, and because the services the Chinese provided were useful rather than crippling. It required from the new rulers a long and determined attempt to oust the Chinese from the Mongol market after the invasion of 1921.

One final although incidental point needs to be stressed. Soviet sources have tried, unsuccessfully, to present Outer Mongolia prior to 1921 as an object of Western imperialist penetration. In a sense it was unfortunate for the new rulers that there had been no stronger Western impact, for it would have lightened the task of the Soviet Union appreciably. A Western trading system based on more extensive use of capital could have been taken over more easily in the conditions prevailing in 1921, and without the attendant difficulties of a large alien, and potentially irredentist, population that was not particularly unpopular among the natives of the invaded territory.

THE SECULAR ECONOMY

Thus far our investigation of possible sources of social friction and grievance among the Outer Mongolians has proved negative. Outer Mongolia in 1921 was, however, an underdeveloped region, and the state of its economy could conceivably have caused widespread discontent. There were problems aplenty: a low standard of living; illiteracy; dominance of an agricultural sector, with low capitalization per worker; a small, possibly zero, rate of investment in the secular sector; extravagant building of monuments and hoarding of resources in the religious sector; heavy dependence on primary exports and on foreign markets for consumption goods in a world of autarkic national policies; a chaotic monetary system; a primitive banking system; lack of an educated elite; a sparse and stationary, if not declining, population located so far from most world markets that transportation costs reached economically unprofitable levels. The last-mentioned feature was the most disabling of all.

Lattimore sums up the economic potential of Outer Mongolia in the following words: "In potential resources, a country like Mongolia ranks with that part of the United States lying west of the Mississippi, east of the Rocky Mountains, and north of Texas. It can combine the exploitation of agriculture, livestock, mining and other industry." [46] Unlike the American West, however, Outer Mongolia lacked one major advantage: she was not part of a larger economic system, itself undergoing economic growth at a rapid pace. Outer Mongolia had to defray the costs of educating her people and of building her schools, roads, hospitals, and other capital facilities out of the slender investment fund her yearly national output guaranteed. Alternately, she would have had to find outside sources of finance, with all the difficulties attending extensive importation of capital from a larger country.

Climate as a Determinant

In regard to climate, Outer Mongolia is as well- or as ill-endowed as the region with which Lattimore compares it. The country lies between the fiftieth and forty-second parallels; Urga (48° N.) has roughly the same latitude as Grand Forks, North Dakota (47° 56′ N.). Its continental position gives the country a harsh climate. During winter the center of the Asiatic anticyclone locates over the country and blankets it with masses of cold, stable air. In consequence, hardly any rain or snow falls, and the atmosphere is still and brilliantly clear. The average temperature in January, the coldest month, is −16.6°F in Urga in the north and 3.2°F in the south (in the town now known as Dalan-dzadagad, lat. 42° N.). In summer Outer Mongolia is subject to the effects of the great cyclone that centers over the Indian continent, but receives little moisture from outside air masses owing to the high mountain barriers over which the air must pass. Hence Outer Mongolia's rainfall originates locally and is caused by unstable, warm air rising off the hot plateau or sweeping over lakes and up mountainsides. The large daily variation in temperature is also responsible for much turbulence. As is characteristic of dry regions, the country is showered with rainfall that is erratic in volume by day, region, and year. The bulk falls in the summer months, but, on average, the country does not receive more than 8 to 10 inches, with only a few areas receiving more than 12. Outer Mongolia's

---

[46] Lattimore, *Inner Asian Frontiers*, p. 76.

continental position and average elevation of some 5,000 feet above sea level help to produce a rigorous winter and to moderate the summer heat. July, the warmest month, produces temperatures of only 64.4°F in Urga and 71.6°F in the south. There are also insufficient consecutive days of sunshine to promote a reliable dryland agriculture. Cold winters and moderate summers combine to bring the annual zero-centigrade isotherm down far below Urga and to scatter permafrost deposits in the coal mines of nearby Nalaikha. The natural fauna and flora specific to this climate are thin. The northern part of Outer Mongolia is sparsely wooded and mountainous, and the east is a land of rolling grass steppe. There are mountains in the center and in the west, the latter also sparsely wooded. The southeast is desertlike.

For a country with an acute transportation problem, Outer Mongolia's rivers are poorly located. Two-thirds drain internally, and of those having external outlets only the Selenga offered in the 1920's the possibility of commercial navigation on some of its stretches. Many of the rivers are large: the Kerulen, the Tes, the Kobdo, and the Dzabkhan. All of them are liable to flash floods, and the Dzabkhan dries up completely in the summer months. All the rivers freeze in winter, the smaller ones completely.[47]

The Dominance of Stock Raising

Type of stock and its uses.—In 1921 Outer Mongolia was still a virtually unexplored and unmapped region. Yet, despite their harsh environment, the country's inhabitants had made a rather impressive adjustment. Given their tastes, the level of their techniques, and their supply of capital and labor, the nomads of Outer Mongolia had made wide use of their country's resources. Maiskii estimated, partly on the basis of the 1918 census, that the Mongols of Outer Mongolia herded 12.7 million head of stock.[48] Although this figure is almost certainly too low, the composition of the herds he gives in millions of animals provides a clue to many aspects of nomadic economic life: horses, 1.5; camels, 0.3; cattle, 1.4; and sheep and goats, 9.5. We must remember that the Mongol consumed not only from his own production but also from the products of trade. Thus the herds he raised reflected the need to produce both trade and subsistence goods.

---

[47] The standard geography of the country is E. M. Murzaev, *MNR: Fisiko-geograficheskie opisanie* (2d ed.; Moscow, 1952). The best Western source is Erich Thiel, *Die Mongolei* (Munich, 1958), which is based mainly on the large number of Soviet studies published since 1921.

[48] Maiskii, *Sovremennaia Mongoliia*, p. 123.

Sheep, for example, provided milk for tea (*manja*), which was the staple of the Mongolian diet and actually was a gruel, or soup, of cereals and tea laced with fat. Cheese and fermented wines also were made from the milk. Wool was used to provide covering and insulation for tents, and dung was used as fuel. Pelts were made into clothing, bone and sinews were shaped into small tools and trinkets, and intestines and blood were turned into sausage. The fat from sheep tails was considered a delicacy; in earlier centuries the Mongolian fat-tailed sheep was probably bred selectively for this feature. Animals were not slaughtered for daily consumption needs, but their carcasses provided food for festive occasions. As trade goods, sheep on the hoof, wool, and fleeces were the major commodities. In general, Mongolian herds concentrated on sheep in a proportion of four to one.

The goat was a poor substitute for the sheep, but was used in the more arid regions, where it could survive better. Camels were primarily transport beasts, but provided such incidental subsistence goods as milk, wool for ropes and thread, and skin for bags. Camel transport and wool were major trade commodities.

Cattle provided subsistence goods and trade transportation services, and were used for plowing and traction. Their main use was to provide meat, milk, and leather, the latter constituting yet another trade good. Some yaks were distributed in the cattle herds. Yaks were found in mountainous regions and served much the same purposes as the Mongolian longhorn cattle, except that yak hair was used for rope and that these animals were not used at plow. There were also some hybrids, crosses between yaks and Mongolian cattle. Yaks made up about 26 percent of the cattle herds, and crosses, about 4 percent. The hybrids were not bred selectively; they were found only in regions where the distribution of yaks and longhorns overlapped naturally, that is, in alpine meadows.[49] Horses provided transportation services and were a valuable trade good; they were exported to China, where they were used to breed mules. Their by-products were hides, and milk for wine production. Mongols of wealth preferred to keep large horse herds.

Share herding and other laborsaving customs.—The herd of the average Mongol, who had not specialized in providing caravan services, would be similar in composition to the majority of herds unless the owner's tastes for subsistence goods were rather out of the ordinary. A Mongol of average income would have about 200 sheep, three mares or more for milking, and perhaps one cow.

---

[49] I. F. Shul'zhenko, "Zhivotnovodstvo MNR," *Trudy Mongol'skoi Komissii*, no. 61 (Moscow, 1954), p. 124.

Naturally, his herds would partly reflect the fact that different animals produced better in different climatic regions. The poorer nomads tended to have more sheep in their herds, but as they grew wealthier their holdings of cattle and horses increased.[50] Inasmuch as both horse and sheep tending in Mongolian conditions required a considerable amount of labor, the nomad of low income used the minimum number of horses to tend his herds.

The nomadic Mongols were short of labor. They could always increase the output of their herds, for example, by special care for lambs and ewes. But this would require a considerable expenditure of labor and would go against traditional standards of leisure. The average nomad thus confined himself to seeking out good pastures for his herds, to caring for his lambs when they were very young, and to standing watch by day over his sheep; cattle and horses grazed unattended.

The way in which herding was conducted shows concern to husband labor. A herding camp (hoton) was composed of family groups (ail's), each usually comprising four to eight families. Normally, the ail was bound by family ties and was a patrilocal, extended family. Some herding groups, however, were composed of friends, and some even included unrelated poor or wealthier persons.[51] Soviet authors tend to stress the latter relationship as the typical one and present the herding camp as a device to exploit surplus labor, an interpretation that seems false.[52] For, when nomads tended herds belonging to others, they were entitled to some of the herd's output. The fact that such "share-herding" agreements were entered into by quite wealthy nomads [53]—that they, too, herded for others—suggests that this arrangement constituted not calculated exploitation but a free transaction of surplus labor for a portion of the output it produced.

In one well-studied area, a herd of 1,000 was the largest that could be grazed as a unit, owing to the fact that larger herds left insufficient pasture for the tail sheep.[54] If a hoton or a group of families had fewer than 1,000 sheep, they could watch a larger herd as easily as a smaller one. The share-herding agreement thus

---

[50] Herbert Harold Vreeland, Mongol Community and Kinship Structure, Human Relations Area Files (New Haven, 1954), p. 32 ff.

[51] Ibid., pp. 10, 34, 35, 51, 88.

[52] V. Maslennikov, MNR na puti k sotzializmu (Moscow, 1951), p. 70; F. S. Tsaplin, "Sel'skoe khoziaistvo," in I. Ia. Zlatkin (ed.), MNR: Sbornik statei (Moscow, 1952), p. 102.

[53] Pozdneev, I, 55, gives evidence that middle-income Mongols were engaged in share herding. Vreeland, p. 101 ff., shows the terms of one agreement: 70 percent of the wool, all the milk, and all the lambs.

[54] Vreeland, p. 32 ff. This is the Narobanchin Temple area.

may be seen as a device assuring a return for minimum additional expenditures of labor. In the average camp all herding duties were merged and rotated, men, women, and all but the smallest children taking part.

Share herding is not the only laborsaving social custom that had evolved in Outer Mongolia. For example, the lambs were separated from the ewes when still very young, for they could not go so far to pasture; joint grazing of ewes and lambs would almost have doubled herding duties. For this reason, two herding camps were set up some distance apart, one tending all the lambs, the other the ewes and the rams; this practice was known as *saahalta*. At night, however, the herds would be separated into ewes and their lambs and rams and brought near the tents, where dogs would guard them.

If the herding camp wished to control lambing time, it would separate ewes from rams, but generally this was not done because of the additional expenditure of labor required. Occasionally, rams were dressed with aprons to prevent mating. No special care was taken of ewes during lambing time, although the freshly born lambs were taken back to the tents of the herding camp. The emphasis thus was on maximizing the quantity rather than the quality of herds, subject to strong social preferences for a normal labor-expenditure pattern.

Sheep were shorn once a year in the spring, or occasionally twice a year. Ewes were milked when young. Slaughtering for food took place as needed, but larger quantities would be slaughtered with the onset of the cold season, when the meat could be frozen. This practice was also rational in view of the fact that Mongolian livestock lost a great deal of weight during the winter and required most of the summer and autumn to be fattened.

Herding camps moved in regular pasturage cycles; that is, the tents and all household inventory would be periodically moved with the herds. This technique is undoubtedly the most important one in nomadic life, for without it pastures would soon be overloaded and destroyed. These cycles generally involved horizontal movement in steppe and desert areas and transhumance in the Altai and Khangai regions. The sparser the vegetation, the longer the distances between stops, and the greater the frequency of moves.[55] The way a herding camp moved embodied much social experience. The nomads of the south, where vegetation was sparser, had a much

---

[55] N. V. Tsapkin, *MNR* (Moscow, 1948), p. 73 ff.

more accurate knowledge of pasture conditions than those in the north.[56]

Animals ranged without veterinary care, although during the period of autonomy the Russians had attempted a measure of inspection of animals to be exported to Russia. As a consequence, herds were liable to rinderpest, anthrax, glanders, epidemic pneumonia, sheep mange, and cattle mange and bloat. Each year, large numbers of animals were lost in snow-, sand-, and windstorms. The worst month was March, when the strong winds and the absence of rains were most dangerous. When hoarfrost covered pastures and the top layer of snow froze, animals could not dig down to food and often starved. In the summer, drought could cause as much damage: predators thinned the herds, and in an average year perhaps as many animals were lost as were slaughtered by the nomads.[57] Because of natural difficulties, the nomads made little effort to construct sheds, to dig wells, to utilize and develop water resources, or to grow, cut, and store hay.

A continual theme among the explorers and scholars who visited Outer Mongolia was surprise at the techniques the Mongols used and at their attachment to the nomadic way of life. We have, however, also seen that their techniques, although primitive, displayed some concern to conserve labor, and that their preference for nomadism probably was reinforced by their inability to move physically to better opportunities, or to find local work offering higher real wages. Whenever opportunities to increase their real wages did present themselves, the Mongols were quick to take advantage of them. It was not always easy for the nomads to innovate. Building shelters, for example, in addition to making demands on labor, required proprietorial claims to plots of land and immovables.[58] Furthermore, owing to the uncertainties of the climate, the chance that any one investment would pay off was extremely low. Off-seasonal slacks of labor needs coincided with the worst weather, and building in summer entailed a direct and immediate reduction in herd output for a return that, adjusted for risks, was low. Given the widespread practice of merging herds, no one person could improve his stock without the collective agreement of the other members of the group.

---

[56] A. A. Iunatov, "Kormovye rasteniia pastbishch i senokosov MNR," *Trudy Mongol'skoi Komissii,* no. 56 (Moscow-Leningrad, 1954), p. 29.

[57] B. Perlin, *MNR* (Moscow, 1941), p. 40.

[58] Property rights in immovables were beginning to be recognized in the early part of the twentieth century (see Vreeland, p. 43; Maiskii, *Sovremennaia Mongoliia,* pp. 115, 229).

Nomadic agriculture had several disadvantages. To begin with, the nomad's need to visit his fields at particular times disrupted his established herding pattern; in addition, agriculture yielded a low economic return. Nevertheless, nomadic agriculture was practiced when times were either very bad or very good. For example, when cattle died in large numbers, agriculture naturally revived, despite its low market return. And, when a Russian grain merchant who wished to encourage agriculture among the Mongols paid a premium of 33 percent above the prevailing price of grain, his granaries were soon filled.[59]

The Nomadic Standard of Living

Despite its limitations, the stock-raising economy was not unsuccessful. Although the nomad's adjustment to his specific environment gave him a low per capita income, this income was by no means intolerably low. Lattimore, for one, believes that in standards of shelter and diet the Mongol was far better off than the Chinese.[60] If this was true, it is necessary to explain why the Chinese did not take up the nomadic way of life to increase their incomes.

There are several possible explanations. For one thing, Chinese law prohibited the Chinese from this way of life, and one may assume that the nomad's self-interest induced him to insist on observance of that law. More important, even if legal exclusion had not prevailed, the inherent difficulties of the nomadic technique of stock raising, with its long periods of isolation and its indispensable requirement of skilled horsemanship, would have had to offer a substantially larger real wage to persuade the Chinese to move into it. Finally, stock raising required a considerable investment in herds and inventory. The average Mongol inherited both, or else was able to trade his labor and skills for a share in output. The Chinese, however, if he had comparable wealth, would return to China proper and invest it there. Thus, social training and tastes led to the formation of two noncompeting national groups (see table 4).

Nevertheless, a nomadic life of sorts had taken hold among the Chinese in Outer Mongolia; Chinese artisans were moving around among the encampments, trading their labor in making implements for subsistence. The Chinese had displaced the Mongols in

---

[59] Pozdneev, I, 20.
[60] Lattimore, *Inner Asian Frontiers*, p. 90, and *Nationalism and Revolution*, p. 30.

lumbering, carpentering, merchandising, retailing, and smithery, but they could not compete with the Mongols in stock raising. The opportunities for trade with the Mongols had also impelled a substantial Chinese population to move northward. Low-income Mongols did not move to China; on the contrary, Chinese moved to Mongolia.

The Mongolian standard of living might have been higher had not the extent of specialization in stock raising been limited by heavy transport costs and the low average income of the stock raiser. Millet, brick tea, and cloth could bear the transport charges from China and would be in natural demand by people with low incomes. The average Mongol, however, could afford more efficient means of transporting his tools and his household, or, for that matter, demand consumption goods such as sewing machines or

TABLE 4

OUTER MONGOLIA'S TOWN POPULATION BY NATIONAL ORIGIN, 1919–20

Town	Total population	Chinese	Mongols who were not seden-tary lamas	Russians
Urga	100,000	70,000	10,000 [a]	3,000
Uliasutai	3,000	2,500	300–400	100
Kobdo	3,000	2,300	300–400	300
Kiakhta [b]	4,000	3,000	[c]	[c]

[a] There were about 20,000 lamas in monasteries in Urga.
[b] Data apply only to the part of Kiakhta in Outer Mongolia.
[c] Data unavailable.
SOURCE: I. M. Maiskii, *Sovremennaia Mongoliia* (Irkutsk, 1921), pp. 70, 88, 104, 106.

stoves which would be easily portable. Eventually, during the period of autonomy, a few wealthy Mongol princes did adopt a sedentary cycle of life, complete with Western gadgets such as telephones and, later, automobiles.

If Chinese real wages in the decade after 1910 were lower in inner China than in Outer Mongolia, and it seems likely then that they were, the light household goods and furnishings produced in inner China could stand the transport costs to the north. Not all Mongolian goods, however, could be so freighted or traded. Because fuel is heavy and thus costly to transport, the Mongols became highly efficient at making their felt tents. Foods needed refrigeration if perishable, and in any event were a by-product of herding. High transport costs prior to 1921 also prevented the utilization of Mongolian mineral resources, chiefly gold, coal, and iron ore. Only impoverished and, presumably, inefficient Mongols could be attracted to labor in mines at wages then prevailing. Heavy costs of exploration and development also prevented mineral utilization. The Chinese demand for minerals was, of course, low, and in the late nineteenth and early twentieth centuries international demands could be met from much cheaper sources. Even if the Mongols had had substantial known undeveloped mineral resources, which they did not, the deposits would not have been exploited because of the absence of transportation means and the distance from railheads and industrial cities.[61]

In one area of the economy high transport costs did not have the same result. There was little, if any, processing of livestock by-products in Outer Mongolia. The Chinese either had cattle and herds driven southward into Inner Mongolia or used caravans to transport hides and skins. Inasmuch as they could have lowered transportation costs considerably, for example by setting up wool washeries (the Mongols dressed wool with dirt in the hope of cheating the Chinese), these practices must have been due either to the legal prohibitions in force or, what is more likely, to the fact that to attract labor, the Chinese would have had to offer substantially higher wages than those prevailing in China.[62] The Russian traders had started some small plants for partial processing of materials, but by 1911 the number of such enterprises was still small.

An economy based largely on subsistence and partly on export of a primary product produced by primitive techniques, and one resistant to technical innovation, could not, of course, guarantee high average incomes. Nonetheless, Outer Mongolia's economy did not produce the lowest average income in the world. We have shown also that the evidence does not refute the view that real incomes were higher in Mongolia than in China.

There are no reliable national income estimates for Outer Mongolia prior to the late twenties, when Soviet economic planners in the country started to develop statistics. The impressionistic data that are available support the view elaborated in the present work. For example, Maiskii estimated the Outer Mongolian national income at the time of his visit to have been 74.5 million 1913 gold rubles, a figure that is an informed guess.[63] Botvinnik's figure for 1927 is 51.0 million tugriks, or roughly 34 million gold rubles.[64] The Soviet Siberian Encyclopedia's estimate for the 1930 national

---

[61] See Friters, p. 50, for a description of the utilization of minerals.

[62] Maiskii, *Sovremennaia Mongoliia*, p. 233 ff. Mongols were employed in these plants (see A. S. Kent, *Old Tartar Trails* [Shanghai, 1919], p. 2).

[63] Maiskii, *Sovremennaia Mongoliia*, p. 231.

[64] E. G. Botvinnik, "Opyt ishchisleniia narodnogo dokhoda MNR," *Khoziaistvo Mongolii*, no. 3(10) (1928), pp. 1–20.

income is 85.5 million 1930 tugriks.[65] More revealing than these rough figures of the national income, however, is Botvinnik's comparison of Outer Mongolia's 1927 per capita income with the 1914 per capita incomes of other countries in gold rubles: [66]

U.S.A.	670
Australia	526
Great Britain . .	486
Canada	390
France	370
Italy	224
Austro-Hungary . .	204
Russia	114
Spain	108
Mongolia	49

This comparison shows Outer Mongolia to be poorer than the other countries listed. But had the comparison included all countries of the world, Outer Mongolia's per capita income probably would not have been the lowest. In short, her economic system guaranteed the Mongol a good diet and adequate clothing and shelter to stand the rigors of his climate. Disease due to malnutrition and vitamin deficiency seems to have been rare.[67]

Population data.—Food and shelter apart, Outer Mongolia shared many of the other ills typical of a low-income country. Illiteracy was the norm, despite the large number of lamas. To the majority of lamas, their recitation of religious texts was a meaningless ritual. Disease was rife, rheumatism, trachoma, syphilis, and epidemic diseases being most prevalent. The first two of these were a result of lives spent in ill-ventilated, poorly heated, and ill-lit tents. Although reliable figures are lacking, one may assume that life expectancy was low and that mortality, especially infant mortality, was high. Kool-Estivend [68] found that of 173 children born to a group of fifty families, 67 died in the first four years of life and 14 between the ages of four and fourteen. As a few of the survivors in his study were still in the critical one-to-four age group, and a larger number were in the group below fourteen, the application of comparable mortality experience suggests that only

---

[65] *Sibirskaia Sovetskaia Entsiklopediia,* III (Moscow, 1938), 535.

[66] Botvinnik, p. 19. The figure for the Mongolian per capita income has been adjusted to make it comparable to the 1914 per capita income in the other countries.

[67] On diet see Maiskii, *Sovremennaia Mongoliia,* p. 165. See also Zenrin Kyokai, *Moko daikan* (Tokyo, 1938), pp. 96–106. This Japanese study was made available to me in an unpublished translation.

[68] I. Kool-Estivend, "O dvizhenii naseleniia v Mongolii," *Vestnik Azii,* no. 35–36 (1915), pp. 3–12. Heavy infantile and general mortality could result from disasters to livestock herds, which in Mongolia occurred about every four sugars.

some 80 of the 173 children reached the age of fourteen. The same observer also found the average size of the fifty families to be only 3.8 (1.8 surviving children plus parents).

Kool-Estivend's study highlights one of the peculiar demographic aspects of Outer Mongolia: Mongol women, prior to the 1920's, were not particularly fecund and had few successful pregnancies over their childbearing span of years. There seems general agreement that the nomads neither resorted to birth prevention nor followed Chinese customs in the treatment of girl infants.[69] Children were, in fact, prized, for they would add to the labor force in the herding economy. The women also enjoyed high status, probably because of their economic productivity. The literature has many explanations, both sound and fanciful, of the lack of fecundity. It is likely that the rigors of nomadic life on the one hand led to many early miscarriages among Mongol women and, on the other, affected the fertility of the Mongol male; moreover, venereal disease, which was rampant, was bound to exacerbate these defects.[70] In addition, a fair percentage of Mongol women were in concubinage to Chinese men, a factor that would discourage procreation. In the monasteries, although sexual morality was free, there was a tendency either to limit sexual contacts, to engage in them sporadically, or to restrict them to homosexual outlets. The implication to be drawn from this combination of factors is that married Mongol women, despite their low fecundity, probably had higher fertility rates than the overall female population of childbearing age.

As a result of high mortality and low fertility rates, the growth of the Mongol population was slow. There was, in fact, considerable speculation that the Mongols as a race were dying out,[71] but Maiskii has concluded that the population remained stationary. This conclusion is speculative, yet one thing is certain: since 1921 the Outer Mongolian population has expanded. Had anything like the post-1921 growth rate been the rule from 1691 to 1911, Outer Mongolia's population in 1691, the year the Chinese took the country over, would have had to be extremely small. As there are no indications that this was so, we may be sure that there was no great growth of population in the Chinese period. There may, however, have been periodic fluctuations, because Mongolian livestock herds suffered disastrous losses about every four years, at times producing famine.

---

[69] Frank Lorimer, *Culture and Human Fertility* (Paris, 1954), p. 96.
[70] V. Daurskii, "Lamaism, the Family and Sex Morals," *Sovremennaia Mongoliia*, no. 1(36) (1938), pp. 60–66.
[71] Maiskii, *Sovremennaia Mongoliia*, p. 67.

These population data give us a clue to many of the Mongol's social practices and to his attitude toward women and children. They also give support to the view that Mongol per capita income and real wages were not exceptionally low. Compared with the Chinese, the average Mongol family did have capital in the form of livestock and inventory and made extensive use of land. Labor, however, was relatively scarce in comparison with China. These facts again argue that the Outer Mongolian per capita income was higher than the Chinese.

Capital and monetary shortages.—The Outer Mongolian secular economy also displayed a total absence of socially owned capital facilities. Social, political, legal, and military administration was centered in the tent of the prince. There were no secular schools. There were no roads, not even one mile of metaled road in the entire region. The first bridge was not built until 1888. When Maiskii visited Outer Mongolia he saw only ten bridges, eight of them in Urga and its environs, all primitive, wooden structures.[72]

Before 1925 Outer Mongolia had no single currency: brick tea, skins, salt, sheep, and other commodities were used as means of exchange or as units of account, in addition to a medley of foreign currencies. Between 1900 and 1921, branches of the Ta Ching Bank and the Russo-Asiatic Bank did operate for a few years in Urga. A Mongolian national bank, sponsored by the Russians in 1915, went out of business during World War I. From 1919 to 1924 the major bank was the Chinese Chun-kuo yin-han. Maiskii sums up the financial picture in these words: "If primitive forms of organization prevailed in Mongol stock raising and transport, then primitive chaos reigns in the sphere of Mongolian monetary conversion." [73]

The picture of Outer Mongolia's secular economy just given illuminates the Mongols' social and political attitudes prior to 1921. An individual usually rates his income by comparing it with that of persons he knows. Hence, despite their underdeveloped economy, the Mongols felt better off than the Chinese, and, thanks to the country's Chinese-imposed buffer status, had little experience of the Russians of Siberia. Since, according to Maiskii,[74] 89 percent of the Mongol national income originated in stock raising, the Mongols' occupational structure was extraordinarily uniform. In addition, personal incomes probably were fairly uniform, without wide extremes. Isolated from the world at large, the average Mongol

[72] *Ibid.*, p. 161.
[73] *Ibid.*, p. 173.
[74] *Ibid.*, p. 123.

enjoying such an income had no strong aspirations toward change.

Almost regularly every four years the Mongols would feel the effects of natural disasters which took a toll of their herds. When, however, both prince and commoner faced the same hazards, and when those hazards were natural rather than social, it was hard for the Mongol to attribute his bad fortune to anything more than the vagaries of nature or perhaps some malevolent deity or spirit controlling nature. The Mongols, in fact, were not well enough informed to be angry at their lot.

THE ECONOMY OF THE RELIGIOUS SECTOR

One other feature is important for an understanding of Outer Mongolia on the eve of invasion. The society in which the Mongol lived had an important safety valve in the religious sector, a fact that becomes evident when one examines the economy of the monasteries and the religious territories. Conventionally they have been depicted as parasitic institutions—a picture that is not accurate.

The average lama was not supported by a monastery; only a few lamas depended on monastery funds. Most of them either were supported by relatives or supported themselves, whether by transfers of income such as subsidies and gifts or by productive output. It was not the custom among Mongols to provide funds for maintaining large numbers of idle people. For the lama without monastic or private support, and he was typical, life was grim if he failed to find a trade for himself. G. Ts. Tsybikov, in describing the Tibetan monasteries, not too dissimilar from the Mongolian ones, comments that whereas in Tibet there were strong built-in incentives for people to enter monastic life, such as the individual's freedom from state taxation (taxes being imposed only on the monastic authorities), nonetheless "stern reality and the continual struggle for existence brings [sic] the poor monks back to their kinsmen to help in the cultivation of the fields or to look for other income." [75] The more successful lamas lived in monasteries by their labor, producing carvings, paintings, icons, and books.[76] So-called medical and veterinary services also were an important source of income.

The economy of a monastery, as opposed to that of the individual

---

[75] G. Ts. Tsybikov, "A Buddhist Pilgrim to the Holy Places of Tibet: Diaries Kept from 1899–1902," unpublished trans. by Robert Shaw, Human Relations Area Files (New Haven, 1952–53), p. 151.

[76] See Robert J. Miller, "The Socio-Political and Economic Aspects of the Monastery in Outer Mongolia" (unpublished Ph.D. dissertation, University of Washington, 1955), esp. p. 173; Vreeland, p. 100 ff.; Baradin, p. 134 ff.

lama, had, of course, to be established by an initial transfer of secular funds in the form of an endowment. Having secured its financial base, each monastery was then able to take care of its prevailing needs by selling services and privileges. Miller describes the monastic financial system: "Economically the monastery may be viewed as a corporation consisting of numerous semi-automatic funds or treasuries, called *jisa* or *tsang*. Individual funds were attached to particular religious departments, to specific religious services, or to the reincarnations resident at the monastery. No lama belonged to a *jisa*, but only to department served by a *jisa*. Each *jisa* or *tsang* bore the name of the unit to which it was attached, and was located near its unit." [77]

Essentially, then, monastic finance was based on a system of decentralized accounting and storage of wealth. Instead of a consolidated system of accounts, specific monastic purposes were given endowments. The treasurer of such an endowment generally could speculate with its capital so long as he retained it intact and fulfilled all the customary patterns of expenditures for which the fund had been set up: "The treasurer could buy and sell for the treasury, send on caravan any animal that might be treasury property, distribute cattle and sheep to be herded by different families, and, in general, use every possible means to increase the wealth of his treasury." [78] As Central Asians tended to use real commodities as stores of wealth rather than as money, the system of decentralized accounting and storehouses overcame the physical problems inherent in storing, guarding, and investing the stocks of goods belonging to the corporate monastic body. Decentralization devolved responsibility and spread the risks occasioned by incompetent and unscrupulous treasurers.

Sanctions were applied against treasurers who failed in their responsibilities. If the funds were diminished by his actions, the treasurer was liable to the extent of his personal wealth; failing personal wealth, he would be forced to pay off losses by his labor. [79]

---

[77] Miller, p. 174.

[78] *Ibid.*, p. 175.

[79] Hermann Consten, "Denominations of Monasteries in Outer and Inner Mongolia," *Collectanea Commissionis Synodalis*, XII (1939); and "The Secular Administration of Mongolian Monasteries and Their Shabinar," *ibid.* In a personal communication to me dated September 2, 1958, Robert J. Miller wrote: ". . . there was a definite feeling that the treasurer's post should be filled, all things being equal, by someone who was capable of making it a paying proposition. Both from the Dilowa Khutukhtu and from our informants in Sikkim and Darjeeling district we obtained an unequivocal statement to this effect. . . . Since in theory any monk who could attract offerings for a particular service or series of services could become a treasurer, and the most successful would thereby give evidence of being a capable person, one might view the position of treasurer as crucial in intramonastic competition, and perhaps the treasurer's status as rising and falling with the status of his department."

If the treasurer was successful, however, he would be reelected for the maximum three terms of seven years each.

This system of endowment funds was used to support resident reincarnations, as well as buildings and monuments in their honor or in commemoration of deceased reincarnations, and also to maintain a few of the more important lamas. Custom sanctioned occasional distributions out of these funds to the population at large, but such disbursements were never significant enough to be considered a form of social security. Chinese subsidies were paid into the jisa of the khutukhtu entitled to them, as were also other gifts and pensions.

Monastery funds were used as primitive banking facilities, providing loans to both Chinese traders and Mongols. Consten claims that the rate of interest was 10 to 30 percent; Miller speaks of rates ranging from 25 to 35 percent or even more; and Maiskii asserts that the rates climbed as high as 60 percent.[80] The funds were built up by grants of trading privileges within the monastic area to Chinese traders; as much as 20 to 100 liang of silver a month was paid for such privileges.[81] Monastic land could be rented to agriculturists, but this source of income was not important in Outer Mongolia, despite the fact that religious prohibitions against agriculture had begun to give way to economic pressures.[82] Itinerant merchants would settle down and build shops around monasteries, using land at rental or by grant of privilege. The horses of the monastery were rented to the local government for horse-relay services and other uses.[83] One high lama provided the Russian consulate with mail service for 20,000 gold rubles a year.[84] Camels were either hired out or used in caravans organized by the lama treasurers. People who rented monastery pack animals for their own ventures shared profits; apparently, the business was conducted in a fair and honest way.[85]

Like the princes, monasteries and prominent reincarnations did have "subjects." These monastic subjects were liable to taxation as in the secular sector, but usually at more favorable rates. They engaged in share-herding monastic cattle, as well as their own livestock. Frequently the labor of the monastic subjects, called

[80] Consten, "The Secular Administration," p. 404; Miller, p. 205; Maiskii, *Sovremennaia Mongoliia*, p. 307.
[81] Consten, "The Secular Administration," p. 404.
[82] Pozdneev, I, 38; Vreeland, p. 198.
[83] Miller, p. 197.
[84] Consten, "The Secular Administration," p. 403.
[85] *Ibid.*, p. 400.

shabis, was used to maintain horse-relay services and to conduct caravans. In this capacity they were financially maintained by the monasteries. The larger stores of wealth of the religious sector, added to the fact that its livestock, being widely dispersed, was less subject to total disaster, meant that those were who so maintained had a much more stable income than, for example, the khamjilga in the secular sector. This factor helps to explain the impressive growth in the number of people who attached themselves to the religious institutions.

This brief description of the economy of the religious sector suggests that it is incorrect to view the monastery as a parasitic institution entirely dependent on taxation or on gifts from the secular sector. The lamas generally managed to live by the services they sold. The monasteries survived because their funds were used for economic activities. It is true that the religious sector probably was able to engage in more saving than the secular sector, and it is also true that it misinvested such savings: the use of monastic funds to construct monastery buildings, schools, and temples might be considered a misallocation from the secular sector. Religious investments in fixed capital gave certain satisfactions to the population at large, but, as the Mongols already had numerous monuments to support, additional expenditures of that kind probably met only ex post facto approval. The marginal social utility of the incremental monument qua monument in Outer Mongolia was low, or even zero, even though private gains may have accrued to the monastic collectivity. Yet it is also a fact that sedentary life— the growth of trade around permanent settlements—came as a result of the formation of monastic centers.

If the religious sector, despite its privileged position, acted as a safety valve, it is owing to the following circumstances. Investment in social goods outside the religious sector was small if not altogether lacking. Private investment in the nonreligious sector largely took the form of accumulation of herds. Only such accumulation, itself mainly dependent upon the accidents of weather, could bring some increase in the personal income of the average Mongol. In the religious sector, investments in buildings and temples benefited some of the resident lamas, but were of little or no advantage to the population at large.

The Mongol upper-income groups had not been exposed to any great extent to the consumption patterns of other countries; travel to Russia and inner China was difficult, if not impossible. Hence only the greater princes, familiar with the court life at Peking, and acquainted with Russia and Russian ways, tended to demand

Western-style goods. Typically, the rich man stored his wealth in livestock.

Let us assume a succession of good years for livestock. Advances in income, if and when they came, would tend to be dispersed throughout the general population because of the widespread practice of share herding.[86] As herds expanded in periods of good weather, the returns to share herding would increase, especially as the demand for share herding was growing.

Of the country's taxes, both those on labor and stock to maintain the horse-relay system and the border guards and those levied to maintain the regional prince and his administration would tend to be constant over time, although probably regressive on income. As average income increased, however, the total burden of taxes relative to total income would fall, for taxation would not increase with income. Thus the Mongol was able to enjoy periods of moderate advances in his standard of living. When adversity came, the herds of all were likely to be afflicted; princes and their serfs, the khamjilgas, alike would suffer a decline in income and wealth. The impoverished noble would once again share the nomadic life with the more fortunate and wealthy commoner. Soon the tax burden would become onerous, and flight to the religious sector, with its attractions, would increase. To recapitulate, these attractions were (1) lower taxes, both in kind and in labor; (2) partial protection against natural disaster through dispersal of herds; (3) more favorable share-herding agreements, because the monastic treasurer, unlike the prince, was held to a customary income and was less affected by Western and other foreign influences; and (4) the opportunity for the Mongol of ability to rise in the religious administration. In short, the advantages offered by the religious sector were substantial and provided the average Mongol with an escape from the natural pressures of his life.

A society endowed with so viable a mechanism of escape from economic pressure was not likely to be one to spawn a revolution. We have commented on the absence of a sense of class division among the Mongols, probably as a result of the cooperative patterns they had evolved for dealing with natural disaster.[87] The whole technique of nomadic stock raising stresses reciprocity of help, and not for immediate gain alone. Thus it was common among the

---

[86] Zlatkin, *MNR: Strana novoi*, p. 180, estimates that one-fifth of all households engaged in share herding.

[87] According to Henning Haslund, *Mongolian Journey* (London, 1949), p. 223 ff., natural challenges led Mongols to judge people by personal qualities rather than by social position. Haslund seems to imply, also, that this characteristic promoted a cooperative spirit among Mongols.

Mongols to help one another to set camp, to break camp, and so on. The princes had not become alienated from their subjects, and the monasteries had not lost their massive popular support. Hence, despite a low level of economic development, although one not so desperately low as to crush any positive enjoyment of life by the Mongol, no lively class antagonisms characterized Mongol society. Neither was there pronounced ill feeling toward the resident Chinese. The nature of Mongol society, however, was such that it could not defend itself. Once China could no longer protect her neutralized buffer and organize the defense of its long border, Outer Mongolia was left open to the world for the taking. The Mongols would not welcome the changes that were coming, but they could do little to prevent them. Despite the underdeveloped state of their economy, they were satisfied with their society and, as deeply conservative individuals, would sullenly contest any attempt at change. In sum, they lived willingly in a society of stable poverty.

From the foregoing it follows that it is quite incorrect to view the Outer Mongolia of 1921 as seething with revolt. Ten years later, after a decade of Bolshevik control, it would be, but in 1921 the Mongols were as passive as Maiskii has portrayed them. The new regime that came in 1921 was a "revolutionary" government without a revolution, and its future would be colored by that fact. To cap it all, this government was composed of a group of Mongols who were not sure themselves why they wanted to ride the Soviet whirlwind.

Now that traditional Russian territorial ambitions had been satisfied by the occupation of Outer Mongolia, the Bolshevik government would proceed to manufacture both a revolutionary government and a revolution. They were going to prove that for those willing to accept heavy social costs and not averse to twisting their policies to suit the day, there was some chance of making history come out the way they wanted it to. For the first time, if not the last, the extension of the power of the victorious proletariat was to be used to promote revolution in a noncapitalist country. Lenin and his followers were, in fact, going to revise Marx, not only in words, but by changing history.

3

BUILDING THE FOUNDATIONS OF THE
MONGOLIAN PEOPLE'S REPUBLIC

One conclusion to be drawn from the survey of Outer Mongolia in 1921 is that any active and organized force could have ruled the country. The Marxists of that day agreed to as much.[1] The Soviet Union, however, could not continue to use the Red Army to supply that force, partly because of the problems she was encountering in her international relations, and partly because she was devoted to a revolutionary program hammered out in Comintern debates which did not countenance such use of the army. There were additional ideological commitments that prevented the Soviet Union from colonizing Outer Mongolia. Unlike the contemporary Chinese, who display no ideological restraints in their treatment of native populations, the Bolshevik leaders of the 1920's did accept the related propositions that national groups have the right to exist, and that outright policies of forced assimilation are reprehensible.[2]

SUBVERSION BY THE COMINTERN AND
NORMAL SOVIET DIPLOMACY
Pro-Soviet Indoctrination of Outer Mongolia

In the light of the restraints imposed by international and domestic considerations, the Soviet Union, in order to rule Outer Mongolia, had to work through the Mongols and create a pro-Soviet govern-

---

[1] I. M. Maiskii used the phrase "any active and organized force" in "Present Day China," *International Press Correspondence*, no. 76 (Sept. 5, 1922), p. 570.
[2] There are exceptions to this generalization: Soviet policy in Tannu-Tuva led to Russification, but not as early as the 1920's.

ment that would enjoy sufficient popular support to guarantee its own continuance in office. To this end the Bolsheviks exerted constant pressure on the Mongol people, and Moscow brought direct pressure to bear on the Mongolian government. For example, the price of Soviet recognition of an independent Outer Mongolia in late 1921 was a commitment by the Mongolian government to speed up social and economic change in accordance with Soviet ideological mandates.[3] Rinchino, as chief Comintern agent in Urga at the time, applied specific pressure on the government there and exploited splits among the Mongols to destroy those who opposed him. At the same time, every effort was being made to build up an organized and active party that would support a pro-Soviet government. Soviet educational institutions played an important role in the implementation of this policy by training young men less conservative in outlook than their elders. The Soviet mentors also placed considerable emphasis on forming a politically indoctrinated army that would be loyal to the regime.

In short, the Soviet government wanted to build in Outer Mongolia a party whose leaders could, and would, implement Comintern directives—directives that came (as we shall see later) to reflect the Soviet Union's national interests. In time the Mongolian leaders arrived at the point where they had to obey Comintern directives, but were quite unable to influence their formulation and content. It should be stressed that this was not a consequence of the change in Comintern leadership from an enlightened Lenin to a tyrannical Stalin. From the very beginning the Soviet national interest triumphed over Mongol interests for the simple reason that the Soviet leaders were dominant in the shaping of Comintern policy. Moreover, the Soviet Commissariat of Foreign Affairs, although itself subject to the guidance of Comintern policy, inevitably conducted itself as any state department or foreign ministry would.

The interests of the Soviet Union thus came to dominate the solution to two problems that came to the fore almost immediately, in fact, at the Kiakhta Congress of 1921: the Mongols' aspiration toward independence, and their desire for a Pan-Mongol settlement. By 1925 both these aspirations had already suffered frustration at the hands of the Soviet leadership. The discussion of Pan-Mongolism is postponed to chapter 4, where it is more appropriate. In 1921, however, the question of Outer Mongolia's independence

---

[3] Ma Ho-t'ien, *Chinese Agent in Mongolia*, trans. John de Francis (Baltimore, 1949), p. 100, specifies seven demands made on the Mongols at this time, all of them involving broad social and economic changes.

was of primary concern. In that year the Bolshevik government, grimly determined to maintain its influence over Outer Mongolia, did its best to prevent the Mongolian government from exercising any of the prerogatives of independence. This Soviet policy of dominance in Outer Mongolia was pursued even at the risk of endangering other paramount objectives.

The Wooing of China

Between 1921 and 1924, a succession of Soviet diplomats (Yurin, Paikes, Joffe, and Karakhan) conducted missions in Peking whose prime purpose was to gain Chinese recognition of the Soviet regime. These negotiations with China had additional objectives, however. The Soviet Union desired to prop up an independent China against the so-called imperialist countries and, at the same time, to obtain opportunities for promoting pro-Communist movements in China. Given such mixed objectives, the Soviet negotiations in Peking had to be conducted with concern not only for their effects on the northern Chinese, but also for their impact on the revolutionary regime of Sun Yat-sen in the south. These preoccupations notwithstanding, the Soviet diplomats were inflexible on the question of Outer Mongolia. The Soviet attitude was: "We've got Mongolia; now let's be friends and go on from there." The Soviet leaders were ready at all times to recognize Chinese sovereignty over the area, but they refused to discuss the right of Soviet troops to be in Urga and the domestic policies being carried out there by Soviet agents. Neither did the Bolshevik government accept discussion of the Outer Mongolian question as a precondition for negotiations on the larger question of Chinese recognition of the USSR. Strange though it may seem, the Soviet approach succeeded; [4] the Sino-Soviet accord of May 31, 1924, accepted the status quo. Chinese sovereignty over Outer Mongolia was recognized, and the situation remained unchanged in all aspects but one: [5] the Soviet government agreed to remove RSFSR troops from Outer Mongolia.

Just what the status quo was will become clearer as this chapter progresses. Essentially, by 1924 the foundations of a puppet state had been laid. Perhaps the Chinese were not fully aware of what was happening, although events on the diplomatic level alone,

---

[4] The reasons for the success of this approach are discussed in Allen S. Whiting, *Soviet Policies in China, 1917–1924* (New York, 1954), pp. 248–262.

[5] Sun Yat-sen also accepted the status quo in Outer Mongolia in an agreement with Joffe in January, 1923. His acceptance was less of a diplomatic triumph for the USSR, for the question of Outer Mongolia's status was quite academic for the Kuomintang regime.

about which the Chinese were well informed, were obvious enough to reveal Soviet intentions.

Creation of a "People's Revolutionary Government of Mongolia" under Chinese Sovereignty

In August, 1921, the Mongolian government requested that Soviet troops remain in Outer Mongolia. This appeal, published in the Moscow *Izvestiia* on August 10, was answered by Chicherin two days later. Chicherin replied, without qualification, that Red troops would stay in Urga until the menace of the White remnants was ended. Both the appeal and its answer were couched in general terms, and the commitment to maintain troops in the area was without time limit.[6] For that matter, the Mongols had to request specific aid just two months later to deal with the White officers Kaigorodov, Bakich, and Kasantsev, who were still operating in the west of Outer Mongolia.[7] Significantly, Chicherin's August 12 note uses the phrase "autonomous Mongolia" repeatedly.

On September 1, 1921, the former Mongolian rulers abdicated and, in a formal edict, officially transferred power to the "People's Revolutionary Government."[8] On September 10 the new government, which had already had de facto control since July, appealed to the Soviet government to act as intermediary in defining Outer Mongolia's relationships with China. In his reply four days later, Chicherin dropped the word "autonomy" and substituted the term "People's Revolutionary Government of Mongolia." He spoke of Mongolia's right of self-determination and offered Soviet services in negotiations with China. The Soviet government, however, never started such negotiations; in fact, it took care not to do so.

A Soviet-Mongol conference held in Moscow in October, 1921, led to conclusion of a treaty on November 5. This treaty recognized the new Urga government as the only legal government of Outer Mongolia and called for an exchange of diplomatic representatives. The RSFSR transferred to the new regime the telegraph and telephone systems, installed in Outer Mongolia at the tsarist government's expense, and canceled the debt incurred by the autonomous Mongolian government during tsarist days. In return,

---

[6] Xenia Joukoff Eudin and Robert C. North, *Soviet Russia and the East, 1920–1927: A Documentary Survey* (Stanford, 1957), pp. 204–205, cites both notes in full.

[7] *Istoriia MNR* (Moscow, 1954), p. 265. The Soviets agreed to the request on October 28, 1921 (see I. Ia. Zlatkin, *MNR: Strana novoi demokratii* [Moscow, 1950], p. 134).

[8] Whiting, p. 170.

the Mongols gave Soviet citizens most-favored-nation trade status and accorded the Soviet government the right to send plenipotentiaries to Outer Mongolia's major cities.[9] This treaty of friendship did not explicitly recognize the Mongolian regime as the government of an independent country, but merely as the legal government of Outer Mongolia—a critically important difference. Neither did the treaty lead to a tripartite agreement among the Russians, the Chinese, and the Mongols, as the Russo-Mongol treaty of 1912 had led to the Tripartite Agreement in 1915. It was far more convenient for the Soviet government to agree to Chinese sovereignty over Outer Mongolia, to leave the exact nature of the relationships legally ill defined, and to exclude third powers from the area by forcing the Mongolian government to negotiate through the Soviet government.

Subsequent to the treaty there was much traffic between Urga and Moscow and between Outer Mongolia and Soviet territory generally. Mongolian delegations visited the Soviet capital, and Mongol delegates attending Comintern and Profintern congresses used the platforms thus provided to make anti-Chinese speeches. At the Congress of the Toilers of the Far East at Moscow, for example, Danzan, in a speech typical of his outspoken manner, made no bones about Mongolia's "suffering" under Chinese rule.[10] Furthermore, on the very eve of Karakhan's negotiations in Peking (January, 1924), the Soviet Union dispatched a minister plenipotentiary, Vasiliev, to Urga. Kalinin, as head of state, received the credentials of a Mongolian representative on January 11, 1924.

The matter of Mongol-Soviet friendship could hardly have been put to the Chinese more plainly. Nonetheless, the Peking government recognized the Soviet Union, on essentially Soviet terms, on May 31, 1924. We might add that the Soviet Union and Outer Mongolia were not magnanimous winners. Once the Soviet Union had won her diplomatic victory, the Outer Mongolians proclaimed the Mongolian People's Republic (MPR) in November, 1924. They left no doubt in Chinese minds just what the situation was. In a manner that, in retrospect, seems singularly ungracious, Chicherin, less than a year after the Sino-Soviet accord had been signed, rubbed the salt into Chinese wounds before the Congress of Soviets which met in March, 1925: "We recognise this republic as part of the Chinese Republic, but we also recognise its autonomy as sufficiently wide to preclude any interference in the internal affairs

---

[9] For the full text of the treaty see Jane Degras (ed.), *Soviet Documents on Foreign Policy*, Royal Institute of International Affairs (3 vols.; London, 1951), I, 484–487.
[10] Whiting, p. 80.

of Mongolia. . . . In Mongolia we have a government completely directing its policy along the lines of a close rapprochement with the USSR." [11]

THE OUTER MONGOLIAN PUPPET GOVERNMENT
Government by Nonrevolutionary Nobles

While Soviet diplomats and the Soviet Commissariat of Foreign Affairs worked to preserve the military gains of 1921, Rinchino in Outer Mongolia sought to secure a puppet government that would follow Comintern directives. Two major purges ensured that Mongolia would accept the legislative changes the Comintern wanted. We should note, however, that those purges by no means increased the so-called revolutionary influence on the government—quite the reverse. The Fourth Congress of the Third International had worked out a formula for Mongolia in late 1922: "Only where the feudal-patriarchal tenor of life has not yet deteriorated so as to completely separate the native aristocracy from the mass of the people, as with the nomads and semi-nomads, can the representatives of these groups appear as active leaders in the struggle with imperialist violence (Mesopotamia, Morocco, Mongolia)." [12]

The language of this resolution is significant. It reflects clearly that the Comintern strategists had accepted a view similar to the one Maiskii had voiced in *Sovremennaia Mongoliia*, namely, that there was little class stratification or identification in Outer Mongolia. They were quite precise in asserting that in Outer Mongolia they were dealing with a national-revolutionary movement rather than with the classic Marxist revolution. To so describe the events of 1921 implies a misreading of the evidence. Be that as it may, the wording of the resolution indicates that the Comintern realized and accepted that the nobility of Outer Mongolia could be used in the new government.

Institutional Purges

In view of the peculiarities of Outer Mongolia's political and social structure and of Comintern views, it is not surprising that after 1921 the Mongolian government was transformed into one composed largely of nobles—nobles made docile by well-publicized purges. The changes in the cabinet illustrate the policy. Distribution of the cabinet posts by the first government in Urga, which

[11] *Ibid.*, p. 234.
[12] *Ibid.*, p. 98.

comprised a prime minister, a vice-premier, and only five ministers, was as follows: Bodo became premier, and Chakdorjab stepped down to the vice-premiership; Sukhe Bator remained as war minister and chief commander of the Mongolian Army. Of the original Kiakhta group, Velik Sai-kahn and Losol were replaced. Iapon-Danzan became minister of finance; despite previous experience in the Ministry of Finance, he seems to have had no special competence or ability.[13] Togtokho became minister of justice. Puntsuk Dorji took over the position of minister of the interior, which he had held during the period of autonomy. So much for the "revolutionaries" and their sympathizers. The only unexpected additions to the cabinet were two princes who occupied positions without portfolio, Tsereng Dorji and Erdeni Zhono Wang, both, as their names indicate, nobles of high Chinese rank.

The composition of the cabinet soon changed, however. In January, 1922, Bodo, Chakdorjab, Puntsuk Dorji, and Togtokho all were removed from office, and a more influential lama, the Jalhansa Khutukhtu, became prime minister. He was acceptable to the Soviet Union for a number of reasons. To begin with, although he had been prime minister under Ungern-Sternberg, he had soon been demoted and sent to the west of Outer Mongolia, where he had entered into negotiations with Shumiatskii concerning the possibility of Bolshevik intervention in the west.[14] He had thus been favorable to the "revolutionaries" from the start. In addition, as he was a reincarnation of the highest Chinese rank, his appointment clearly threatened the influence of the Urga Khutukhtu. Finally, while in the west he had made common cause with Maksarjab, a noble who was later to become war minister. Maksarjab, too, had at first joined Ungern-Sternberg's cause and had later changed sides. He had participated in the fighting against the White remnants in the western part of the country. Maksarjab, who had a powerful

---

[13] I base this judgment on Iapon-Danzan's speeches before the Third Congress of the Mongolian National Party (see the transcript of the Third Congress of the Mongolian National Party in *Tretii s'ezd MNP* [Urga, 1924]). Hereafter, unless a specific judgment is made about a person, in which event the source of the judgment is footnoted, I do not indicate my sources for changes in appointments, purges, and names of officeholders, for they are matters of record. Iapon-Danzan, who acquired his nickname as a result of his trip to Japan, should not be confused with Danzan.

[14] D. P. Pershin, "Baron Ungern, Urga and Altan Bulak: An Eyewitness' Account of the Troubled Times in Outer (Khalkha) Mongolia during the First Third of the Twentieth Century" (MS in Library of the Hoover Institution, Stanford, Calif.), p. 80; *China Year Book, 1924*, p. 580; Amor and Doksom, "Istoricheskie uroki 15 let revoliutsii," *Tikhii Okean*, no. 3(9) (1936), p. 84; V. I. Iudin, "U istokov mongol'skoi narodnoi revoliutsii," in A. T. Iakimov (ed.), *Mongol'skii sbornik, ekonomika, istoriia, arkheologiia*, Akademii Nauk SSSR, Institut vostokovedeniia (Moscow, 1959), p. 112.

and colorful personality, was to become one of the heroes of the new regime, one who surpassed even Sukhe Bator in popular esteem.[15] It is likely that his military exploits were far more important to the new regime than Sukhe Bator's. The Jalhansa Khutukhtu, then, had done well in befriending Shumiatskii and Maksarjab. The Tsetsen Khan, Navan-Nerin, became minister of the interior. As one of the four khans of Outer Mongolia, he was of the highest rank. Tsereng Dorji, the prince, took over the Ministry of Foreign Affairs.

These cabinet changes illustrate that the January, 1922, purge had affected mostly the original Kiakhta group of conspirators. There was one exception: Danzan became vice-premier. For a while the purged government leaders were permitted freedom, but not for long. In August, 1922, the Soviet secret police arrived in Urga to compensate for the fact that Soviet troops there had been reduced from a division to a battalion.[16] On August 30, 1922, eleven months after the invasion, Bodo, Chakdorjab, Togtokho, Puntsuk Dorji, Dindub, and ten others were shot.

It is instructive to analyze the reasons for the purge of Bodo, how it was justified, and how conducted. Ma Ho-t'ien asserts that the real cause for the purge was that Bodo and his colleagues opposed the demands the Soviet government had made as a condition for recognition of the new regime in late 1921.[17] These demands, as we have learned, were for a program of change in Outer Mongolia along Soviet policy lines. There seems little doubt that Ma Ho-t'ien's assessment is correct. He was a Koumintang agent who visited Urga in 1926 and 1927 and was well informed about the situation there. At that time the Koumintang was viewed as a friendly revolutionary party, and Ma Ho-t'ien's visit to Urga was quasi-official.

Bodo, however, was not directly charged with opposition to Soviet wishes. It is, indeed, difficult to establish what he actually was charged with, thanks to the custom of Soviet and Mongol commentators to change the crimes of purged individuals to suit the party line at given times. There seems reason to believe that during his tenure of office Bodo had attempted to promote Western-

---

[15] For an interesting assessment of Maksarjab, see Walter Kolarz, *The Peoples of the Soviet Far East* (London, 1954), p. 133.

[16] *China Year Book, 1924*, p. 578. This was not the first appearance of secret police in Outer Mongolia. The Mongolian Department of State Internal Affairs had been set up on July 10, 1922. Choibalsan had the prime role in organizing the secret police (see P. P. Staritsina, "Marshal Choibalsan (iz zhizni i deiatel'nosti)," *Kratkie soobshcheniia instituta vostokovedeniia*, no. 6 [1952]).

[17] Ma Ho-t'ien, p. 101.

izing reforms, such as a change in women's dress and orna-
ments.[18] In addition, it is not unlikely that he was also blamed for
the mistakes of Butkevich, the Soviet financial adviser at that
time. Butkevich was removed in August, 1922, because his reforms
had provoked strong local antagonism.[19]

As there was probably much discontent with Bodo in the capital,
Rinchino must have found it easy to unseat him. The official
history of Sukhe Bator shows that Rinchino, in order to help unseat
Bodo, sided with Western trade interests that were alarmed by
Bodo's actions. Rinchino apparently exploited not only the evidence
of popular discontent but also the reactions of foreign firms
interested in Outer Mongolia, to convince the Mongolian cabinet of
the need to destroy Bodo. The communiqué that was released to the
world to describe the Bodo "plot" was unusually frank: it made
quite clear that those who confessed did so "under torture." [20]

The next disappearance of one of the Kiakhta group of "revolutionaries" is puzzling to interpret. Sukhe Bator is supposed to have
been poisoned on February 2, 1923. According to the official
histories, he was poisoned by the Urga lamas, but the Dilowa
Khutukhtu, a prominent Mongol and a reincarnation of high rank,
asserts that Bator was poisoned by Soviet agents. Lattimore, in
turn, suggests that Bator's death may have been due to natural
causes.[21] There is, unfortunately, no way to decide whose version
is the correct one. The evidence for natural death is that Sukhe
Bator actually had fallen ill in Irkutsk in 1921. Furthermore, it is
somewhat hard to understand why the lamas should poison Sukhe
Bator but not Rinchino or the Jalhansa Khutukhtu. In his capacity
as war minister, Bator could hardly have been held responsible
for the social reforms that injured the lamas. Thus, the evidence of
poisoning is not entirely convincing, and the allegation of a natural
death depends on unverifiable assertions.

In any event, Sukhe Bator's timely death, which (as we have remarked earlier) was most fortunate for his posthumous prestige,
led to an advancement in fortune for Danzan. It increased Danzan's
authority, for in addition to the vice-premiership, he took on the
duties of war minister and chief commander of the army. Given the

---

[18] *Istoriia MNR*, p. 268.

[19] *China Year Book, 1924*, p. 579; J. Lévine, *La Mongolie: Historique, géographi-que, politique* (Paris, 1937), p. 147.

[20] Lévine, p. 147, cites the communiqué in which the words "Sous la torture" occur.

[21] Bazaryn Shirendyb, *Narodnaia revoliutsiia v Mongolii i obrazovanie MNR* (Moscow, 1956), p. 9; see also Sh. Nachukdorji, "Life of Sukebator," in Owen Lattimore, *Nationalism and Revolution in Mongolia* (New York, 1955), p. 176. See *ibid.*, p. 175 n. 8, for Lattimore's and the Dilowa Khutukhtu's views.

reduced size of the Soviet garrison in Urga and the growing strength of the Mongolian Army, his new responsibilities made Danzan powerful indeed. A man of his courage and independence could not but be a threat to Rinchino. Events followed the expected course. Danzan did, in fact, make the mistake of attempting to use his power, and as a consequence was shot together with his closest supporter, Bavasan, in August, 1924. We shall take up the circumstances of Danzan's death in a more relevant context. For the moment, it is sufficient to say that after Danzan's death, Tsereng Dorji, who had previously taken on the prime minister's position, became the most important puppet of the Soviets. It is clear from the following observation what manner of man had risen to power in comparision with Danzan: ". . . the earnest and rather intelligent Tsereng-dorji . . . was an official of the Chinese school who always kept his nose to the wind, and would at any time sell anybody anything if he found it advantageous to do so." [22] Incidentally, Rinchino had to go to much trouble to preserve this pliable instrument. We know from the transcripts of the Third Mongolian National Party Congress that he came under severe criticism from young Mongols of pro-Bolshevik persuasion for doing so.

Danzan's demise was largely attributable to his own character. A man of considerable ability and ambition, he undoubtedly made a bid for personal power and contested Rinchino's authority. That was Danzan's real crime. The debates of the Third Mongolian National Party Congress disclose that, among other charges, he was accused of intriguing with the Russian Comintern agent, Starkov, against Rinchino while the latter was in Russia [23]—a charge that appears ridiculous for reasons to be discussed later.[24] We can understand Danzan's "crime" when we examine the views he expressed at the Third Party Congress. Those views, combined with his ability to influence the Urga garrison of Mongols, made him an obstacle Rinchino had to remove. "The provincial masses are backward," he commented on Rinchino's demands for self-government of the masses, "and are so passive that they cannot make use of their freedom." When Rinchino and others demanded action against the hereditary princes, Danzan retorted: "Do the nobles in the provinces still wear spheres with the feather on their hats or not? . . . Why should we seek to destroy that which is falling to pieces of its own accord? We have more serious problems to attend

---

[22] Pershin, p. 80.
[23] Tretii s'ezd, p. 185.
[24] Rinchino's charges and complaints about Danzan are available in ibid., p. 177 ff.

to." When Rinchino demanded laws to restrain capitalists, Danzan replied with telling accuracy: "But we have no capitalists in Mongolia; that question is not today's but tomorrow's." Next, with considerable bravery—or was it foolhardiness?—he remarked: "I think a heedless repeating of our friendship for the U.S.S.R. without a leading point is useless." Danzan's final words were prophetic: "Rinchino is sitting on my head, take him off! Today Rinchino devours me, and tomorrow you." [25]

Even at this late date and after one purge, Danzan showed a certain lack of understanding of the realities of power in Urga. Rinchino lost his role as chief Comintern adviser in 1925, and he, too, would soon fall in a purge; he had always been under Soviet supervision. Korostovets, the able tsarist minister to Outer Mongolia, asserts that a Soviet spy, Ratgebern, succeeded Rinchino as chief adviser,[26] although other sources mention two Letts, Otkhin and Berezin, as being influential.[27] We have already learned that the arrival of the Soviet secret police in 1922 led to a stiffening in the treatment of the Mongols. We know also that Rinchino maintained a close relationship with Vasiliev, the Soviet minister. Vasiliev appeared before the Third Party Congress with Rinchino to tell the shocked Mongols shortly after Danzan's death that "sometimes we must let a little [blood] to save a lot." [28] Clearly, Rinchino did not have an entirely free hand in shaping Comintern policy and was something of a puppet, although the strings that pulled him are harder to discern.[29] Essentially the Comintern devoured Danzan, not Rinchino.

This brief account of the purges that took place to ensure the foundation of a Mongolian puppet people's republic reveals one striking fact: most of the purge victims were members of the Kiakhta group. By 1924, approximately half the Mongols who had met at Kiakhta in 1921 had been shot. Their place in the government had largely been taken by men of noble rank, who were pliable instruments and likely to be more obedient, given the salutary warnings of other men's deaths. Incidentally, after Tser-

[25] All quotations are taken from the J. Attree translation of the minutes of the Third Congress of the Mongolian National Party, which is available in the Hoover Library, Stanford, Calif. I have checked all quotations against the original transcript of the proceedings of the congress, *Tretii s'ezd*, and have made such changes as were necessary.

[26] Iwan J. Korostovetz, *Von Cinggis Khan zur Sowjetrepublik* (Berlin and Leipzig, 1926), p. 330.

[27] Lévine, p. 147; *China Year Book, 1924*, p. 579.

[28] *Tretii s'ezd*, p. 225.

[29] Western visitors to the region showed Rinchino as undisputed ruler (see, for example, Marguerite E. Harrison, *Red Bear or Yellow Dragon* [London, 1924], for a vivid sketch of Rinchino).

eng Dorji replaced the Jalhansa Khutukhtu, no lama remained in a position of authority. The fact that so many of the original Kiakhta group soon met death is clear testimony to the fact that they were nationalists rather than Bolsheviks.

LEGISLATIVE AND ADMINISTRATIVE CHANGES

Before the institution of the Mongolian People's Republic (MPR) in late 1924, three major steps were taken to secure a regime whose objectives would accord better with those of the Comintern. First, a state structure was designed which imitated that of the Soviet Union, and care was taken to staff it with men whose ambitions served Comintern objectives. Second, considerable emphasis was placed on building up a Mongolian army that was deeply pene- trated by members of the Mongolian National Party. Third, the MNP was increasingly transformed from a group of men dedicated to Pan-Mongol and nationalist policies, with a flavor of Westerniz- ing reform, to a party of men who would accept Comintern direction. Not one of these steps was fully completed by 1924 (as we shall learn in subsequent chapters), although substantial progress had been made.

Creation of a Sovietized State

In taking the first step, Rinchino and his advisers used a shrewd policy: they first attacked the nobility, the traditional leaders of Outer Mongolia, but made no outright assault on the religious institutions of the country. The nobility were, after all, few in number, and their source of authority had been the Chinese power of appointment, which implied backing by the Chinese imperial government; moreover, the nobility had no great wealth. In con- trast, the religious organizations were economically powerful and well organized, and had a powerful hold over the life of the individual Mongol. The nobles thus were the lesser enemy. It is of interest that this attack by the Rinchino group was pursued with much greater energy and competence after Bodo's execution in late 1922. Prior to that event, the new administration had tended to make specific attacks on particular individuals—to prohibit, for example, a certain noble from using the horse-relay service, or to harass a particular lama—and changes were confined to Urga, by- passing the country at large. Still, despite this greater application of energy, legislation passed before 1923 concerning affairs outside

Urga was largely declaratory in nature, as no effective enforcement mechanisms existed.

In September, 1921, the titles, ranks, and special subsidies to the Urga Khutukhtu, his wife, the former ministers, and other important princes were abolished.[30] These perquisites were Chinese in origin, but they had continued during the period of autonomy and had, in fact, been a considerable charge on the autonomous government's budget. On November 1, 1921, a law was promulgated prohibiting princes and higher lamas from collecting money or labor dues from Mongols formerly subject to them.[31] In May, 1922, khamjilgas were ordered not to render any of the customary services to their princes.[32]

The most important piece of legislation, the statute on local organs of power, became effective on January 5, 1923. This statute set up local councils (*khural*'s analogous to the Russian soviets), each of which was elected from ten households. Indirect elections were held for higher councils at the district (*bag*), area (*somon*), region (*hoshun*), and subprovincial (*aimak*) level. In essence, this reform applied Soviet theories of political organization to the old political structure of the Mongols. That such theories could be applied so easily in Outer Mongolia gives us an important insight into the adaptability of the Soviet political structure. The local councils had wide powers: they were to conduct censuses, organize schools and hospitals, help the disabled and sick, collect taxes, and enforce government orders. The vote on persons to be elected to the councils was secret, and wealthy persons were prohibited from standing for election. Higher organs could annul elections that allowed the wrong persons to gain power in subordinate organs. Regional and subprovincial councils were given the duty of conscripting men for the army and of acting as courts of appeal.[33] Broadly speaking, the allocation of responsibilities was not too dissimilar from the Chinese military-administrative system in Outer Mongolia, which itself had been adapted from the organization of the armies of Genghis Khan.

On March 22 legislation complementing the January statute was announced. The statute on ruling and nonruling nobility (regional princes and so-called free princes) ended the hereditary rights of princes and affirmed the elective process already set up.

---

[30] Zlatkin, p. 138.
[31] *Ibid.*, p. 129.
[32] Shirendyb, p. 81.
[33] *Ibid.*, pp. 84–85.

Zlatkin, a Soviet authority on Outer Mongolia, comments: "now
. . . the overturning of power of the feudal class, achieved in the
center of the country in 1921, was also definitely accomplished on
the periphery." [34]

It was one thing to announce a new system of government but
quite another to staff it with men favorable to the new regime. The
elections that took place in 1923 returned the representatives of
the "feudal class" in three out of four aimaks.[35] The elections were
promptly revoked and, after a special course had been held to train
party members as election supervisors, fresh elections were held.
Consequently, the elections for the Great People's Council (Khural)
held in November, 1924, returned a body of delegates 90 percent
of whom were drawn from classes acceptable to the regime.

Although the power structure of the new government was built
in, it was still weak in operation. For example, the statute on ruling
and nonruling princes was reaffirmed in December, 1923.[36] As late
as 1924 the government abolished taxes paid to the religious
authorities, thereby confirming existing legislation.[37] Legislation
still tended to be declaratory in nature. Above all else, in the
countryside the religious leaders conducted a massive campaign of
passive resistance to the laws of the new regime.[38]

Reform of the governmental structure aroused little direct opposition.[39] It is true that small disturbances against the new regime
were not lacking, but there seems to have been no organized outcry
in favor of the princes. In fact, the reverse was true, for, although
the Mongols continued to elect the nobility to office, there was no
organized group to support them. The resistance of the religious
leaders *had* to be passive, for by temperament and philosophy they
could hardly incite the population to forceful action. Thus, power
passed from the princes to the local soviet-type khurals relatively
easily and smoothly, even though the loyalties of the population at
large did not.

[34] Zlatkin, p. 149.
[35] I. Ia. Zlatkin, *Ocherki novoi i noveishei istorii Mongolii* (Moscow, 1957), p.
189.
[36] *Istoriia MNR*, p. 273.
[37] Shirendyb, p. 132.
[38] Roland Strasser, *The Mongolian Horde* (London, 1930), p. 137, gives an
example of passive resistance.
[39] Yasuo Misshima [sic] and Tomio Goto, *A Japanese View of Outer Mongolia*,
translated and condensed by A. J. Gradjdanzev (New York, 1942), gives the fullest
account of uprisings in Outer Mongolia under the Soviets. As this work, despite a
poor translation, is in general highly reliable, I assume that its account of the
uprisings is accurate. The uprisings before 1924 do not seem to have resulted from
the overthrow of the nobility. One gets the same impression from Shirendyb, pp.
103–105, and from *Istoriia MNR*, pp. 268–270.

Creation of a Sovietized Army

If the new khurals were to be effective, they needed instruments of
coercion to back them up. The use of the secret police and of purges
was only partly conducive to making the population at large heed
the new regime. Thus, the creation of a politically indoctrinated
army had great importance in perfecting the governmental power;
in turn, military affairs became a matter of some importance.

One of the first acts of the new administration was to make all
citizens liable to military service.[40] By 1923, the Mongolian Army
numbered 2,560 and, by 1924, 4,000. Although this seems a small
force, by 1924 it was already four times as large as the army of the
autonomous period. Support of the army placed a heavy burden on
the finances of the new regime: it absorbed 60.4 percent of all
expenditures, if extraordinary expenditures (credit operations and
debt repayments) are included, and 41.8 percent if they are
excluded.[41]

Political indoctrination of the new army was given high priority.
Rinchino and Zhamtsarano themselves gave lectures to the troops.
The army was given a political administration as early as August,
1921.[42] More than one-third of its personnel were actually members
of the MNP, the number having risen from 650 in 1923 to 1,445 in
1924.[43] Most of the members of the new regime who were leftist in
sympathy and occupied prominent positions in the party were also
connected with the army. Genkin's assertion that by 1925 the
Mongolian Army was an important political force is a correct
judgment of the situation.[44]

Creation of a Revolutionary Party

A final step, education of the young, was needed to ensure that the
administration, the government, the party, and the army would be
composed of men who would obey the Comintern. Consequently, as
many young Mongols as possible were sent to be trained in Soviet
schools.[45] Political reeducation of older Mongols was too difficult,

    [40] Shirendyb, p. 80.
    [41] F. D. Holzman, "The Financial System of the MPR," in *MPR*, Human Relations
Area Files (New Haven, 1956), III, Ec. 26. See also N. N. Tugarinov, "Biudzhet
MNR," *Novyi Vostok*, no. 15 (1926), pp. 168–177; Zlatkin, *MNR: Strana novoi*, p.
145; Zlatkin, *Ocherki novoi*, pp. 186, 193.
    [42] Shirendyb, p. 82.
    [43] *Tretii s'ezd*, p. 27.
    [44] I. I. Genkin, "Dva s'ezda MNP," *Novyi Vostok*, no. 12 (1926), p. 184.
    [45] For a description of these schools, see N. N. Poppe, "MNR," *Vestnik institut po
izucheniiu istorii i kul'tury SSSR*, no. 4(11) (1954), p. 15.

but it was likely to be effective among the young. The young Mongols, once educated, came back to compete for positions of authority. There is no doubt they had taken to Marxism-Leninism with enthusiasm, and had caught the "revolutionary spirit" from their Soviet friends, for they exerted continuous pressure on their elders. Part of the reason is that their personal ambitions had been fired, because under the new regime they could aspire to positions denied them during the period of autonomy, except in the religious sector. These young revolutionaries constituted a significant political force.

By the time the Third Party Congress was held, 81 of its 95 delegates were below thirty-five years of age, and 24 were below twenty-five. Some of these young men had formed a new party called the Revolutionary Union of Youth (Revsomol). By 1924 it had reached a strength of 4,000 and was as strong as the senior party; [46] one-third of its members had been trained in the Soviet Union. In its activities, Revsomol was under the direction of, and given assistance by, the Executive Committee of the Comintern of Youth.[47] So successful had the educational program of their Soviet mentors been, so imbued with the desire for change were these young Mongols, that they attempted to take over control of affairs from the senior party. Their leader, Buin Nemkhu, took complaints about the MNP to both the Comintern and the Comintern of Youth. Finally the divisions between the two parties became so severe that the issue of which of the two was the true revolutionary party was considered at the Fourth Congress of the Comintern itself, in 1924. The congress decided that the Revsomols must subordinate themselves to the senior party—a typical decision, given the Communist fear of dual parties. Nevertheless, Revsomol pressure forced such a degree of change in the older party that in 1924 its name was changed to the Mongolian National Revolutionary Party (MNRP). It is interesting to observe how this pressure was applied, for it gives us an insight into both the Mongolian politics of the period and the circumstances that brought about Danzan's downfall.

The Second Party Congress had been held in July, 1923 (the first was, of course, the meeting held at Kiakhta in 1921). By 1923 Revsomol had already been formed with the assistance of Starkov, the Russian.[48] Many Mongols tried to prevent the convening of this congress but, according to a modern Soviet account, they were

[46] Anatolii D. Kallinikov, *Revoliutsionnaia Mongoliia* (Moscow, n.d.), p. 90.
[47] Zlatkin, *MNR: Strana novoi*, p. 133 ff. Zlatkin thinks the Revsomol was an effective party by 1924.
[48] Eudin and North, p. 127. This Starkov is possibly the one who later played an important role in turning Tannu-Tuva into a satellite.

overruled by the Executive Committee of the Comintern.[49] It appears that Buin Nemkhu, Starkov, and Damba Dorji (the telegrapher) manipulated and controlled the proceedings of the Second Party Congress. It was at this congress that the decision was made to revoke the elections of early 1923, because the delegates who had been elected to organs of power were too rightist. Rinchino's absence at the time also helped to make the scene ripe for a move from the left.[50]

Left-wing moves continued in the earlier sessions of the Third Party Congress in 1924. Buin Nemkhu's representative, Gombojap, a Buriat Mongol trained at the University of the Toilers of the East, continually pressed for more radical change. At the same time, indirect pressure was applied in the crudest manner. Ja Damba, Damba Dorji, Bavasan, and Dorchi Palim, the last three being secretaries to the congress, were arrested by the Urga City Committee of the Revsomols. Bavasan was a member of the Revsomol Central Committee, a protégé of Danzan's, and secretary to the Military Council. The sheer irresponsibility of Bavasan's arrest becomes apparent when we consider that at that very time the administration was considering Chinese mobilization threats against Outer Mongolia.

Danzan, hearing of Bavasan's arrest, attended the Third Party Congress to prorogue it and threatened to call in the Urga garrison. Thirty armed members of Revsomol, led by Badarkho and Choibalsan, thereupon immediately occupied the meeting place of the congress. Under their guns the congress was quickly turned into a court to try Danzan and Bavasan, with Rinchino as prosecutor. Needless to say, the two accused were found guilty and sentenced to death; they were shot within twenty-four hours of sentencing. Ironically, even Buin Nemkhu himself was arrested, and by the very Revsomols he had led. Genkin, the Marxist historian of the period, frequently refers to Buin Nemkhu as an able and talented person.[51] Nemkhu's downfall seems, therefore, to have been due to his inability to control his own party rather than to his threat to the senior party.

As a result of the direct attempts to influence its course, the purging of Danzan and Bavasan and the setback to Buin Nemkhu,

---

[49] Zlatkin, *Ocherki novoi*, pp. 148 ff., 188.

[50] Danzan also made his bid for power at this time, but his asserted alliance with the Left seemed rather suspect. He certainly opposed Rinchino, as did Buin Nemkhu and Starkov. The fact that they all challenged the Comintern representative presumably was enough to make them allies in the eyes of Communist commentators.

[51] See Genkin's introduction to *Tretii s'ezd*, and his articles in *Severnaia Azii*, no. 2 (1928), and *Novyi Vostok*, no. 12 (1926).

the Third Party Congress showed a general shift to the left in its appointments of party officers: Badarkho, already the leader of Revsomol in fact, was now made so by law; Choibalsan was made chief commander of the army, although Maksarjab retained the post of war minister; Gombodjap became president of the Economic Council; and Damba Dorji succeeded Iapon-Danzan as chairman of the party. Only the durable Tsereng Dorji hung on as premier to represent the right wing, despite cries for his arrest; it was Rinchino who saved him at the time.

It is of interest that this opportunity to head the party was seized by Damba Dorji. Of the original Kiakhta group Sukhe Bator, Danzan, and now Damba Dorji had achieved prominence. Choibalsan's time still had not come.

With the shift in leading personalities and the political complexion of the Mongolian National Revolutionary Party, as it was now called, the pressure of Revsomol was alleviated and its official subordination as a party to its political parent was ensured. Nonetheless, it was to maintain continuous pressure on the MNRP in the years to come. We may be sure that Rinchino's handling of the situation leading to the crisis, prompt though it was, in the end helps to explain why we find another Comintern agent supplanting him and attacking him at the next party congress.

Subsequent to these events, the calling of a great khural, its acceptance of the establishment of the Mongolian People's Republic, and the adoption of a new constitution—all in late 1924—were really only formalities constituting a ratification of the Soviet Union's demands of 1921, formerly blocked by Danzan and his supporters.

Creation of Cooperatives

It is not surprising that when the Outer Mongolians visited Lenin in 1920 and listened to his advice to form a "national-revolutionary party," implementation was fairly rapid. The Bolshevik Party, with its substantial traditions and experience of party organization, was the model; the period of underground activity and of the Civil War had introduced into Bolshevism a quality of ruthlessness in achieving goals and in building organizations. The Comintern ably directed and supervised the Mongols' efforts.

Lenin's recommendation to introduce peasant cooperatives among the Mongols was less successful. His advice was interpreted to mean a single trade cooperative rather than many producers' cooperatives. In addition, the trade cooperative had a peculiarly

Mongolian flavor: it started as little more than a trade venture, in which the Urga Khutukhtu became a prominent stockholder. This arrangement was in full accord with Mongol and Chinese customs, which permitted political leaders to feather their own nests in economic institutions under the control of the state.

As the Revsomols built up their strength, they pressed for conversion of the Mongolian Central Cooperative into one similar to the Soviet model. The Second Party Congress of 1923, under their manipulation, passed a resolution that the cooperative be made a mass organization.[52] At the Third Party Congress in 1924, Zhamtsarano remarked of the Mongolian Central Cooperative: "Is it not a cooperative of ten to twenty rich men? Is it not a corporation of Chinese firms, who are remaining in the shadow?" [53] By 1923 it accounted for only one-half of 1 percent of the trade circulation in the country and, by 1924, for only about 4 percent.[54]

The lack of success in making the cooperative system work was owing to the fact that there was not enough trustworthy Soviet and Mongolian personnel to manage its affairs. Only the Soviet representatives in Urga and the Revsomols really wanted drastic changes. For example, under Butkevich, and until August, 1922, there was a degree of energy in economic policy: Butkevich set up high tariffs, established price ceilings, and imposed an income tax on merchants. These taxes were, indeed, sufficiently heavy to arouse the merchants' fear of eventual total governmental control. Butkevich also seems to have made heavy, almost confiscatory, levies on livestock to finance government operations. His policies are strongly reminiscent of those of Soviet War Communism. As we know, the changes Butkevich made led to widespread resentment.[55]

After Butkevich's dismissal in 1922, Rinchino directed economic affairs briefly. He was president of the Economic Council until replaced by the more radical Gombojap in 1924. Rinchino seems to have instituted few reforms. He made hardly any changes in the Ministry of Finance: for example, by 1924 it still had no statistician; [56] the government did not have a report on the 1923 budget until 1925 and never knew whether the country had an import or an export surplus in its balance of payments; and budget surpluses

---

[52] Zlatkin, *Ocherki novoi*, p. 184.
[53] *Tretii s'ezd*, p. 9.
[54] *Protokoly zasedanii 4-go s'ezda upolnomochennykh paishchikov Mongol'skogo narodnogo kooperativa* (Ulan Bator, 1925), p. 2.
[55] *China Year Book, 1924*, p. 579.
[56] *Novaia Mongoliia: Economiko-politicheskoe i kul'turnoe sostoianie strany, Protokoly pervogo Velikogo Khuraldana MNR* (Ulan Bator, 1925), p. 140.

accrued until 1926 more by chance than by plan.[57] By 1924 only twenty-three schools serving a mere 400 children were in operation. Nothing was done to develop either industry or transportation. Essentially, the bulk of governmental expenditures was funneled into party organization and buildup of the army, activities that were both Soviet-supervised.

Consolidation of the Satellite Relationship

When Soviet representatives took the initiative, things were accomplished in Outer Mongolia. For example, in 1924 Vasiliev, the new Soviet minister to Urga, brought an agreement to set up a Mongolian national bank, a joint Soviet-Mongol company. The bank commenced operations rapidly and fairly effectively. If, however, domestic reasons prevented Soviet participation in implementation of Mongolian policies, nothing was accomplished if progress depended on Mongol initiative and resources. A good example is provided by the conduct of foreign trade.

Promotion of Revolution through Foreign Trade

The Soviet Union had given considerable thought to trade policy. The Bolshevik leaders, once they realized that revolutionary upheaval was unlikely in Western countries, arrived at the view that trade with Eastern countries was an essential part of revolutionary policy. At the Second Congress of the Comintern in 1920, Lenin laid down the broad principles for Far Eastern trade. Trade with capitalist countries was considered bad, as was trade with countries like Japan, which pursued a policy of national aggrandizement. In contrast, trade with countries that might rebel against Western control and influence was considered important in promoting revolution. Naturally, to be effective such trade—the Bolsheviks agreed—must be conducted along lines different from those of capitalist trade. This broad policy, however, had to be translated into the decrees of the Commissariat of Foreign Trade. Just what was to be "socialist" trading? And just how was it to be better than "capitalist" trade? In real terms, the problem came down to trading with countries on Soviet Russia's borders: Turkey, Afghanistan, Mongolia, Tannu-Tuva, and Sinkiang. How were countries such as

---

[57] Zlatkin, *MNR: Strana novoi,* p. 143 ff. According to Misshima and Goto, p. 40, however, the budget surplus was accumulated to finance monetary reform in 1925–1928.

these to be dealt with in trading matters? In 1920, these five countries and their traders were exempted from the Soviet state monopoly of foreign trade to enable them to deal directly with Soviet economic organizations and, to some extent, with individuals.[58] This exemption released their merchants from the onerous and costly business of negotiating through the Commissariat of Foreign Trade if they wished to do business in the Soviet Union. In 1923 the Second All-Union Congress of Foreign Trade Commissars enunciated principles for trade with Eastern countries which were essentially an elaboration of Lenin's 1920 policy position. Goods sold to the East were to be priced lower than similar goods going to other markets. Joint-stock companies with stock owned by both the RSFSR and an Eastern country were to be encouraged on terms more favorable than those stipulated by Western countries. The general Soviet requirement that foreign trade with a specific country had to show an export surplus did not apply to trade with the Soviet Union's neighbors to the east.[59]

Outer Mongolia was to have a privileged position among the five. The Soviet-Mongol treaty of friendship of 1921 had, in fact, already given Outer Mongolia most-favored-nation treatment, and trade was later conducted along the lines discussed. In substance, however, these privileges amounted to little. For one thing, Outer Mongolia had no trading class of her own to benefit from the privileges; she was dependent on Soviet organizations. Furthermore, until 1928 no joint Soviet-Mongol companies were set up, with the exception of the bank. When Soviet trade organizations did appear in strength in Outer Mongolia, which did not happen until 1923, they concerned themselves with procuring goods from the Mongols without supplying commodities in exchange. Tsentrosoiuz, which had been in Outer Mongolia since 1919, expanded to branch offices outside Urga in 1923. In 1924 this agency was reorganized and taken over by Sibgostorg, which became the most important Soviet trade organization in Outer Mongolia. As its name suggests, it was concerned with procuring Mongolian commodities for the Siberian population. Sherst' (wool), Torgpredstvo USSR (the commercial section of the Trade Delegation of the USSR), and Nephtesyndicat all were procurement organizations. By 1924, Soviet exports to Mongolia had not reached the 1913 levels of tsarist trade.

---

[58] See Violet Conolly, *Soviet Economic Policy in the East: Turkey, Persia, Afghanistan, Mongolia and Tana Tuva, Sin Kiang* (London, 1933), pp. 116–117, the best study available on the six exempted countries' relationships with the Soviet Union.

[59] *Ibid.*, p. 11.

The Soviet Union, even at the existing level of trade, had a substantial import surplus on the Mongolian account.[60]

Modern Soviet sources assert that the Soviet trading agencies in Outer Mongolia sold commodities at 10 percent below, and purchased goods at 10 percent above, world price levels.[61] This could have benefited the Mongols as sellers, but it could have had no influence on them as buyers; the volume of goods the Soviet Union sold Outer Mongolia was too small relative to total Mongolian consumption to make much difference. Lenin's thinking on trade policy, then, was not successfully implemented in Outer Mongolia owing to domestic difficulties in the Soviet Union. Needless to say, the Mongols did not take over the business of trading themselves.

To sum up, prior to 1924 politics were of predominant importance in Outer Mongolia. They were so, primarily in the sense that the only important change that had taken place in the country up to that date was the slow buildup of an active and organized force that could govern. But politics may have been predominant in a broader sense. It is likely that Soviet representatives in Urga, before 1924, had been instructed not to press for too many changes. To have done so, and to have inspired mass discontent thereby, would have destroyed the fiction the Comintern had attempted to manufacture: namely, that Outer Mongolia was led by a group of progressive nobles demanding national autonomy. Insistence by the Soviet government on rapid change would certainly have provoked adverse reactions from the Chinese government at a time when Soviet-Chinese negotiations were in progress. In any event, during that entire period the Soviet government displayed a sure sense of priorities: in Peking, Soviet diplomats maneuvered to gain time; in Outer Mongolia, Bolshevik agents and supporters destroyed the Chinese political apparatus and started to substitute their own, and a loyal army was built up, permitting withdrawal of the Soviet troops stationed there. Finally, to make sure that these policies would bear fruit, enough Mongolian leaders were purged to make their successors extremely sensitive to Soviet wishes.

---

[60] Zlatkin, *MNR: Strana novoi*, p. 283; Kallinikov, p. 55 ff.; Conolly, p. 100.
[61] Zlatkin, *MNR: Strana novoi*, p. 169, for example.

4

THE SHIFT TO THE LEFT, 1924 TO 1929

Soviet Policy toward Mongolia

The institution of the Mongolian People's Republic in November, 1924, constitutes not only a sharp break in the history of Outer Mongolia but also a significant success of Soviet Far Eastern policy. Nonetheless, this event brought no fundamental change in Soviet policy toward her recently acquired satellite, nor in the processes that were already under way in the MPR owing to the implementation of the broad policies formulated by Lenin and, more widely, by the Comintern. In fact, until 1929 events proceeded along predictable lines, although they were critically affected both by the wider course of events in the Far East and by domestic politics in the Soviet Union.

Relation to International Events

In January, 1925, Chicherin sent a note to the government of the MPR announcing his intention to withdraw Soviet troops in accordance with the Sino-Soviet agreement of 1924. Tsereng Dorji "acceded" to this proposal on January 27, three days after dispatch of the note. In March of the same year these facts were communicated to the Chinese by Karakhan, then in Peking,[1] and the troops were withdrawn shortly thereafter.

In retrospect, this action amounts to an empty gesture, consider-

---

[1] The two notes and Karakhan's communication are available in Jane Degras (ed.), *Soviet Documents on Foreign Policy*, Royal Institute of International Affairs (3 vols.; London, 1951), II, 7–19.

ing the Peking regime's steadily growing weakness and the diminishing political significance its friendship had for the Soviet government. True, the Kuomintang regime in the south of China was gaining in importance, and the Soviet government probably desired its friendship also. But, even though the Kuomintang turned anti-Soviet in 1927, at no time thereafter did Chiang Kai-shek, who controlled it, have either the chance or the military means to reoccupy Outer Mongolia. Thus in the end it mattered little whether the Soviet troops remained in the area or withdrew. In 1925, however, when the friendship of both the Peking government and the Kuomintang still were important to the Soviet Union, the true picture could not have been so readily apparent to her. Hence, Soviet foreign policy toward China continued to demand some caution in promoting domestic change in Outer Mongolia.

In 1927, when Comintern policy in China collapsed and the southern border of the MPR became the effective limit of the Soviet sphere of influence in the Far East, caution became less important. After that date, when defense of the Mongolian border could no longer be entrusted to diplomatic means, a major rethinking of Soviet Far Eastern policies must have ensued.

Relation to Domestic Events in the USSR

Despite the demands of foreign policy, domestic events in the Soviet Union prevented the emergence of any firm policy toward her satellite. Throughout the early 1920's, Stalin and the right wing of the Bolshevik leadership were in a temporary alliance to destroy Trotsky. While this power struggle for dominance of Soviet political life was going on, the New Economic Policy (NEP) instituted by Lenin continued unchanged, and the Soviet political leaders were far too preoccupied to formulate new and bold policies in external affairs. Even had one of them done so, no agreement would have been reached on implementation.

Thus, until 1928, the old policies continued in effect in the MPR. The leftist elements in the MNRP were being strengthened by an inflow of young men trained in Soviet schools, while the Comintern assisted by nibbling away at the rightist elements in the party. The political complexion of the Mongolian government and the political apparatus of the country underwent similar changes. Soviet trade interests in the region were slowly building up; the Mongolian Central Cooperative was gradually expanding; the Mongolian Army was steadily growing in manpower and armament; and the power of the leading lamas was being gradually eroded.

Cost to the Mongols

Certain features of the Soviet NEP were introduced in the MPR: a limited amount of free enterprise was permitted. But, whereas in the Soviet Union the limited restoration of private trade and industry brought an increasing measure of economic recovery, Outer Mongolia suffered a contrary effect. The Mongols had no traders or capitalists of their own; yet, Comintern policy required them to destroy Western and Chinese economic interests in the MPR. Moreover, as Soviet organizations operating in the MPR were overwhelmingly concerned with the purchase of Mongolian raw materials for the Soviet market, the Mongols were practically forced to ruin part of their economy without any clear balancing gain or reward.

The Mongols' relationship with the Soviet Union also implied special sacrifices in another area. It is no exaggeration to assert that the USSR shifted some of her defense costs onto Outer Mongolia. The Mongols were encouraged to specialize in cavalry in order to supplement Soviet armor and infantry. The evidence suggests that the rising total cost of the Mongolian defense arm was largely borne by the Mongols themselves. The Mongolian Army did, of course, help to preserve the MPR from the evils of Chinese warlordism during this period, but it was, in effect, part of the Soviet military establishment in the East. There was also another, more subtle, shifting of costs. As Japan's threat to the Soviet Union grew, it was obviously in the Soviet interest to fight the Japanese forces in Outer Mongolia rather than on Soviet soil, and plans were made accordingly.

Whether by oversight or plan, the Soviet government did not compensate the Outer Mongolians for the special sacrifices they were being asked to make for defense at the expense of economic development. Apart from political assistance and a small amount of technical aid, itself largely misdirected, the Mongols gained little from their relationship with the Soviet Union. In the late thirties, the party line would be quite frank in its rationalization of the Soviet lack of concern with the MPR; it would stress that there had been little point in building up capital facilities in Outer Mongolia when these might be lost to the Japanese. During the period we are considering, however, this was not so frankly admitted.

In summary, the relationship of the MPR with the Soviet Union, although entailing sacrifices, made no new and special demands on the Mongols until 1929. Few new policies were formulated by either the Comintern or the Soviet Commissariats of Foreign Trade and Foreign Affairs, while the old policies steadily continued to take effect. Apart from some possible military rethinking in 1927, the Outer Mongolians continued to live within the framework of policies discussed with Lenin in 1920.

MONGOLIAN DOMESTIC POLICIES AND POLITICAL GROUPS

In the field of Mongolian domestic politics, the purge of Danzan had permitted a step to the left. This is not to say that the Mongolian government and the MNRP had made the complete turn to the left. Generally speaking, until 1929 there were three major groups in Mongolian affairs, of which only one was truly leftist.

The first group comprised Mongols who had supported the original "revolution" of 1921 and were for the most part in favor of some reform and social change. The most rightist among them was undoubtedly Tsereng Dorji, who managed to retain the premiership until 1928. His membership in this group is attributable largely to his opportunism. The most influential member of the group, and its leader, was Damba. He was strongly disliked by the Revsomols and antagonistic to the Soviet Union. According to Ma Ho-t'ien, Damba favored closer links with the Kuomintang in order to lessen Soviet influence.[2] Damba does not seem to have been hotly opposed to Buddhism. We can understand Tsereng Dorji's exhortation to the First Great Khural "to bear in mind that the nation's moral and spiritual welfare was also in their keeping and that the Church must therefore be protected."[3] Damba's slogan, "For a pure Buddhism," is, however, a little more surprising.[4]

Anna Louise Strong found Damba a "genial revolutionist." Judging by the charges brought against him when he was subsequently purged, he seems to have believed in accomplishing change with moderation. Ja Damba, Damba's friend and protégé, vice-chairman of the party, and president of Revsomol, was of the same general persuasion. Amor, a Mongol of noble birth, possibly a participant in the First Party Congress at Kiakhta in 1921 and later premier, held right-wing views.[5] So did Doksom, one of the original

---

[2] Ma Ho-t'ien, *Chinese Agent in Mongolia*, trans. John de Francis (Baltimore, 1949), p. 115. At that time the Kuomintang was still leftist.

[3] Ladislaus Forbath, *The New Mongolia: As Related by Joseph Geleta*, trans. Lawrence Wolfe (London, 1936), p. 196.

[4] Reported by Anna Louise Strong, *China's Millions* (New York, 1928), Bk. II, p. 394.

[5] "Biographies of Key Personalities," in MPR, Human Relations Area Files (New Haven, 1956), II, 646; I. I. Genkin, "Dva s'ezda MNP," *Novyi Vostok*, no. 12 (1926), p. 188.

Kiakhta group, who would also attain prominence later. It is important to stress that "right wing" is used only in reference to the then existing range of opinions in Outer Mongolia, for in general the whole of Mongolian political opinion had shifted to the left. One commentator suggests that the Rightists were tinged with Bukharinist views; [6] certainly their personal experience would influence them to accept this interpretation. It would have been difficult for Rightists to think of a class stratification that included a kulak and a bourgeois class, for no such stratification existed in Outer Mongolia. Furthermore, for a country without a national bourgeoisie and without traders and middlemen, Bukharin's view that such elements should be encouraged would have seemed entirely sensible and economically sound. In any event, in the party congresses this group apparently adopted a conservative position in discussing such national questions as (1) the continuance of Buddhism, (2) the rights and roles of lamas, (3) the relationships with capitalist countries, (4) the relationships with the Kuomintang, and (5) the extent of necessary social, economic, and administrative change.

The viewpoint of the second group was not too different from that of the first. We already know that Rinchino and Zhamtsarano represented a Buriat-Mongol force in Outer Mongolian politics, and that they were animated by Pan-Mongol sentiments. It is not unlikely that Rinchino may have attempted to strengthen what we will show to be his declining political position by introducing other Buriats into the government. Erdeni Batukhan, a member of Maiskii's expedition, became minister of education quite early in 1924. Anna Louise Strong describes him as a "man of kindly philosophic sentiment." [7] Dashi Sampilon, after serving the MPR in Moscow, France, and Germany, became minister of trade in 1927. [8] He was a well-educated and intelligent, if not very forceful, man. Zhamtsarano continued to play an active part in politics and was an important member of the MNRP, but in his work he concentrated on a scholarly role in the Committee of Science. Most of the Buriats were intelligent, reasonable, and moderate, and much to the right of Rinchino. Damba, Sampilon, and Batukhan as ministers of education seem to have attempted to do something to lessen Soviet influence. Batukhan, together with Damba, visited Europe. Mongolian students went to France and Germany, although in small numbers compared with those going to the Soviet Union. An

---

[6] N. N. Poppe, "MNR," *Vestnik institut po izucheniiu istorii i kul'tury SSSR*, no. 4(11) (1954), p. 15.

[7] Strong, Bk. II, p. 394.

[8] Serge M. Woolf, "Mongol Delegations in Western Europe, 1925–1929," *Royal Central Asian Journal*, XXXII (1945), 289–298; XXXIII (1946), 79–92.

educational and economic mission visited France, Germany, and Sweden. Representatives of the MPR bought German equipment and started talks on the possibility of German technical assistance to the Mongolian government.[9]

The General Shift to the Left

Despite these restraining influences, the Mongol left wing, the third group, progressively gained in strength. In 1924, the Soviet diplomat Vasiliev was accredited to the MPR and took part in the country's internal affairs. His successor, Nikiforov, was equally active. In addition, Amagaev, whom Strong describes as a "zealot," increasingly assumed the influential role of chief Comintern agent in the MPR,[10] taking over the chairmanships of both the Economic Council and the Military Council. Rinchino lost his post as secretary of the MNRP to Dugarjap, whom we may assume to have been Amagaev's man. In addition, other Leftists began to occupy important positions: Khayan Khirva became head of the secret police, until he himself was displaced by a Russian, Konorov;[11] Gendun, who by 1926 had become president of the little khural, also was left wing.[12] Ma Ho-t'ien, our Kuomintang observer, reported of the years 1926 and 1927 that

Since Outer Mongolia has become independent, all important organs have had Russians as advisers. To put it bluntly, it is the Russians who are directing everything. The Ministry of Finance, for example, has four Russian advisers. The Ministry of War has eight military advisers, with K'ang-ko-la-li as chief of staff. The secret police, which sees to the suppression of internal disorder, has six Russian advisers and is actually headed by one. All the military training officers are Russian. The rest is manifest. Even the managers and drivers of the motor company, which concerns itself with matters of communication, are all Russians.[13]

At this time also, the major political organizations of the country were being packed more and more with extremist sympathizers. The rank and file of Revsomol was strongly leftist, and the Association of Labor Unions, which was growing as a political force, was dominated by its secretary, Chizhiia, a Mongol of strongly leftist views.[14] In addition, the MNRP itself at the intermediate level, in the

---

[9] *Ibid.*; Gerard M. Friters, *Outer Mongolia and Its International Position,* ed. Eleanor Lattimore, intro. by Owen Lattimore (Baltimore, 1949), pp. 269, 347; I. Ia. Zlatkin, *MNR: Strana novoi demokratii* (Moscow, 1950), p. 183.

[10] Strong, Bk. II, p. 394.

[11] Verbal communication from N. N. Poppe.

[12] V. A. Maslennikov, *MNR na puti k sotsializmu* (Moscow, 1951), p. 54.

[13] Ma Ho-t'ien, p. 95.

[14] Chizhiia was purged as a "left deviationist" in 1932 (see *Istoriia MNR* [Moscow, 1954], p. 288).

aimak and the hoshun, was quietly assuming an entirely leftist complexion. Later, these intermediate party officers were to help the top
Leftists destroy the Right. In the modern commentaries, this is
misnamed the "khudon" opposition, or the countryside opposition.
We shall show later, with the help of Soviet sources, that this
modern attempt to represent the countryside as being in broad
opposition to the Left is just as much a fiction as the claim that a
revolutionary situation existed in 1921. What was happening was
that the young men educated in Soviet schools were slowly gaining
control of the political apparatus of Outer Mongolia. In 1926, the
year when links with Europe became important, only 36 Mongols
went to the West for education compared with 180 who went to
the USSR.[15] Furthermore, education of Mongols in Europe was a
temporary policy of two or three years' duration, whereas education of Mongols in the Soviet Union was a policy persistently carried
out from 1920 on. Those Mongols who did go to the Soviet Union
for training received a political education, not a professional
or technical one; [16] they went there simply to be indoctrinated.
Another source of leftist strength was the army. As pointed out
earlier, the army was thickly laced with party members, and was
controlled by Amagaev and led by Soviet officers. By 1927 it had
attained a strength of 17,000 men.[17]

The Constitution of 1924

The rising power of the Left based on the party and the army was
used to the full, and successfully. Whereas in China Comintern
agents and Soviet sympathizers played only an advisory role, in
Outer Mongolia they held positions of authority. Moreover, they
used the powers they had without any inhibitions save those
imposed by Comintern policy. We know how Danzan and his
supporters had been summarily removed. This restraint gone, the
Left proceeded to direct the already handpicked First Great Khural.
Intimidated as the khural was by the previous purges, there was
little difficulty in getting approval of the new constitution and the
state structure it provided for. The Constitution of 1924 national-
ized lands, mineral wealth, forests, and water resources; it canceled
individual and hoshun debts to foreign traders, and abolished the

---

[15] Dugardzhap, "Zadachi narodnogo prosveshcheniia MNR," *Khoziaistvo Mongolii*, no. 4(17) (1929), p. 36.
[16] Robert Smith, "Political, Economic and Trade Conditions in Outer Mongolia"
(MS in Library of the Hoover Institution, Stanford, Calif.), p. 69.
[17] Ma Ho-t'ien, p. 104.

system of mutual guarantee of debts (*krugovaia poruka*); it established a state monopoly of foreign trade, to be introduced gradually; and it declared the determination of the state to end the "feudal theocratic regime" of Outer Mongolia.

The new state structure was closely modeled on that of the Soviet Union. There was constitutional provision for a great khural, indirectly elected from subordinate councils, which were themselves indirectly elected. The great khural in turn was to elect a small khural of thirty members to act as the supreme executive organ between meetings of the great khural. The little khural elected a presidium of five members and a council of ministers composed of twelve members. These changes amplified those that had been instituted by the 1923 decree on local organs of power. The vote was given to all over eighteen years of age, irrespective of race, religion, or sex, provided the prospective voter lived by his own labor or was attached to the army. Traders, moneylenders, those who lived by the labor of others, former princes, khutukhtus, and permanent residents of monasteries were disqualified from electoral rights.[18] This change had been heralded by the nullification of the 1923 elections.

Yet, as testimony to the nonrevolutionary viewpoint of the average Mongol, the First Great Khural did not behave as expected of it. For instance, it raised the question whether Chinese merchants should be restricted, a matter that constitutional provisions had already settled in favor of the Soviet Union. Opinions on the desirability of abolishing the personal and tax privileges of the shabis varied considerably. In other words, when broad policies had to be implemented in concrete pieces of legislation during the khural's session, the Rightists usually adopted a conservative stance while the Leftists pressed for results the MNRP was already committed to in principle.[19]

After the First Great Khural, the Central Committee of the MNRP, whose composition had shifted much farther to the left during the Third Party Congress, took the hint. A party purge was ordered, and the party ranks were thinned from 6,200 to 3,200.[20] The explicit purpose of this move was to clear out supporters of Danzan, former princes, lamas, and wealthy commoners so that the strength of the Right would be diminished.

---

[18] The constitution may be found in *China Year Book, 1926*, pp. 795–800.

[19] T. Ryskulov, "Velikii Khuraldan Mongolii," *Novyi Vostok*, no. 8–9 (1925), pp. 215–219. See also Bazaryn Shirendyb, *Narodnaia revoliutsiia v Mongolii i obrazovanie MNR* (Moscow, 1956), p. 131.

[20] Genkin, pp. 184–195.

The Fourth Party Congress

As a consequence, the composition of the Fourth Party Congress, which met from September 23 to October 2, 1925, was much more leftist than that of the third. Amagaev put the issues clearly, noting that loyalty to the Comintern had paid off:

The National Revolutionary Party, which is struggling for the political and economic enfranchisement of the Mongol masses, has acted and has worked from the first days of its existence in absolute agreement with the Comintern. . . . The national revolutionary movement of the Mongol masses could not have progressed had it not maintained contact with the Comintern and followed Comintern leadership.[21]

Amagaev, stressing that such loyalty must continue, indicated that the major task of the party was to strengthen its divers relationships with the masses.

Rinchino played no role of importance in the Fourth Party Congress; in fact, it was made clear to him that his views were out of order. Amagaev pointed out in no uncertain terms that Pan-Mongolism did not square with Comintern policy. A basic tenet of Comintern policy, Amagaev noted, was "the principle of self-determination of nationalities, and this must underlie the policy of the party on nationalities." This principle, however, raised a serious problem: Supposing that the various Mongol groups wanted to unite? Was such unification permissible? Amagaev, in full accord with Comintern thinking, pointed out that the question could not be answered without some qualification. It was all a matter of timing in revolutionary strategy: "The problem of uniting the Mongol race is a matter of future voluntary agreement of the workers themselves, business for the day after the victory of the national-revolutionary movement."[22] The basic Comintern objection to "pan" movements was their support by reactionary forces; therefore, to encourage such movements strengthened rather than weakened reaction.

It is undoubtedly true that Amagaev was speaking under instruction. In March, 1925, a prospective platform for the fourth congress was submitted to the Executive Committee of the Comintern; it had as its intent a revision of the Kiakhta platform. The Executive Committee of the Comintern returned the prospective

---

[21] *Chetvertyi s'ezd MNRSP* (Ulan Bator, 1925), p. 8. In the original, *Mongol* reads *arat*, which is the Mongol equivalent of *worker* and refers to the average nomad. As *arat* is, however, a meaningless term, I have not translated it literally.
[22] *Chetvertyi s'ezd*, p. 47.

platform with the comment that it was obsolete, particularly with regard to Pan-Mongolism. The committee also ordered that the writing of a new platform for the MNRP be postponed to a later party congress.

It seems safe to conclude that the rejected program had been written under the guidance of Rinchino. It had obviously brought about his downfall as chief Comintern agent in the MPR, for it was Amagaev who dominated and controlled the Fourth Party Congress, not Rinchino. The reason for the timing of Rinchino's loss of power seems clear: by 1925 the Pan-Mongol question was no longer a theoretical one, but one that touched the interests of the Soviet Union. In 1921 the Chinese had been driven not only from Outer Mongolia but also from Urianghai. The Soviet Union then imposed on Urianghai a new status, that of a satellite under Soviet protectorship, and gave the area a new name: Tannu-Tuva. When the inhabitants of Tannu-Tuva in 1924 wished to affiliate with Outer Mongolia, the Soviet government moved quickly to nip this threat of a Pan-Mongol movement in the bud. Soviet troops were dispatched to the area, and a revolt was put down. Subsequently, the government of the MPR was forced to accept Tannu-Tuva as an "independent" people's republic.[23] The question of the nationalities of Tannu-Tuva voting for absorption into the MPR "after the victory of the national-revolutionary movement" was never to arise, for in 1944 the area was incorporated into the USSR.

Although the action of the Soviet Union was highly unpopular among the Mongols in Urga, they had no choice but to accept the solution dictated to them. We may wonder what enabled the Buriats to retain any influence at all in Outer Mongolian affairs after 1925. The following explanations may provide an answer. In the first place, this was a period in which genuine, if limited, debate on Comintern policy was permitted. In a sense, Rinchino had been foolish to go against a policy that had been shaped by leading theoreticians like Lenin and Roy. But that Rinchino felt able to do so at all is indicative of the state of affairs: he could suffer relative loss of power for taking the losing side of the argument, without being purged completely. Second, there was an absolute shortage of trained men capable of running the affairs of the MPR, men who were politically suitable and who knew the Mongolian language. The Soviet minister plenipotentiary Vasiliev, for example, had sat through the stormy and critical debates of the Third Party Congress without being able to follow them, because he had no knowledge of

---

[23] Friters, p. 130 ff.

Mongolian; he had to depend on Rinchino for information. The lack of a literate class in Outer Mongolia guaranteed the survival of the Buriats for some time, until Mongols could be trained to supplant them. Finally, we may be sure that the Buriats themselves held on to office because they believed they might salvage something in the days to come, a belief encouraged by the facts that debate on Comintern policy was still permitted, and that the ministers in the Mongolian government still had some authority for administrative action and could thus modify Comintern policy.

But the lesson of the Fourth Party Congress was clear: the Comintern made and broke people, and there was danger for those inside as well as those outside its ranks. Small wonder that the Fourth Party Congress had the air of being well stage-managed, with little debate.[24]

In the interval between the third and fourth party congresses, leftist elements tightened their grip. In fact, the only division of opinion in the Fourth Party Congress was on a major item of business—religious property—and even this division is hard to discern. The Urga Khutukhtu had died in May, 1924, but a search for a ninth reincarnation was forbidden by law. Consequently, the issue of the disposal of his not inconsiderable property arose. A reading of the transcript of the Fourth Party Congress (unfortunately not a verbatim account) leaves the impression that the Mongols were doing largely what they were told to do. Genkin, the contemporary Soviet commentator, professes to see splits in opinion between Right and Left. The most extreme proposal was made by Choibalsan, who advocated that the Khutukhtu's property be assigned in equal shares to religious purposes, state cultural expenditures, and public health. Khayan Khirva, later head of the secret police and loyal to the Soviet Union, merely suggested that the division be based on monetary, not physical, valuation. So-called rightist opinion, as represented by Ja Damba, was that, although the threefold division was acceptable, items of religious use should be given to the religious authorities. In other words, the debates were largely concerned with minor objections to leftist proposals.

The threats of the Right to the Left after 1925 were largely that members of the Right could use executive governmental powers to obstruct the Left, and that the Rightists could attempt to follow their own policies. For example, they had started negotiations with Germany for technical assistance.

---

[24] For example, a delegate who attempted to raise the whole issue of religious policy was ruled out of order (*Chetvertyi s'ezd*, p. 47).

The Fifth Party Congress

At the Fifth Party Congress in 1926, Amagaev repeated the familiar theme that it was imperative to increase the party's links with the masses. Nikiforov, the Soviet ambassador (who had also taken part in the Fourth Party Congress), promised Soviet aid should an external threat develop. The resolutions passed emphasized the need to break trade links with China and to liquidate the semi-independent estates of the monasteries.[25] Such resolutions seem highly orthodox and prompt this question: Where was the Right during the Fifth Party Congress? The only indication of rightist activity during its debates was Damba's remark that the Mongolian nobility was not a threat and that Buddhism was not a problem.[26]

Throughout this period the Left was becoming more urgent in its demands for change. It pressed for confiscation of the property of the "feudal class" and for a progressive income tax, and protested that the new Mongolian bank was extending credit to the wealthy instead of the poor. These protests were definitely inspired by the Executive Committee of the Comintern, which pressured not only the Left but Amagaev to stir the Mongols to action. If the Comintern was demanding that the Left make some move,[27] so were the young men of Outer Mongolia. The MPR Congress of Trade Unions, at its first session in August, 1927, was the scene of an open attack on the Right by Chizhiia, its secretary, himself a newcomer to politics.

The Sixth Party Congress

At this point, it would seem, a firm, experienced, and bold hand took hold of Outer Mongolian politics, if only for a short time. Michael Borodin, in late 1927, chose to return to the Soviet Union via the MPR, after failing to meet success in his mission to the Kuomintang. While in Ulan Bator he attended the Sixth Party Congress (September 22 to October 4). By then Borodin knew that Comintern hopes of a revolution in China, with the Kuomintang as

---

[25] Smith, p. 51.

[26] Poppe, p. 15. The Fifth Party Congress is scantily reported. I was unable to find transcripts of party congresses after the fourth, although transcripts of very recent ones are available.

[27] The demands of the Left are given in *Istoriia MNR*, p. 281 ff.; Zlatkin, *MNR: Strana novoi*, p. 180 ff.; I. Ia. Zlatkin, *Ocherki novoi i noveishei istorii Mongolii* (Moscow, 1957), p. 209 ff. Zlatkin, *MNR: Strana novoi*, states definitely that the Executive Committee of the Comintern was involved in the proceedings of the Left.

the vehicle, were dead. He must also have realized that now the MPR was the basis of the Soviet position in the Far East. Hence he advised the Mongols to strengthen the Left politically, to concentrate on building up cavalry forces to supplement Soviet infantry and armor, and to intensify political control of the army.[28]

The extent of Borodin's influence is unknown, nor is it known whether his recommendations were embodied in subsequent Comintern directives. The collapse of Soviet policy in China called for a rethinking of the USSR's course of action in the Far East, and others besides Borodin must have given serious thought to Outer Mongolia. But whether it was Borodin or other policy makers in the Comintern who were responsible, the Left began to exert more pressure.

The 1928 Central Committee Plenum and Its Aftermath

In April, 1928, a plenum of the Central Committee of the MNRP called for expulsion of the Rightists from both party and government.[29] A few months later, in September, the Congress of Trade Unions again expressed sharp criticism of the Right. The next month a plenum of the Central Committee of Revsomol added its voice to the rising volume of adverse comment. That its voice was the deciding one in this campaign may be seen from the fact that the Central Committee of the MNRP used Revsomol resolutions to frame a platform for the Seventh Party Congress, which started on October 23, 1928. After forty-seven days of debate the Left carried the day. The congress expelled the Rightist and called for more direct action against "feudalism," for lower taxes on the poor, for a party purge, and for party reorganization.[30] These moves took place under Comintern direction.[31]

Both Damba and Ja Damba were removed on the charge that they had used their positions to engage in "rightist opportunism." Damba was quoted as saying that the former feudal classes were "political corpses" and that the nobles and religious leaders who had fled the MPR, apparently with the cognizance of the government, constituted no threat to the state. In addition, Damba was blamed for the

---

[28] Anna Louise Strong accompanied Borodin to Ulan Bator. Borodin's views on military matters are reported by Yasuo Misshima and Tomio Goto, *A Japanese View of Outer Mongolia*, translated and condensed by A. J. Gradjdanzev (New York, 1942), p. 54.

[29] The time lag between the Sixth Party Congress and the April plenum suggests that the Mongols, though willing to listen to Borodin, needed orders from Moscow before attempting a major change in policy.

[30] Zlatkin, *MNR: Strana novoi*, p. 187 ff.; Zlatkin, *Ocherki novoi*, p. 213 ff.

[31] Zlatkin, *MNR: Strana novoi*, p. 186.

MPR's trade and educational links with Europe, for the fact that the extent of share herding had not declined, for the increase in the number of lamas, and for the fact that the presidents of regional administrations still included a leaven of former nobles. Also attributed to Damba was the increase in the cattle holdings of monastic estates, while those of the poor had decreased.

There is little doubt that this was the state of affairs in the MPR of the late twenties. The journal *Khoziaistvo Mongolii*, started in 1927 and edited and largely written by Soviet contributors, supported these accusations with statistical data.[32] Although one has to examine all but the most recent Mongolian statistics with a rather cautious eye (Damba himself complained of the difficulty of making the average Mongol report accurately to census takers), the statistics of the time nonetheless did support the factual truth of the leftist position. In any event, Damba Dorji, Ja Damba, and Rinchino were all exiled to the Soviet Union in 1928. With the decline of Rinchino, the Buriats lost their protector. Dashi Sampilon in 1929, Batukhan in 1930, and Zhamtsarano in 1932 were also exiled to the Soviet Union. Some, if not all, of these men died in the purges of the late 1930's.[33]

The collapse of the Mongolian Right preceded the collapse of the rightist leaders Bukharin and Rykov in the Soviet Union. Those who pressed for left-wing policies—Gendun, Chizhiia, Badarkho, and Dindub—seem to have taken over important roles, and new men became prominent: El'dby-ochir as first secretary of the MNRP, and Damdin-surun as president of the Revsomol.[34]

The purge of the late 1920's had another significant result. Previously, purges had steadily moved the center of gravity of political opinion toward the Left. They had reduced the willingness of the Mongols to think or act for themselves and had narrowed the range of Mongol political opinion. The latest purge, however, brought to the fore young men whose opinions were highly sympathetic to the type of changes the Comintern wished to implement in Outer Mongolia. The idea of obedience to a Comintern interest rather than to the Mongolian national interest was now accepted; it no longer had to be enforced, but was a spontaneous attitude.

---

[32] Anon., "Imushchestvennoe rassloenie skotovodcheskogo naseleniia MNR," *Khoziaistvo Mongolii*, no. 5(18) (1929), pp. 15–25.

[33] Zhamtsarano was accused, among other things, of supporting Buddhism (*Istoriia MNR*, p. 282). See also Robert A. Rupen, "The Buryat Intelligentsia," *Far Eastern Quarterly*, XV (1956), 397.

[34] Maslennikov, p. 54, describes Gendun as leader of the "left deviationists."

LOCAL ADMINISTRATIVE ORGANIZATION
AND FINANCIAL REFORM

What was true of the MNRP at top levels was not true of its organs
at the grass roots. For example, local plenipotentiaries who supervised monastic estates often were not even party members.[35]
Throughout this period there was constant stress on the problems
posed by local separatism. Party cells, where they existed, frequently used local administrations to further their own ends rather
than those of the national party.

The Need for Centralization

In 1927 the University of the Toilers of the East sent an expedition
to the Tsetserlik aimak to study a tax reform introduced a year
earlier; the expedition was designed in part to bring local administrations under closer central supervision.[36] It studied two hoshun,
eight somon, and thirty bag administrations. As the Tsetserlik
aimak was a central region, the conditions uncovered by the
expedition undoubtedly represent better rather than average circumstances.

The situation they found must have distressed the investigators.
Aimak and hoshun offices were located in monasteries, and somon
and bag offices usually were situated in the tent of the elected
president, who naturally moved with the other stock raisers.
Communications among all the units were poor, for there were no
telephone and telegraph lines, and all messages had to pass by
courier. Under favorable circumstances, it took four days to reach
Ulan Bator from aimak headquarters. An average time for getting
to hoshun headquarters might be two days, and there were twenty-
one hoshuns in all. Naturally, it took less time to visit lower
administrative units but it was virtually impossible for one man
alone to visit all the headquarters at aimak level within a year.

Had an investigator visited all the lowest administrative units, he
would have found few people loyal to the new regime. Leftist policy
was partly to blame. It made a great deal of sense for the Leftists to
place their men in the intermediate and top administrative offices
and, as the number of leftist followers grew, to assign them to new
institutions being formed along socialist lines. These men had
received an expensive education and by inclination and ambition
were not likely to wish to return to the life of a stock-raising camp.

---

[35] *Chetvertyi s'ezd*, p. 31.

[36] F. T., "Mestnye organy vlasti Tsetserlik aimaka," *Revoliutsionnyi Vostok*, no.
4–5 (1928), p. 390 ff.

Younger people predominated in the higher administrative units, and there were few former nobles and hardly any lamas at the top. The converse was true in the lower administrative units. The older people who staffed the primary administrative units were illiterate, and did not belong to the party. As one descended the ladder of authority, financial record keeping, financial and administrative responsibility, and continuity of personnel in administrative offices all declined.

The implications of the policy of using Leftists in higher organs of power were that party members would be forced to continually supervise the lowest administrative ranks and to find ways of ensuring obedience to government decrees. Although the upper ranks could nominate new leaders at the lower levels, it is possible that the older administrators, with experience and traditions behind them, remained the de facto leaders. There were, however, positive factors: as the great khurals and party congresses were elected indirectly, the Left naturally came to predominate. Moreover, encouragement of women and young people to take part in the administration tapped new sources of leadership.

The report of the expedition of the University of the Toilers of the East reveals that Outer Mongolia in 1928 was much the same as the one described by Maiskii in 1920. "It is necessary to note the slow tempo of work," the report remarks cautiously. It observed that the "separation of church and state" had not been accomplished, a generalization based on the fact that the expedition had found a somon administration devoting an entire meeting to complaining that it was always entrusted with preparing the tent for the yearly religious festival (Nadom); it felt that some other somon should bear the cost. The expedition found some administrations still discussing whether they should tax monasteries. When administrative officers were asked why there were no schools, they replied, "The people do not send their children," or simply, "No money." When asked why no one read the propaganda literature sent out, the answers were "No one can read," or "There is no time." One conclusion may be drawn from the expedition's report: the opposition of the countryside—the khudon opposition that is reputed to have destroyed the Right in 1928—is a figment of the imagination of modern Soviet and Mongol commentators.

The 1926 Reform of Taxes and Local Budgets

The reform the Soviet expedition had come to study was the 1926 law on taxes and local budgets. Prior to 1926, all local governments except that in Urga had financed themselves, each levying different taxes on the population; for instance, taxes on cattle varied as much as ninefold among regions. Local administrations had been following their own initiative in the matter of office personnel, remuneration, and duties.

The reform took the tax initiative away from the localities. A standard rate of taxation was introduced, a table of organization was set up for the various administrative units, and sources of income and permitted expenditures were rigidly defined. Budget estimation was initiated, and estimates for lower units of administration had to be confirmed by higher ones. Monastic herds were subjected to progressive taxation. The taxes levied on the shabi were similar to those the lay population was assessed. To ensure the compliance of the local administrations with the center's wishes, standard percentages of the taxes they collected were permitted them as deductions to finance their operations, a device also used in the Soviet Union at that time.[37]

Given the political reform and the fact that the upper layers of the administration were manned by Leftists, the population at large could now be subjected to taxation to finance the central government and to help destroy the economic power of the monasteries. For the first time in Outer Mongolia's history, the population was subjected to a centralized and standardized tax system. Adverse reactions were sharp, especially in the monasteries.[38] Only one fact saved the new regime from a widespread uprising. As we have learned from the expedition of the University of the Toilers of the East, local administrative units in 1927 were still discussing whether to tax religious institutions. In short, the habit of obedience to central government had still to be learned. Hence, the impact of the reform was substantially lessened.

IMPLEMENTATION OF GOVERNMENT POLICIES

This review of the period 1924–1928 suggests that, at the cabinet level, a division of opinion on major policy goals, combined with a shortage of men of experience and a high level of personal ability, caused policy to be less than vigorous. Below the cabinet level, the administrative system became less reliable the broader its base. Although the right wing of the cabinet represented the wishes and

---

[37] See *ibid.* for details of the reform. See also Zlatkin, *MNR: Strana novoi,* p. 171 ff.; Zlatkin, *Ocherki novoi,* p. 203 ff.

[38] Zlatkin, *MNR: Strana novoi,* p. 173; Zlatkin, *Ocherki novoi,* p. 204; Misshima and Goto, p. 18.

goals of the broad masses more closely, it was beginning to be separated from them by leftist control of the administrative system.

Reduction of the Resident Chinese

The Leftists were continually vexed by the seeming apathy or the lack of desire for change on the part of the Rightists who dominated the cabinet and the top administrative posts. Although Mongols of all shades of opinion were united in their desire to run their own country, their government had left the problem of the large, and potentially irredentist, Chinese population largely untouched. For example, by 1928 the Mongolian Central Cooperative still commanded only 29.6 percent of the country's trade circulation, despite the fact that it had been made the political duty of each party member to join the cooperative and introduce new members.[39] Yet Chinese traders continued to operate largely unhindered.[40]

Such administrative steps as were taken led, essentially, only to the eviction of the larger Chinese firms. For example, the total number of trade licenses issued to both Chinese and other foreign firms was steadily reduced. (By 1928 most, if not all, American and European firms had suspended operations.[41]) Another device used

---

[39] Maslennikov, p. 122; Anatolii D. Kallinikov, *Revoliutsionnaia Mongoliia* (Moscow, n.d.), p. 59.

[40] Before World War I, Russia had an import surplus with Mongolia, and the percentages of Mongolian exports and imports received and sent by Russia were similar to those of 1927 and 1928. It is worth noting that the Soviet Union was of little help in the Mongols' balance of trade. By 1928, when Outer Mongolia's trade levels had been restored to those of 1910–1913, the Soviet Union still was responsible for a mere one-fifth of the available Mongolian imports, despite the fact that between 1925 and 1928 her share of total exports to Mongolia had risen from 24.1 to 57.8 percent, thus giving her dominance of the Mongol export market. Strong (Bk. II, p. 391) quotes Onishchenko, head of the Soviet trading organization Stormong, to the effect that the 1910–1913 trade levels were so restored. For other data see N. T. Vargin, "Torgovlia," in I. Ia. Zlatkin (ed.), *MNR: Sbornik statei* (Moscow, 1952), p. 206. Onishchenko also said that in 1926 the Soviet trading organizations in Mongolia were combined into Stormong, which must have created the basis for Sovmontorg. Zlatkin (*MNR: Strana novoi*, p. 169) dates the beginning of Stormong's operations from July 1, 1927.

[41] I. G. Iur'ev, "K voprosu ob inostrannom kapitale vo Vneshnei Mongolii do narodno-demokraticheskoi revoliutsii 1921 g. i v pervye ee gody," *Kratkie soobshcheniia instituta vostokovedeniia*, no. 6 (1952), p. 56. Iur'ev also notes that of 19 foreign firms in Urga in 1925, 15 were English and American and 4 were German. In the same year there were 56 private Russian traders (many from Harbin), as against 166 in 1924. According to *China: A Commercial and Industrial Handbook*, U.S. Department of Commerce, Bureau of Foreign and Domestic Commerce, Trade Promotion Series, no. 38 (Washington, 1926), p. 688, there were no Americans and only three American firms in Urga in 1925. In 1932 a German firm, Wostwag, opened communications between Kalgan and Urga. This exception was owing to the disruption of Mongol trade caused by interruption in the operation of the Chinese Eastern Railway (see *China Year Book, 1936*, p. 19).

was the imposition of a 20 percent duty on gold and silver exports. Also, the Mongolian National Bank was given power to manipulate foreign exchange conversion at will. These fiscal measures made it more difficult for Chinese (and other foreign) firms to repatriate their earnings. The imposition of arbitrary customs procedures added to the large Chinese trader's difficulties. Ma Ho-t'ien asserts that customs officers were not only intentionally slow in dealing with Chinese traders but also used their power to value commodities to discriminate against the Chinese. Although the general customs rate levied on imports and exports was 6 percent, some commodities were subjected to higher rates than scheduled: the rate on tarbagan pelts was 9 percent; on tobacco, 12 percent; and on some luxury goods, 30 percent and, according to Ma Ho-t'ien, as much as 100 percent. Finally, foreign merchants were forced to buy internal passports and residence permits, to pay for passport inspections, to pay a business tax assessed proportionally to a firm's capital, and to submit to inspection of their mail and their scales and measures. And they were subjected to petty harassments:

Another grievance has to do with the theatre which is set up in every banner [region]. For this, a contribution of ten dollars is exacted from each Chinese firm. Then the theatre shows plays depicting the oppression of the Mongols by Chinese officials like Ch'en I. The Chinese officials are forced to attend; if they fail to do so, each one is fined sixty dollars, and if they leave after seeing half the play, they are also fined. Thirty bricks of tea are demanded of each firm attending the performance.[42]

Faced with such difficulties, the larger Chinese and Western firms vacated the Mongolian market, but the small Chinese trader remained. In terms of prices then current, the Chinese retained their volume of foreign trade. As inflation in Outer Mongolia's prices during this period was slight, the total Chinese trade position was not seriously reduced. Hence, there could have been no great decline in the total number of Chinese traders, even though the large firms had left the market.

The small Chinese trader was the average Chinese resident in Outer Mongolia. Chinese troops had left the country in July, 1921. In 1922 all Chinese without settled occupations had been expelled. A small number of Chinese agriculturalists remained, despite the introduction of legislation discriminating against them. But they probably numbered only some two or three thousand, and together cultivated very few acres.

It is understandable that the Chinese trader of small means

---

[42] Ma Ho-t'ien, p. 20.

should have tried to hang on. The large firms, with interests in areas other than the Mongol market, were able to cut their losses. Also, they could more accurately appraise their chances for the future. The small Chinese trader, however, had special investments in skills, local knowledge, and experience. If he left the market he faced heavy capital losses, and had no immediate alternative opportunity. Usually, therefore, he tried to ride out what he must have thought was another temporary storm.

Religion and Education

In areas where Rightists had stronger inhibitions against change, policy shifts were less pronounced. In religious matters, the Mongolian government restricted itself to forbidding the search for the reincarnation of the Urga Khutukhtu, placing lamas on call for military service, and imprisoning and liquidating some of the higher lamas. (Liquidation, as the responsibility of the secret police, did not reflect the temper of the cabinet.) Moreover, the shabi was freed from his tax obligations to his monastic superior. These administrative measures, combined with the taming of the religious leadership through purges, would in time have solved the religious problem. The financial and economic base of the religious sector would have been destroyed, and young men, especially those of military age, would have been exposed to indoctrination in the army.

Nevertheless, the Leftists had strong complaints. They argued that the shabi, though legally freed by the Mongolian government, still remained a de facto serf of the monastery. Furthermore, what statistical evidence there was—and it was published in the influential *Khoziaistvo Mongolii*—suggested that monastic wealth in livestock herds was actually increasing. Finally, the influence of the religious sector was strongest where that of the Leftists was weakest—among the common people. The religious retained a powerful hold on the beliefs of the average Mongol, a situation that was intolerable to the Left.

In education (and other areas of public policy) the story of languishing progress was the same. By 1925 only 1,500 of 79,000 young people of school age received any formal education whatsoever. The budget, although a rising and substantial share of it went to education, was used primarily to train party cadres. The allocations for genuine education were usually 5 percent of the total budgetary expenditures. From descriptions given by Ma Ho-t'ien and the expedition of the University of the Toilers of the East,

it seems that the education provided by Outer Mongolian schools
was minimal.

Implementation of Economic Policy and
Soviet Technical Assistance

In agriculture and stock raising the situation was just as bad. By
1928 the total of veterinary workers, at all levels of skill, was only
fifty-three. Even the highest level of competence was low, as none
of the workers had had formal training. By 1927, after much
discussion of the problem, only 80,000 acres had been put to hay,
acreage that was small indeed for livestock herds of 20 million
head.[43] In 1930 an agricultural expedition of the Academy of
Sciences of the USSR found no trace of change in stock raising.
I. F. Shul'zhenko, an agricultural authority, remarked at the time that
"techniques have not changed from those of the twelfth or thirteenth century." [44] The Third Party Congress in 1924 had stressed
the need to construct a state veterinary service, to develop winter
fodder by use of stockpiles, and to protect stock by building corrals
and wells. Little attention had been paid to carrying out these
directives.

The economic and social technical assistance the Mongols received was not of great help. There was, for example, a categorical
prohibition on the publication of reports of some Soviet expeditions
(e.g., geologic expeditions), because they might provide information of use to a potential enemy.[45] A Soviet medical mission which
included a branch for veterinary work did tackle some of the
diseases endemic in the MPR.[46] Beginning in 1924, the Academy of
Sciences of the USSR, sometimes in conjunction with the Mongolian Committee of Sciences, sent a series of expeditions to survey the
flora, linguistics, archaeology, geography, geology, and mineral
resources of the country.[47]

Much of this research was, however, of questionable value to a

---

[43] F. S. Tsaplin, "Sel'skoe khoziaistvo," in Zlatkin (ed.), MNR: Sbornik statei, p.
107.
[44] I. F. Shul'zhenko, "Miasnoe khoziaistvo Mongolii," Trudy Mongol'skoi Komissii,
no. 8 (Leningrad, 1933), p. 6. See also Ia. Ia. Lus, N. N. Kolesnik, I. F. Shul'zhenko,
et al., "Domashnie Zhivotnye Mongolii," Trudy Mongol'skoi Komissii, no. 22
(Moscow and Leningrad, 1936).
[45] Verbal communication from N. N. Poppe.
[46] Strong, Bk. II, p. 353.
[47] For an account of some of the expeditions see E. M. Murzaev, Geograficheskie
issledovaniia MNR (Moscow and Leningrad, 1948), p. 120 ff.; A. D. Simukov, "Rol'
SSSR v dele issledovaniia Mongolii," Khoziaistvo Mongolii, no. 5(18) (1929). Many
of the expeditions contributed monographs to the series Trudy Mongol'skoi
Komissii.

truly underdeveloped country, as the Soviet experts themselves came to recognize. The issue of the proper nature of technical assistance had by no means been resolved in the Soviet Union. Most of the aid to Mongolia was in the nature of very basic research. An adequate catalog of plant life is, however, a luxury easily foregone if the resources devoted to its compilation are diverted from more useful purposes, such as increasing the output of agricultural foodstuffs.

Banking and Currency

In banking and currency some initiative was shown, but only because the Soviet Union took matters into her own hands. The introduction of banking and of a new currency, the tugrik, was carried out successfully. The Mongolian National Bank was set up as a joint company in June, 1924.[48] In December of that year it started issuing the tugrik to supplant the various media of exchange: liang, Mexican dollars, rubles, and commodities such as tea and cattle. In February, 1925, the bank was given the monopoly of note issuance. It issued notes rather slowly, and in the first years permitted their conversion into silver. The currency was backed by 25 percent precious metals and 75 percent short-term obligations and easily salable goods.[49] No explicit charge was made for currency conversion, an important inducement because Chinese moneylenders and currency changers did make such charges. As branch offices of the bank were scattered throughout the country, a single currency reduced the costs of doing business. Demand for the new currency exceeded its supply, however; because of rumors that tugriks might appreciate in terms of silver, there was some desire to hold them speculatively. By April, 1928, all foreign currencies had been withdrawn from circulation, as the bank did not reissue foreign currencies it had exchanged for tugriks.

The reform was skillfully handled; there seems no convincing evidence that it caused strong inflationary pressures or noteworthy depreciation in the foreign exchange rate of the tugrik. Further, it led to the displacement of foreign currencies. To prop up the reform, the government apparently attempted to promote moneti-

---

[48] *China Year Book, 1926–27*, p. 800.
[49] On monetary reform see E. Breiter, "Denezhnaia reforma i narodnoe khoziaistvo Mongolii," *Novyi Vostok*, no. 25 (1929), pp. 127–146; L. Zolotarev, "Denezhaia reforma v Mongolii," *ibid.*, no. 13–14 (1926), pp. 234–236; N. N. Tugarinov, "Denezhnoe obrashchenie Mongolii," *ibid.*, no. 20–21 (1928), pp. 241–257. See also F. D. Holzman, "The Financial System of the MPR," in *MPR*, Human Relations Area Files (New Haven, 1956), III, Ec. 105–115; and *Izvestiia Ulan Bator Khoto*, May 16, 1925.

zation of the economy by ordering taxes to be paid in money. As no law or administrative decree on this matter seems to be available, the precise requirements are not known. In any event, the attempt failed; by 1928 the bulk of the taxes were still being paid in kind, and were being collected by the Mongolian Central Cooperative. Disagreements among Soviet commentators suggest that the degree of monetization effected by the monetary reform itself was not substantial. The nomad still lived primarily in a barter economy.

It is apparent, from this brief but comprehensive survey, that until 1928 the Mongol government had a largely neutral, and possibly negative, effect on economic matters. From 1924 to 1928 most of the budgetary resources were devoted to financing such administrative reforms as were necessary to fasten the regime's hold on the country. Between 1926 and 1928 the budgetary expenditures of the government increased from 10.4 to 15.7 million tugriks.[50] Although some of the growth may reflect inflationary effects, it may also represent an increase in government control over social resources.[51] In 1926, 44.2 percent of budgetary expenditures were for administrative expenses, and in 1928, 45.9 percent,[52] a substantial portion representing the costs of instituting effective local government.

By 1928 the data on budgetary expenditures are fairly reliable, for the administrative reform had had some time to take effect. In that year, of a total of 10.9 percent of the budget expended on the national economy, only 2.9 percent was allocated to industry. Defense spending during this period was large, about 25 to 30 percent of all budgetary expenditures.

PRELUDE TO EXTREMISM

Whether by policy and design, or by chance and neglect, the Soviet Union, apart from technical assistance, contributed little to Outer Mongolia during this period. At the same time, the Outer Mongolian government was apathetic when not prodded. In combination, these circumstances led to the rising pressure by the Mongolian Left, which was fueled by the Leftists' anger at the slowness of change. They accused the Right of delaying social change, of protecting the monasteries and lamas, and of sheltering the former feudal class. Yet the Leftists lacked popular support and, until the

[50] Holzman, in *MPR*, Human Relations Area Files, III, Ec. 25.

[51] Holzman estimated that the ratio of budgetary expenditures to national income increased between 1927 and 1930. But see his qualifications and also his strictures on Mongolian budgetary data of the time (*ibid.*, III, Ec. 2–11).

[52] *Ibid.*, III, Ec. 27.

collapse of the Soviet government's policy toward China, seem to
have lacked Soviet support for sweeping measures involving social
and economic change. Soviet support, however, was not long in
coming.

After 1927 the international position of the MPR changed. It was
no longer necessary to be cautious to prevent Chinese reactions. By
1928 Stalin had triumphed over his chief political foe, Trotsky. To
do so he had had to rely on the support of the right wing of the
Bolshevik Party in the Soviet Union. After his success in destroying
Trotsky, Stalin proceeded to duplicate this feat among his erstwhile
right-wing supporters, notably Bukharin and Rykov. Stalin then
instituted in the Soviet Union a broad program of change, which
essentially embodied the thinking of the Bolshevik left wing. The
Soviet Union planned a similar program for the MPR. The government of that country was asked to institute planning and social
change, of a kind similar to that introduced in the Central Asian
union republics of the USSR.

Some commentators have presented those changes the Outer
Mongolian government did finally attempt to institute as evidence
of a Trotskyite deviation. In the next chapter we consider these
changes in the light of this assertion. We can, however, state one
preliminary conclusion: the Mongolian left wing, which had been
built up by the Comintern, did not have freedom of action until
both the international and domestic circumstances of the Soviet
Union were ripe for it.

5

EXTREMISM

Major Policy Changes Instituted by the Left

The Left, on securing power, made fundamental changes. The Seventh Party Congress, held in late 1928, not only had destroyed the Right but had also called for confiscation of feudal property, lowering of taxes on poor and middle-income Mongols (part of the introduction of a general progressive tax on the basis of class principles), and speedy implementation of the Soviet trade monopoly. State and cooperative trading agencies had been ordered to take the place of Chinese traders.[1] The Fifth Great Khural, in January, 1929, had given formal assent to these mandates. The Eighth Party Congress which met in 1929 (followed by another rubber-stamping great khural, the sixth) called for collectivization, elaboration of a five-year plan, and the immediate end of trade with the Chinese.[2] Owen Lattimore was so struck by this change in direction that he attributed it to a left-wing deviation in the government, a deviation led by the young men of Revsomol.[3]

The new plans were drastic, especially in view of the state of affairs in the MPR in 1929. The economic wealth of the church, the

---

[1] *Istoriia MNR* (Moscow, 1954), p. 284; Erdeni-Ochir, "Na puti k sotsialisticheskomu stroitel'stvu (VIII s'ezd MNRP)," *Khoziaistvo Mongolii*, no. 3(21) (1930), p. 65 ff.

[2] E. G. Botvinnik, "K voprosu o kontrol'nykh tsifrakh na 1931 god," *Khoziaistvo Mongolii*, no. 1(25) (1931), p. 7, states that the plan was started in 1930, whereas the years actually covered were 1931–1935. Whether there was a delay in setting up the plan is not clear.

[3] Owen Lattimore's introduction to Gerard M. Friters, *Outer Mongolia and Its International Position*, ed. Eleanor Lattimore (London, 1951), p. xxxvii. N. N. Poppe, in his review of Friters' book (*Yale Review*, XXXIX [1950], 567), has strongly criticized Lattimore's view.

nobility, and rich citizens remained essentially untouched. The traditional sources of authority still had social support, although there was growing dissatisfaction in the monasteries because of the new taxes and the delay in finding a reincarnation for the Urga Khutukhtu. The population was almost totally illiterate, with only 2 percent in secular schools. There was no "proletariat" to act as the "vanguard" in radical moves, and the MNRP was still weak at the grass-roots level. Nor had the Soviet Union yet been able to supplant the Chinese in trade relations. Not least of all, there was an almost total lack of knowledge of planning statistics; there was also no planning apparatus, no experience with yearly plans, and no cadres to implement such plans.[4]

Reliance on Soviet Guidance

Adoption of Soviet political and socioeconomic policies.—It is not difficult to appreciate why the Outer Mongolians selected the policies already outlined. From the events then taking place in the Soviet Union, it becomes evident that the Mongolian policy changes were part and parcel of a major change in Soviet economic policy, which itself went along with a major shift in Comintern thinking. In this period, "leftist adventurism" generally characterized Comintern policy.[5] There need be no doubt that the Mongols listened to the Comintern; they made it quite clear that they were following Comintern directives.[6] In addition to Mongolian admissions on this score, Soviet historians concede that the Mongolian policy changes were due to a mechanical transposition of Soviet domestic policy to Outer Mongolia.[7] It could hardly have been otherwise, for there was

[4] The articles on planning which appeared, beginning in 1929, in the journal *Khoziaistvo Mongolii* describe the absence of favorable conditions for transition to planning. See, for example, the articles by I. L. Baevskii in no. 4(17) (1929), Dugarzhap in no. 4(17) and no. 5(18) (1929), Iu. B. Eskin in no. 3(21) (1930), Sodnom and Kurash in no. 1(25) (1931), etc. See also Robert Smith, "Political, Economic and Trade Conditions in Outer Mongolia" (MS in Library of the Hoover Institution, Stanford, Calif.).

[5] In the Chinese Communist Party, for example, there was a period of leftist deviationism (1928–1932), the so-called Li li-san line.

[6] Chapter 3 illustrates this tendency. A Comintern directive to the MPR (Jan. 24, 1927) is available in *Kommunisticheskii Internatsional*, no. 31(209) (Aug. 29, 1929), pp. 38–47. Robert A. Rupen, in his review of Owen Lattimore, *Nomads and Commissars: Mongolia Revisited* (New York, 1962), in *Journal of Asian Studies*, XXII (1963), 222, quotes from the proceedings of the Eighth Party Congress: "Thanks to the brotherly leadership of the Comintern we have attained great successes. . . . before everything are needed close ties and the direct leadership of the Comintern. . . . All the resolutions and decrees of the Comintern and plenum of the International Committee of the Comintern which are concerned with our Party must be carried out completely."

[7] *Istoriia MNR*, p. 286, rather soberly comments: "Such a policy was incorrect and contradicted the Marxist-Leninist thesis on the necessity of strictly accounting for the concrete historical conditions and peculiarities of each country."

a strong Soviet presence in Ulan Bator which guided and directed events. This is not to deny that when the order "March!" was given, the Mongolian Revsomols marched willingly. They pushed on with zeal and committed all the mistakes of intolerant and inexperienced zealots. Excess, intolerance, and inexperience were the rule also in the Soviet Union during this period; it was not only in Mongolia that the Left was impatient for orders.

Put simply, Stalin had come to accept the Soviet leftist viewpoint on industrialization, planning, and social change. With the loss of power of the prominent Rightists—Bukharin, Rykov, and Tomsky —in 1929–30, Stalin and his supporters initiated a major change in economic policy by instituting five-year planning and collectivization. The conclusion of the political power struggle was also reflected within the Comintern, thereby enabling the Stalinists to dominate this body also. Thus, leftist policy in the MPR was attributable not to Trotskyite deviationism but to the application of Stalinist views. The facts about collectivization and the commencement of planning in the Soviet Union are well known. When the changes in Mongolia are detailed, it will be easy to recognize similarities in policy. There was, however, a special aspect to the Mongolian economic system: its widespread reliance on nomadic stock raising. It seems evident that the Soviet experts who planned Mongolian affairs gave no special thought to Mongolian problems; they merely applied to the MPR policies that were then being implemented in the Soviet Union.

Adoption of the Soviet solution to the nomadic problem.—In 1929 the Soviet Union had many nomadic populations of her own to contend with. The Soviet nomads were distributed on the southern borders of the USSR in Central Asia and along the northern arctic coastline. The Soviet authorities failed to recognize that the settlement and collectivization of the nomads constituted a problem distinct from the peasant problem. The resolution of the Central Committee of the All-Union Party (Bolshevik) on May 27, 1929, which called for the settling of nomadic peoples, admitted its own considerable ignorance: "Despite the great significance of stock raising in the Republic, until recently the prevalence of nomadic ancestral relations has not been studied nor reflected in practical work such as the settlement of the stock raisers, the transition to more advanced forms of economies, the struggle with kulak bondage, or the forms of collectivization of such stock raisers." [8]

---

[8] Cited by M. I. Pomus, *Buriat-Mongol'skaia ASSR* (Moscow, 1937), p. 190.

The course of events inside the Soviet Union had affected different nomadic groups unevenly. In some areas (e.g., Kazakhstan), owing to an early penetration of Bolshevik control in settled areas of cultivation, land reform had taken place by 1929. In remoter areas such as Buriat Mongolia, the Far North, and the eastern Far North, there had been virtually no action in regard to nomads and their hereditary aristocracy by 1929. For that matter, even in Kazakhstan in 1929, although the leaders of the villages had been removed by familiar techniques, on the steppe and in the mountains "there even remained vestiges of an aristocracy." [9] The position of the MPR thus was not too distinct from that of areas in the Soviet Union remote from Moscow.

In the Soviet Union the same directives that set in motion the collectivization drives among the peasants applied without qualification to the nomads. In addition, the nomads were to be forced to accept a settled way of life in permanent communities. The methods used to accomplish this objective were heavy-handed, provoking the nomad, with his traditional authorities still in power, to a strong reaction, probably one stronger than that shown by the peasant. This reaction took the form of destruction of the herds which were the basis of their economy. Caroe cites estimates of livestock losses for the whole of Kazakhstan between 1924 and 1928 at 73 percent of all the cattle, 87 percent of all the sheep, and 83 percent of all the horses.[10] An agricultural expert comments: "In some regions, livestock numbers declined more than in others during forced collectivization, and recovery was only partial by 1928. A glaring illustration of this failure to recover was in the important livestock region of Kazakhstan, with its extensive grazing lands and pastoral population." [11] Walter Kolarz claims that Soviet policy had an even more disastrous result in Kirghizstan.[12] The reindeer nomads of the Far North also suffered; for example, in the Koryak National Area the number of reindeer fell from 264,000 to 127,000 between 1926 and 1934.[13] By and large, in the Soviet Union the nomads' losses were heavier than those sustained by the peasants. The nomads in the MPR suffered similar losses.

The views of Soviet planners in the MPR.—It is clear by now

[9] Olaf Caroe, *Soviet Empire: The Turks of Central Asia and Stalinism* (London, 1953), p. 175.

[10] *Ibid.*, p. 183 ff.

[11] Lazar Volin, *A Survey of Soviet Russian Agriculture*, U.S. Department of Agriculture, Agricultural Monograph no. 5 (Washington, 1951), provides data showing livestock losses to be far larger in areas of predominantly nomadic stock raising than in other areas.

[12] Walter Kolarz, *Russia and Her Colonies* (London, 1952), p. 272.

[13] Walter Kolarz, *The Peoples of the Soviet Far East* (London, 1954), p. 71.

that the major policy changes in the MPR mechanically reflected those effected in the Soviet Union. Soviet representatives in the MPR who directed the changes also did the detailed planning. It is not known how they were instructed from Moscow, but it is of interest to note that among the Soviet experts in Ulan Bator the Stalinist doctrine of "revolution in one country" had apparently emerged and did, in fact, shape plans for the Mongol future. We can trace this development by examining the articles in *Khoziaistvo Mongolii*, published in Ulan Bator, the vehicle in which the Soviet experts in the MPR made their views known. Until 1929, the publication was devoted to questions of economic, administrative, and social policy as well as to historical topics. But beginning in 1929, planning received increasing attention in its pages. In 1931 an article contributed by A. A. Simukov expressed, although in extreme form, a view that was gradually becoming dominant.[14] He argued that the geographic distribution of livestock in the MPR could be explained by variation in the natural environment. From this statement he then inferred that it was not so much social as environmental factors that were important in shaping the economy of the nomads. This thoroughly un-Marxist position provoked strong disagreement from the editor. But Simukov was merely exaggerating a viewpoint generally held and expressed by the Soviet representatives in Ulan Bator. I. L. Baevskii, for example, noted that the MPR must remain an "agrarian-livestock" economy.[15] The plan itself, as described by Baevskii, E. G. Botvinnik, and Shleifer, reflected continuance of this type of economic specialization. Baevskii was also quite frank about the role assigned to the MPR by the Soviet Union: "The five-year plan must be constructed to permit maximum utilization of the resources of the MPR in the industrialization of the USSR." [16] Shleifer was equally outspoken. He maintained that the Mongols should develop an export surplus to the Soviet Union.[17] These views cannot be dismissed as mere expressions of opinion, for they were uttered by men who were in the MPR to direct its life.

Simukov was, in a sense, only rationalizing a decision his

---

[14] A. D. Simukov, "Skotovodstvo MNR v sviazi s geograficheskimi landshaftami strani," *Khoziaistvo Mongolii*, no. 1(25) (1931), pp. 57–75.
[15] *Khoziaistvo Mongolii*, no. 4(17) (1929), p. 28 ff.
[16] *Ibid.*, p. 29.
[17] I. O. Shleifer, "Osnovnye problemy piatiletnego plana khoziaistvennogo i kul'turnogo stroitel'stva MNR," *Khoziaistvo Mongolii*, no. 3(21) (1930), p. 33. Shleifer also believed that Mongolian import levels were determined by export levels. His projections for trade levels during the Five-Year Plan did not call for a sizable export surplus, although they did call for a substantial increase in the level of exports.

compatriots in Ulan Bator had already made: the MPR was to be a raw-material exporter dovetailed into the economy of the Soviet Union. In addition, although it was the economically poorer country of the two by far, the MPR was to extend credits to the USSR. Yet, the Soviet Union seems to have offered no quid pro quo to offset the visible export surplus in the trade of the MPR.

THE ABORTIVE ECONOMIC AND SOCIAL PLAN OF 1931–1935

Targets: Collectivization and Livestock Growth

Before examining how the Outer Mongolians implemented Soviet thinking and directives, we must take a close look at the MPR's economic and social plan of 1931–1935 and some of the problems implicit in its goals which led to failure. The plan projected

TABLE 5

MAJOR TARGETS OF OUTER MONGOLIA'S ECONOMIC PLAN
OF 1931–1935

Target	Actual (1930)	Planned (1935)
National income (in millions of tugriks)	85.5	138.3
As percentage of national income		
Stock raising	64	61
Agriculture	6	13
Industry	30	26

SOURCE: *Sibirskaia Sovetskaia Entsiklopediia*, III, cols. 533–535; I. O. Shleifer, "Osnovnye problemy piatiletnego plana khoziaistvennogo i kul'turnogo stroitel'-stva Mongol'skoi Narodnoi Respubliki," *Khoziaistvo Mongolii*, no. 3(21) (1930), p. 21.

ambitious increases in all sectors of the national economy except that industry, by the end of the five-year period, was to produce a smaller share of the national income than at the beginning (table 5). Among national plans for socioeconomic development, the MPR plan must be truly unique in this respect. The more detailed figures on the planned national income given in table 6 reveal the extent of industrial growth projected for the entire country.

According to the plan, the Mongols were to breed more livestock, market more output, and be initiated into new activities such as agriculture, haymaking, and crafts while they were being collectivized and converted to sedentary life. The intent of the government was to incorporate the majority of Mongol families in collectives of one form or another by the end of the plan. Seventy-five percent of the poor Mongols (those owning less than 600 tugriks each) and 50 percent of the middle-class Mongols (those owning between 600

TABLE 6

PROJECTED STRUCTURE OF OUTER MONGOLIA'S NATIONAL INCOME, 1931–1935

(In millions of tugriks)

Receiving sector	Actual (1930)	Planned				
		1931	1932	1933	1934	1935
Stock raising						
Marketed products	19.6	20.8	22.6	25.7	29.9	33.3
Nonmarketed products	20.8	21.9	23.0	24.3	25.7	27.3
Total ᵃ	40.4	42.7	45.6	49.9	55.6	60.6
Agriculture and haymaking	3.5	4.1	6.0	8.1	10.2	12.5
Crafts, hunting, transport, and woodcutting	19.0	20.2	21.5	24.0	24.7	25.9
State industry	1.6	3.0	3.5	4.0	4.0	5.0
Trade	9.0	10.5	11.2	12.6	14.1	15.7
Budget revenue	6.6	7.1	7.7	9.2	10.8	11.3
Construction	6.0	6.5	7.0	6.5	6.0	6.0
Income from foreigners	0.3	0.3	0.3	0.3	0.3	0.3
Grand total ᵃ	85.5 ᵇ	94.4	102.9	114.6	125.7	138.3 ᵇ

ᵃ Totals may not add up because of rounding.
ᵇ These totals are incorrect. They should read 86.4 (1930) and 137.3 (1935).
SOURCE: I. O. Shleifer, "Osnovnye problemy piatiletnego plana khoziaistvennogo i kul'turnogo stroitel' stva Mongol'skoi Narodnoi Respubliki," *Khoziaistvo Mongolii*, no. 3(21) (1930), p. 21. It should be noted that the Western method of computing national income differs from that used by Shleifer.

and 3,000 tugriks each) were destined for collectivization.[18] Calculated from data on property distribution among the social strata, these figures meant the collectivization of at least 55 percent of the population.[19]

The projected increase of livestock which was to support the plan was from 17.6 to 25.0 million head.[20] Exports were to increase from 32.2 to 50.0 million tugriks, and imports, from 27.0 to 47.0 million.[21] The activities of Montsenkoop, the state trading organization, were to be expanded to deal with all imported goods and 85 percent of retail turnover to city dwellers. The number of state farms was to grow from five to twenty-six,[22] cultivating an area to be expanded from 3,500 to 355,000 dessiatines.[23] The total cultivable area was to expand to 500,000 dessiatines.[24] Transportation

[18] I. Ia. Zlatkin, *MNR: Strana novoi demokratii* (Moscow, 1950), p. 193.
[19] This percentage may be inferred from the anonymous article, "Imushchestvennoe rassloenie skotovodcheskogo naseleniia MNR," *Khoziaistvo Mongolii*, no. 5(18) (1929), p. 18.
[20] Shleifer, p. 33.
[21] Shleifer, "Osnovnyeproblemy . . . ," *Khoziaistvo Mongolii*, no. 2(20) (1930), p. 19.
[22] A. P. Tsirniuk, "K predstoiashchemu sostavleniiu piatiletnego perspektivnego plana razvitiia Mongol'skoi narodnoi kooperatsii," in *ibid.*, p. 82. The remaining 15 percent of retail turnover was to be supplied by Soviet organizations.
[23] Shleifer, "Osnovnye problemy . . . ," *Khoziaistvo Mongolii*, no. 3(21), p. 31.
[24] *Ibid.*, p. 29.

was to grow substantially in ton-miles of loads carried, and its capital budget was to be increased tenfold.[25] The least ambitious part was the industrial plan, which largely contemplated the expansion of the existing, pitifully inadequate industrial facilities. Finally, the budget was to increase both in overall size and as a percentage share of the national income.[26]

Benefits and Faults of the Plan

Naturally, there were political benefits to the plan. First, establishment of a Soviet trade monopoly would permit the ousting of the Chinese domiciled in the MPR. Second, collectivization would strengthen party control, weaken the former nobility and the religious leaders, and indoctrinate the population in new habits, loyalties, and skills.

Although unrecognized at the time, there were also dangers in the plan. To begin with, collectivization of the nomads would inevitably affect the level and the marketing of agricultural output. This might be only a short-term problem, provided a new structure of incentives could be developed. But meanwhile any Mongolian economic activity that was projected to grow out of the real savings from planned given levels of income in the agricultural sector (where most of the income was generated) would suffer when it came to financing in real terms. A less important consideration was that new industry would sensitively reflect fluctuations in its material input. In addition, the export plan depended on the rate of collectivization. If the export plan failed, so would the import plan. The latter encompassed the inflow of both the capital tools and goods needed to build up industry and the consumption goods essential to keep the nomads producing. Thus, should the import plan fail, the nomads could be expected to react to both collectivization and the drop in their standard of living due to failure of the plan.

The livestock-producing sector was the nexus of critically interdependent factors in the economy of the MPR. Consequently, if collectivization was a grand folly for the Soviet Union, it was an even greater one for the MPR. In the MPR, unlike the USSR, one could not expect a nondeveloping agriculture to be forced into providing an iron ration for the population at large while the gross

---

[25] *Ibid.*, p. 7.

[26] The budget expenditures were to swell from 21.7 million to 34.8 milion tugriks. The proportion of the budget to the national income was to increase from 23.7 to 25.0 percent. More detailed breakdowns are given in *ibid.*, p. 29 ff.

national product was growing because of expansion in the nonfood commodity sectors.

Collectivization of the Outer Mongolian nomads did prejudice agricultural output, the investment plan, and the export plan. At first, the export plan was met by confiscation of cattle. As a policy, this measure was irresponsible, because it was tantamount to destruction of capital stock. The import plan also failed, because the Soviet Union did not meet her commitments.[27] The consequences of these failures are discussed later.

Implementation by Expropriation

In retrospect, the plan was highly unrealistic. In the MPR, however, there was a willing proponent of Soviet goals to drive through the major policy of collectivization and settlement of the nomads and its corollary, expropriation of the wealthy to endow the collectives with capital stock. Choibalsan, as president of the little khural and as head of the commission in charge of expropriation of the wealthy, was precisely the kind of unquestioning servant of Comintern policy to put through the projected changes, heedless of the consequences.[28]

In 1929, 699 feudal estates (comprising herds and fixed property rather than land) were distributed to lay Mongols and to lamas who wished to leave their monasteries. In 1931 and 1932 the property of 837 clerical and lay lords was expropriated.[29] This measure was carried out in two waves, the secular group being expropriated first and the religious next. The second wave of expropriations reflected a hardening in leftist policy toward religion and destroyed the economic base of the Buddhist monasteries. The figures for ownership of livestock in table 7 illustrate to what extent the monasteries had been economically crippled by 1934.

After conclusion of the Eighth Party Congress, an outright attack was launched on Buddhism and its institutions. Concomitantly with expropriation, and, in fact, highly dependent on it, came the formation of collectives of various types. In 1929 and 1930, 152 communes, 135 artels, and 122 collectives were instituted.[30] By

---

27 Botvinnik, p. 9.

28 *Noveishaia istoriia stran zarubezhnogo vostoka*, Moskovskii gosudarstvennyi universitet (2 vols.; Moscow, 1955), II, 83. Similar commissions were set up in local organs of power (*ibid.*).

29 Zlatkin, p. 189. Erdeni-Ochir, p. 66, shows that by the time of the Eighth Party Congress, 669 feudal households out of 729 had been expropriated, netting 4,450,351 tugriks, or an average of 6,650 tugriks per household. Feudal households were not wealthy ones.

30 Erdeni-Ochir, p. 66.

TABLE 7

COMPOSITION OF LIVESTOCK HERDS OF OUTER MONGOLIA'S
MONASTIC TREASURIES IN 1927, 1933, AND 1934

(In thousands)

Animal	1927	1933	1934
Camels	56	8.3	5.8
Horses	227	31.5	19.6
Cattle	249	21.4	11.2
Sheep	2,822	305.3	171.4
Goats	244	25.8	16.5

SOURCE: A. Rish, "Mongoliia na strazhe svoie nezavistimosti," *Tikhii Okean*, no. 4(6) (1935), p. 103.

1931 the total of collective institutions had reached 700 and comprised 35 percent of all stock-raising households.[31] The criteria and procedures of the expropriation policy give some indication of the levels of wealth in the MPR at the time. Persons owning 3,000 tugriks or more were classed as kulaks and, together with owners of 2,400 to 3,000 tugriks or more, were subjected to confiscatory taxation and administrative harrying.[32] Monasteries were subjected to stepped-up tax rates.[33] A progressive war tax, affecting those not subject to military service, was levied with lamas in mind.[34] Ordinary lamas were to be forced to abandon their religion, those of middle status were to be placed in concentration camps, and those of highest rank, such as khutukhtus, were to be liquidated.[35]

The Eighth Party Congress.—The Eight Party Congress took the actions discussed despite the fact that it had had ample warning that the leftist policy initiated at the time of the seventh congress in late 1928 was under stress. As the eighth congress convened in 1929, uprisings were taking place in Ulankom and the Togus Buiantu hoshun.[36] In its deliberations, the Eighth Party Congress recognized that the country was unprepared for collectivization, and that the difficulties this procedure created were greater in the MPR than in the Soviet Union. In fact, the analysis made by the

---

[31] A. Rish, "Mongoliia na strazhe svoei nezavistimosti," *Tikhii Okean*, no. 4(6) (1935), p. 107. Kolarz, *The Peoples of the Soviet Far East*, p. 136, and Botvinnik both give the figure of 35 percent.

[32] Zlatkin, p. 191.

[33] *Ibid.*, p. 190; Ia. Ryzhik, "Khoziaistvennoe i kul'turnoe stroitel'stvo MNR," *Planovoe Khoziaistvo*, no. 6 (1936), p. 177.

[34] Zlatkin, p. 210.

[35] N. N. Poppe, "MNR," *Vestnik institut po izucheniiu istorii i kul'tury SSSR*, no. 4(11) (1954), p. 16. See also William B. Ballis, "The Political Evolution of a Soviet Satellite: The MPR," *Western Political Quarterly*, IX (1956), 307 ff.

[36] Erdeni-Ochir, p. 69.

congress is surprisingly complete and realistic.[37] Yet the response of
the MNRP to opposition was to strengthen leftist policy rather than
weaken it. The congress thus proceeded to attack the Buddhist
church, to decry Pan-Mongolism, to purge the party, and to call for
the use of former army men in forcing collectivization.[38] As
if determined to destroy itself, the congress continued to attack the
entire lama class, the nobility, the nomads, and the nationalists. It
also suppressed craft shops, forcing their workers to join artels, and
subjected to punitive taxation (up to nearly one-half of net
income) persons engaged in private trade, crafts, and cartage.[39]
Foreign and domestic trade and transportation were declared state
monopolies. Not surprisingly, the growing impoverishment of the
country was attributed to foreign intervention rather than to the
policies of the party.[40] Prime Minister Amor, dismissed as too
rightist, was replaced by Gendun.[41]

Evaluation of Results

The period of extremism had produced some irreversible consequences. The economic base of the Buddhist monasteries had been
destroyed, as had been the Chinese trade position, and the country
was generally closed to Western nations. But the costs were heavy.

Prime Minister Gendun, who survived the debacle, gives a fairly
full account of the effects of the "leftist adventurist" policy. "The
Sixth Great Khural," he remarked in 1934, "conducted an erroneous
state policy not answering the peculiar needs of our country." [42] He
condemned the great khural (proxy for the Eighth Party Congress)
for indulging in collectivization and for the "mechanical transfer-
ence" from the Soviet Union of higher forms of socialist organization such as communes and artels, which were unsuitable to the
Mongolian economy. He also assailed the liquidation of prosperous
Mongols by taxation and administrative order. The net result of
these measures was the slaughter of some 7 million animals in
three years by disaffected nomads.

---

[37] *Ibid.,* p. 96 ff. The congress recognized the problems of cadres, of illiteracy, of
Buddhism, of the lack of a proletariat, of the lack of an adequate administrative
apparatus to supervise collectives, of the severe natural conditions of the MPR, of
the relative lack of preparation in comparison with the USSR, and of the faster
tempo of planned change.
[38] *Ibid.,* p. 74 ff.
[39] N. T. Vargin, "Finansy," in I. Ia. Zlatkin (ed.), *MNR: Sbornik statei*
(Moscow, 1952), p. 226.
[40] Smith, p. 190.
[41] Erdeni-Ochir, p. 69; see also Smith, p. 186.
[42] Gendun, "Iz doklada prem'er ministra MNR Genduna, VII Velikomu Khuralu,"
Tikhii Okean, no. 1(3) (1935), p. 250.

The liquidation of private trade, according to Gendun, led to a goods famine.[43] In 1931 and 1932 the Mongols were in "great need," the situation in the western and southern provinces being especially bad. "Trade was essentially converted into supply," noted Gendun, "being conducted under the slogan 'take what is given.'" As pointed out earlier in this chapter, Montsenkoop did not command a very large share of the market in 1928. Thus, the tasks assigned to it under the plan were quite beyond its capacities.

Collectives formed for pack and load transport also failed to work efficiently. The officers of Mongoltrans had thought that more emphasis should be placed on automotive transportation, a policy that led to collapse of transportation services.[44] Gendun also mentioned that, although craft (kustar) cooperatives had been conceived and private industry banned in 1931, by 1932 there were neither craft cooperatives nor artels; productive work was being carried on only in Chinese workshops in Ulan Bator.

In agriculture the plan had stressed self-sufficiency in cereals. As part of the ambitious target mentioned, six grain and three livestock state farms had actually been created; they were not experimental and were expected to produce immediately. In view of the overall picture of unredeemed failure, Gendun's comment that all these farms accomplished was to involve the state in serious financial loss need not surprise us.[45] As for the conception of the MPR as an exporter of raw materials, Gendun thought that the exports during the period of leftist adventurism had been clearly exaggerated and did not correspond to the potential of the MPR. This comment is highly significant, especially because the Soviet Union had failed to meet her export commitments to the MPR.

In his analysis Gendun also assailed the religious policy of the

[43] It was obviously not the liquidation of private trade alone which led to a goods famine; slaughtering of animals, inflation, loss of confidence in the government, and many other factors were also operative.

[44] At the time of the declaration of the transport monopoly, only 13 percent of all freight was moved by Mongoltrans (see F. S. Tsaplin, "Transport i sviaz'," in Zlatkin (ed.), MNR: Sbornik statei, p. 181). Owing to the emphasis on pack and load transport, the amount of freight carried by pack and load fell steadily (ibid., p. 182). The camels absorbed in transport collectives were badly cared for (Yasuo Misshima and Tomio Goto, A Japanese View of Outer Mongolia, trans. and condensed by A. J. Gradjdanzev [New York, 1942], p. 12). The automobile sector declined in output because of a shortage of trained personnel, the rough use of machines, and poor maintenance. To cap it all, in 1932, Mongoltrans had a bank indebtedness of 4.5 million tugriks, as it could not operate more cheaply than camel caravans.

[45] The Five-Year Plan had called for the cultivation of 100,000 hectares, plus freedom from the necessity to import cereals (see F. S. Tsaplin, "Sel'skoe khoziaistvo," in Zlatkin (ed.), MNR: Sbornik statei, p. 129). The plan called for agriculture to advance from 6 to 13 percent of the national income. There was no conspicuous success, however, for the target set up for the farms was only 20,000 dessiatines sown, which they failed to meet.

Left and pointed out that, in implementing the several policies of the government, control had been lost over the local organs of power, and that the government itself had lost all trust in the eyes of the people. Each person interpreted the law as he saw fit.

Gendun might have extended his analysis. The years 1929 to 1932 witnessed a severe inflation, causing loss of confidence in the tugrik.[46] The goods famine, then, may be explained in part by the flight to goods typical of galloping inflation. The source of the inflation was overissue of paper money. Much of the ambitious plan had been financed by government note issue and by lending from Mongolbank.[47]

It is possible to gain further insights into the situation from the orthodox articles published in *Khoziaistvo Mongolii*. Mongols who settled in the towns and engaged in sedentary work were usually marginal workers. These inefficient workers crowded into collectives to get their share of expropriated cattle; [48] needless to say, they contributed to the failure of the collectives. Mongoltrans, in an attempt to bolster the inefficient collectives, gave them transport subcontracts and thereby shared in their losses.[49]

With the plan failing on all fronts, and with the country in revolt,[50] one cannot doubt the truth of Misshima and Goto's statement that during the four years 1929–1932 "Outer Mongolia endured the most tragic, most gloomy period of hunger, commotion, violence, and terror." [51] In a land of strong solidarity, even *bezprizornyi* (children without parents) appeared.[52] Misshima and Goto assert that members of the MNRP and Revsomol and sections of the army actually participated in uprisings during these years, and that it became necessary to use Soviet airplanes and tanks to quell the disturbances, a charge Soviet scholars have denied.[53] Gendun, however, admits that the Mongolian Army and the Mongolian secret police (GVO) had to be called upon to put down the uprisings. Thus the plans made for Mongolia with Soviet advice and implemented with Soviet help led to conditions as bad as, if not worse than, those that had emerged in the Central Asian union republics of the USSR during her first five-year plan.

---

[46] Zlatkin, *MNR: Strana novoi*, p. 211.
[47] *Ibid.*, p. 194.
[48] B. M. Belen'kii, "Voprosy kolkhoznogo stroitel'stva," *Khoziaistvo Mongolii,* no. 2(20) (1930), p. 40 ff.
[49] Botvinnik, p. 10.
[50] Gendun, p. 264, admitted that the country was in revolt.
[51] Misshima and Goto, pp. 10–12.
[52] Belen'kii, p. 39.
[53] For example, Professor I. Ia. Zlatkin, at one time a Soviet diplomat assigned to Ulan Bator, denied the use of Soviet planes and tanks at a public meeting of the 25th Congress of Orientalists.

Soviet Reactions to Failure of the Plan

Despite the sharp reactions occasioned by them, the policies of the Soviet Union toward her own nomadic peoples did not change appreciably. In contrast, the policies pursued in the MPR underwent basic alterations. The difference, however, should not be taken as a sign of independence of action on the part of the Mongols; international considerations supplied a reason for dissimilar responses to similar situations.

By 1932 Japan had already become a power to be reckoned with in the Far East. As China grew weaker, Japanese ambitions for empire had grown. The Soviet government could not fail to take account of the changed international picture in relation to the MPR. The grave situation that had resulted from the loss of control by the Outer Mongolian government was worsened by the fact that in 1932 the Japanese advanced their troops to the borders of the MPR. Mass disaffection in Outer Mongolia was thus likely to hand the Japanese authorities a good excuse to come to the Mongols' aid and to advance Japanese influence to the Altai. Pro-Japanese Mongols were eager for such a move. It was the Japanese threat, far more than the slaughter of livestock, the loss of life, or the turmoil and misery in the MPR, which called a halt to the leftist policy.

According to Kolarz, Stalin personally intervened to ensure that the "Left-wing adventurers" of Mongolia were ousted from both the MNRP and the Mongolian government.[54] So urgent was the need for action that the requests of Moscow were implemented, not by a regular party meeting, but by an extraordinary meeting of the Central Committee of the party and an extraordinary meeting of the little khural.[55] The Leftists Chizhiia, Badarkho, and Dyndyb were expelled;[56] they were, of course, mere scapegoats for Gendun and Choibalsan and, ultimately, for Stalin. To restore order, plenipotentiary committees were set up in the aimaks.[57] The socioeconomic plan was dropped, collectivization and the creation of state farms were forgotten, worker cooperatives were abandoned, the monopolies on domestic trade and transport were relaxed, the assault on the church was modified, and the onerous tax on cattle was reduced.[58] Only the foreign-trade monopoly was retained without

[54] *The Peoples of the Soviet Far East*, p. 136.
[55] P. P. Staritsina, "O narodnykh khuralakh MNR," *Kratkie soobshcheniia instituta vostokovedeniia*, no. 5 (1952), pp. 3–16.
[56] *Istoriia MNR*, p. 288.
[57] *Ibid.*, p. 299.
[58] *Ibid.*, p. 292.

change. In sum, the leftist policies that had been initiated were completely abandoned. The reversal did not stem from Soviet detection of counterrevolution in its Asian dependency; Stalin intervened in the MPR not to destroy Trotskyites but to curb his own supporters, just as he partially reversed his own policies in the Soviet Union.

6

GRADUALISM

THE PROS AND CONS OF GRADUALISM

Benefits to the Soviet Union.—In the light of the failures attending the policy of extremism and the MPR's abortive first attempt at socioeconomic planning, Soviet policy toward the satellite country underwent rapid change. It was decided to halt all measures likely to cause disaffection among the population. Surprisingly, some time elapsed before the Mongols themselves openly discussed the new policy. Not until 1934 did Gendun define it:

. . . our county is a people's revolutionary, anti-imperialist, antifeudal, bourgeois-democratic republic of a new type, laying the basis for gradual transition along the road of noncapitalist development. . . . our country is still not socialist in that its economy is based on private property and in that it is only preparing to become socialist in the future; at present it is creating the premises that will lay the foundation for the transition to noncapitalist development.[1]

Gradual is the key word in analyzing the change in policy. In a complete reversal of the policy that obtained in the period 1928–1932, the whole emphasis now was on gradual change. One mark of the reversal is the fact that until 1940 the MPR maintained an import surplus with the USSR. By 1938, it is claimed, Mongol indebtedness to the Soviet Union had reached 35 million gold rubles.[2] This state of affairs was the opposite of what the Soviet

---

[1] Gendun, "Iz doklada prem'er ministra MNR Genduna, VII Velikomu Khuralu," *Tikhii Okean*, no. 1(3) (1935), p. 255.

[2] Yasuo Misshima and Tomio Goto, *A Japanese View of Outer Mongolia*, trans. and condensed by A. J. Gradjdanzev (New York, 1942), p. 82.

planners in the MPR had considered desirable, although it did not prevent continued trade dominance of the MPR by the Soviet Union.

Another important decision was apparently made during this period of policy change. The decision makers in Moscow seem to have concluded that it was senseless to locate capital facilities— a salient ingredient of Soviet power—in the MPR, where they were likely to be lost to the Japanese. Hence the Soviet government gave the Mongols hardly any capital-goods assistance, nor did it encourage the MPR to develop her own facilities.[3] Soviet assistance was confined to investments that either had a military purpose or produced an immediate yield in scarce materials without creating an economic potential of possible use to an enemy.

This is not to say that the Soviet decision makers—it is not known precisely who made the decisions—were ready to abandon the MPR to Japan on first threat. The missions to Peking had fought too stubbornly for this prize in the first place. Furthermore, as industrial buildup continued in the Soviet Union proper, the MPR became vital to the USSR as protection for the vulnerable Siberian flank. The territory of the MPR was an excellent base for armored warfare and would enable Soviet troops to fight, if need be, without sacrificing their own cities and villages.

The gentlemen's agreement of 1934 between the USSR and the MPR and the Soviet-Mongol Protocol of Mutual Assistance of 1936 made the stand of the Soviet Union unequivocal: the USSR would protect the MPR. To dispel any doubts on that matter, Stalin, in an interview with the American publisher Roy Howard just before the signing of the protocol, emphasized that the USSR deemed the MPR a vital part of her sphere of influence.

When the Japanese later put Soviet intentions to the test at the battle of Khalkhin-gol in 1939 (a major engagement in the eastern part of the MPR), they were dealt a resounding defeat by Soviet armor and infantry under Major General (later Marshal) Zhukov and Mongolian troops led by Choibalsan. This decisive setback cured the Japanese government and Japanese militarists of ambitions for expansion in Soviet Siberia and turned their attention southward to China.

A final policy decision may possibly have been forced on the Soviet Union. In 1934 a revolt in the MPR was instigated by persons formerly loyal to Soviet policies. (The details of this event are given elsewhere in this chapter.) Whether or not this uprising

---

[3] For a frank expression of this view see G. D. R. Phillips, *Dawn in Siberia* (London, 1942), p. 149.

was the cause, in 1934 the Soviet Union handed control over joint Soviet-Mongol companies to the Mongols. For example, Mongoltrans, Mongolsherst, Mongsovbuner, and the Ulan Bator industrial combine passed into Mongol hands. This action muted the evidence of the Soviet presence in the MPR, introducing a policy that has been continued without exception to the present. As Mongols were trained to take jobs held by Soviet citizens, the latter were withdrawn. Nevertheless, Soviet influence over decisions taken by the Mongols did not wane; in fact, the reverse was true.

These, then, were the major policy decisions of the period of gradualism. Some of the policies originated in 1928 were, however, left unchanged. There was continued Soviet dominance of Mongolian trade, and the antireligious policy went on, although at a slower pace. Also, the Mongolian Army remained largely a cavalry force, without heavy arms and equipment.

Once we understand the Soviet government's fundamental policies toward the MPR, the pattern of events until 1948 becomes comprehensible. In substance, the Soviet Union chose for the MPR a status not unlike the buffer status the Chinese had assigned to Outer Mongolia prior to 1911, with Mongol levies acting as the Soviet flank guard. The Mongols' loyalties were secured by creating a social elite that benefited from Soviet favors. The army was made as effective as Mongol forces in the early Manchu period had been. The centers of resistance to Soviet control, the monasteries, were slowly reduced. But little else was done which might provoke the Mongols into becoming pro-Japanese.

Mongolian opposition.—The new political strategy did not succeed without considerable opposition. Unfortunately, we do not know enough of the facts of Outer Mongolia's history to establish whether nearly all Mongols opposed the policies in force. The monastic lamas and many of the people certainly did, for the years that followed were punctuated by minor rebellions and uprisings. In addition, elements more closely identified with the Soviet cause became disaffected. Misshima and Goto record rebellions in Ulan Bator, Bain Tumen, and Tamsk (1934) which incriminated the minister of justice and members of the Revsomol and of the army.[4] These rebellions, engendered by dislike of Soviet advisers, probably were responsible for the advisers' withdrawal. Finally, it is a fact that Outer Mongolian political leaders, one after the other, fell to purges in the late thirties. But no one knows whether these purges were due merely to unfounded suspicions in

---

[4] Misshima and Goto, p. 19.

the mind of Stalin, or whether they constituted a deliberate Soviet response to the Mongol leadership's firm dislike of the policies of gradualism and neutralization.

CHOIBALSAN: TOOL OF THE COMINTERN

On the subject of purges, it is interesting to examine Choibalsan's role as he steadily advanced in power as a willing agent of the Comintern. As minister of the interior, Choibalsan had the task of liquidating Gendun, then prime minister.[5] In fact, in that year (1937) not only the prime minister but the chief commander of the army and all the higher lamas of Ulan Bator were eliminated.[6] Choibalsan is also credited with the liquidation, between 1937 and 1939, of the succeeding prime minister and minister of foreign affairs, Amor, and of others, including Lubsan-Sharap, Lubsan Dorzhi, and Basanzhap.[7] During this period practically all the personnel of the state apparatus were purged,[8] and it undoubtedly fell to Choibalsan's lot to help effectuate this policy. When, in 1939, Choibalsan emerged at the top as prime minister, he had displayed the qualities necessary for the period of gradualism: obedience to the will of the Soviet Union and willingness to see his country neutralized. Furthermore, as defense minister he executed the only policies calling for vigor in the conduct of Mongol affairs—those connected with safeguarding the Soviet flank.

Whether those Choibalsan helped to purge were patriots or not we do not know. If they had protested Soviet policies, they had cause enough to justify their actions. After all, the MPR contributed to the defense of the Soviet Union, but in return received worse treatment than the most disfavored union republic of the USSR. No Mongol leader who had genuine concern for the interests of those he governed could have accepted this state of affairs.

After 1932 it is increasingly difficult to trace the relationship

---

[5] Owen Lattimore, *Nationalism and Revolution in Mongolia* (New York, 1955), p. 74. Gendun was accused of pro-Japanese sentiments, with some reason, Lattimore thought, though V. A. Maslennikov called Gendun a "left-deviationist." Gendun had replaced Amor as prime minister in 1929, thus taking office during the general shift to the left.

[6] I. Ia. Zlatkin, *Ocherki novoi i noveishei istorii Mongolii* (Moscow, 1957), p. 90, asserts that the executions were carried out through the agency of the Ministry of the Interior, though he mentions no names. For the strange details of the elimination of Demid, the war minister, see Walter Kolarz, *The Peoples of the Soviet Far East* (London, 1954), p. 130.

[7] *Istoriia MNR* (Moscow, 1954), p. 305.

[8] Misshima and Goto, p. 22; see also I. Ia. Zlatkin, *MNR: Strana novoi demokratii* (Moscow, 1950), p. 277. Misshima and Goto give details of the purge of cabinet ministers and lower executive officers at this time.

between the views of the Moscow government and the Comintern, on the one hand, and the issues ventilated and the policies formulated in Mongolian political bodies on the other. Partly this difficulty is due to a decline in useful political comment about the MPR in the Soviet press. But in part it also stems from the fact that Mongolian political life ceased to have even the semblance of independence. Until the Eleventh Party Congress (December, 1947) reversed the policy of gradualism, only two party congresses were held, and neither accomplished much. The Ninth Party Congress (September–October, 1934) seems to have initiated no major change, but instead emphasized the specifics of the new course taken after the policy reversal. The Tenth Party Congress (March, 1940) introduced a new constitution, but its purpose seems to have been mainly propagandistic. The great khural met only twice. Political life thus centered in the small khural, which met more or less annually; this body was, however, little more than a council of ministers.

It may seem puzzling that the MPR was permitted to retain formal independence, but a closer look suggests that only the years 1944 to 1946 remain to vex one's curiosity. Prior to 1944 the Soviet Union had always had good reasons for not annexing the MPR. At first the Soviet government's desire to win recognition from China, and then the threat posed by Japan, were important reasons. In addition, the costs of bringing the MPR up to union republic level, the fear of a widespread Mongolian rebellion, and the desire for positive Mongol loyalty in World War II may have had considerable weight in the minds of Soviet policy makers. After 1946 the rise of Communist China and the possibility of an Outer Mongolian vote in the General Assembly of the United Nations undoubtedly became major considerations arguing for formal independence. In 1944, when Tannu-Tuva was incorporated into the USSR, the time was also ripe for annexation of the MPR; yet, it did not happen. On the contrary, at Yalta, on January 5, 1946, Soviet negotiators laid the ground for Chinese recognition of an independent Mongolian People's Republic. In a sense, then, Choibalsan's passive acquiescence in Stalin's wishes may have gained the Outer Mongolians the benefit of a formal state of independence.

THE RESULTS OF GRADUALISM

Defense

It seems logical, considering the overall framework of Soviet-Mongolian policy, that the major energies of the regime had to be directed into building up the army. It has been estimated that by 1944 the Mongolian Army numbered 80,000.[9] This force had given a good account of itself at Khalkhin-gol.

By 1938 defense expenditures in the MPR amounted to 46.8 million tugriks, or more than 50 percent of all budgetary expenditures.[10] In the preceding five years, defense expenditures had totaled about 200 million tugriks.[11] Expenditures this large could have only financed the operating costs of a military arm the size of the 1944 estimate. As the Mongols did not build their own military equipment, and as foreign trade statistics show no sign of military imports, the heavy equipment of the army may have been a gift from the Soviet Union, although direct evidence to substantiate this suggestion is lacking. By the evidence of budgetary data, the Outer Mongolian population at large seems to have supported the upkeep of an army of considerable size relative to the population. Whatever the truth, "gifts" of arms to the MPR should not be viewed as unqualified generosity on the part of the Soviet Union.

The only other known sizable act of assistance in capital-goods formation by the Soviet Union to the MPR during this period was construction in 1939 of a rail spur from the Trans-Siberian Railroad at Solovevsk to Choibalsan in eastern Mongolia. As this small community was neither populous nor endowed with natural resources, the narrow-gauge rail spur was unquestionably military in purpose. During this period military incidents were frequent on the eastern border of the MPR.

As a consequence of the emphasis on defense and of the policy of gradualism, no important advances were made in stock raising and industry. The percentage of budgetary expenditures for defense climbed from 34.7 in 1936 to 49.3 in 1937 and to 52.6 in 1938. In contrast, the percentage spent in the period 1934–1939 on the national economy, which comprised industry, stock raising, transport, and trade, was 26.4 in 1934 and thereafter did not exceed 18.8, with a low of 13.0 in 1938. Sociocultural expenditures were slightly lower still. Unfortunately, the figures presented in table 8 include the costs of upkeep and hence are not truly indicative of the amount of capital formation in the various sectors of the economy of the MPR.

---

[9] Edgar Snow cited by Gerard M. Friters, *Outer Mongolia and Its International Position*, ed. Eleanor Lattimore, intro. by Owen Lattimore (London, 1951), p. 297.

[10] F. D. Holzman, "The Budget Expenditures of Outer Mongolia," *Finances Publiques*, XII (1957), 41.

[11] Estimated from F. D. Holzman, "The Financial System of the MPR," in *MPR, Human Relations Area Files* (New Haven, 1956), III, Ec. 29.

TABLE 8

BUDGETARY EXPENDITURES OF THE MONGOLIAN PEOPLE'S REPUBLIC, 1934–1939

Purpose	1934		1936		1938		1939	
	Millions of tugriks	Percentage of total	Millions of tugriks	Percentage of total	Millions of tugriks	Percentage of total	Millions of tugriks	Percentage of total
National economy	9.9	26.4	7.3	15.1	11.6	13.0	18.4	18.8
Sociocultural services	5.0	13.3	7.0	14.5	14.4	16.2	17.1	17.5
Administrative	3.7	9.9	3.9	8.1	4.4	4.9	a	a
Defense	13.0	34.7	23.8	49.3	46.8	52.6	a	a
Other	5.9	15.7	6.3	13.0	11.7	13.3	a	a
Total	37.5		48.3		88.9		97.8	

a Data unavailable.
SOURCES: F. D. Holzman, "The Financial System of the Mongolian People's Republic," in *The Mongolian People's Republic*, Human Relations Area Files (New Haven, 1956), III, Ec. 30; and "The Budget Expenditures of Outer Mongolia," *Finances Publiques*, XII (1957), 41.

Industry

As a consequence of budgetary limitations, the growth of industry in the MPR was negligible. In 1934 the first large-scale plant in the MPR, the Choibalsan industrial combine, was opened. Prior to World War II its work force did not exceed 1,500. Built with Soviet assistance as a joint company, the Choibalsan combine started the production of cloth, saddlery, fur coats, and footwear, all designed for military consumption; in addition, it processed the by-products of livestock.[12] By 1938 the MPR could boast only fourteen enterprises of various types.[13] Physical output data provide a clue to the magnitude of these enterprises. For example, the State Construction Trust produced 4.5 million bricks, 5,376 tons of lime, and 22,400 cubic meters of lumber in 1939.[14] In 1940 the production of castings amounted to 128 tons, the Ulan Bator power station generated 14.2 million kilowatt-hours of electricity, and the Nalaikha mines near the capital city produced 173,100 metric tons of coal. In 1936 the printshops of the country put out 12 million pages of printed matter, and in 1938 the Khatkhyl wool-washing plant processed 3,000 tons of wool.[15] These are extremely small outputs by any standard.

The growth of gross industrial output, measured in prices then current, is shown by the figures in table 9. This series, however, because it represents gross industrial output and thus involves double counting, gives an inflated notion of the true output. It does suggest that the upper limit of per capita industrial output in 1940 was 50 to 75 tugriks. (At that time the tugrik was at par with the ruble.)

Much of the increased output in 1937 and 1938 was due to the incorporation of large numbers of lamas into artels (see table 10); that is, cooperative industrial output grew. But, since these lamas in all likelihood had been craftsmen in their monasteries, the increase in output probably reflects a substitution of goods (secular for religious) rather than addition to real output. To achieve this spurious increase, only a small labor force was needed. The most significant statistic is that state industry employed only 5,000 workers by the outbreak of World War II.

---

[12] V. A. Maslennikov, *MNR na puti k sotsializmu* (Moscow, 1951), p. 94.
[13] I. G. Iur'ev, "Gosudarstvennaia i kooperativnaia promyshlennost'," in I. Ia. Zlatkin (ed.), *MNR: Sbornik statei* (Moscow, 1952), p. 158.
[14] *Ibid.*, p. 157.
[15] *Ibid.*, pp. 155–157.

TABLE 9

OUTER MONGOLIA'S GROSS INDUS-
TRIAL OUTPUT IN CONSTANT
PRICES,[a] 1927–1940

Year	Millions of tugriks
1927	1.8
1929	1.8
1930	1.9
1934	8.7
1935	15.6
1936	20.8
1937	28.0
1938	41.5
1939	47.4
1940	52.1

[a] Soviet sources for the data do not always give the year of the price weights used. This series probably uses 1940 constant prices.

SOURCE: George G. S. Murphy, "Industrial Potential," in *The Mongolian People's Republic*, Human Relations Area Files (New Haven, 1956), II, 860.

Stock Raising and Agriculture: Mechanization

The policy of gradualism implied minimum disturbance of agriculture and stock raising. With the abandonment of collectivization, emphasis on the expansion of agriculture was dropped, and it was recognized that the MPR's advantage lay in range stock raising. Consequently, the tax and credit structures of the country were partly changed to promote the rebuilding of individual farms. Nomads could obtain state credit to purchase implements and equipment. Individual private farmers were allowed both to hire labor to tend their herds and to retain the herds as private property.

TABLE 10

THE DISTRIBUTION OF OUTER MONGOLIA'S LABOR FORCE IN
SELECTED YEARS BETWEEN 1932 AND 1940

Year	Total workers and salaried employees	Workers in state and cooperative industry	Workers in artels [a]
1932	2,335	b	b
1934	10,979	3,293	1,091
1939	31,098	12,785	7,337
1940	b	13,300	9,336

[a] Cooperative craft workshops.
[b] Data unavailable.
SOURCE: George G. S. Murphy, "Labor Force," in *The Mongolian People's Republic*, Human Relations Area Files (New Haven, 1956), I, 400.

"We do not forbid or hinder wealthy households," remarked Gendun, "but we are oriented mainly toward helping the middle and poor households."[16] Tax privileges were given the poorer peasant, and rewards were bestowed on owners who showed special care for their livestock.[17] An extraordinary speech at the Tenth Party Congress in 1940 documents this return to private enterprise: "The development of the stock-raising sector must be based on the private economic initiative of all laboring stock raisers. The party and the administration must implement the policy of checking and suppressing only those persons who use hired labor for purposes of profit."[18] This criterion obviously could not be taken literally, for it implied that only inefficient stock raisers—those who failed to make a profit—could employ hired help.

The government did attempt, in rather lukewarm fashion and merely as a face-saving device, to promote socialist forms of organization in agriculture. It sponsored the growth of "mutual aid" (*vzaimopomoshch*), a rudimentary form of socialist economic organization which entailed collective labor by nomadic families in clearing pastures of snow, constructing wells, destroying predators, and helping one another at times when their labor hours were not fully employed. Mutual assistance and cooperation, as we have seen, had deep roots in Mongolian society, for reciprocal aid was essential to the conduct of the nomadic economy. During the period of "leftist adventurism" such reciprocal aid had been viewed as an instrument of social exploitation, to be replaced by such cooperative institutions as the commune, the *toz*, or the artel. During the period of gradualism, however, this attitude was reversed, although only temporarily. As Maslennikov comments, "In the egalitarianized hoton [herding camp], the element of exploitation is removed and joint labor yields a positive result which is peculiar to collective forms of labor: economy of labor and the raising of its productivity."[19] This admission did not save the hotons in the collectivization drives of the late 1950's.

From 1935 on, the government sought to promote the growth of the previously mentioned producers' cooperatives, a new form of artel which took account of the special conditions in the MPR. As has been mentioned, this cooperative was an association of stock raisers who paid a small entrance fee in livestock, which then became collective property, a member's other animals remaining

[16] Gendum, pp. 255–256.
[17] F. S. Tsaplin, "Sel'skoe khoziaistvo," in Zlatkin (ed.), *MNR: Sbornik statei*, p. 109.
[18] N. V. Tsapkin, *MNR* (Moscow, 1948), p. 71.
[19] Maslennikov, p. 73.

his private property. In theory there was supposed to be a considerable difference between the Soviet Union's artel and the Mongolian producers' cooperative, but in fact the differences were not significant. In the USSR, the Model Statute of the Artel allowed stock raisers substantial private herds, but with a limit. There was no such limit in the MPR, but, as only poorer persons joined the artels, the lack of a ceiling on ownership had no practical significance.[20] Membership in the Mongolian cooperative, however, was voluntary. These institutions were given tax privileges and incentives, which probably explains why poorer Mongols, or at least those in moderate circumstances, joined them rather than the wealthier stock raisers. Prior to the 1950's such cooperatives represented little more than a government experiment; they had no influence on the countryside at large. In 1938, three years after they had been introduced, there were thirty-four of them, with a membership of 190;[21] by 1941 there were ninety-six, with 2,023 members.[22]

Only a few state farms were started during the period of gradualism or survived the collapse of the leftist-adventurist policy. Until 1940, however, such farms were concerned with agriculture only,[23] and could have contributed nothing in the way of technical assistance or research and little in the way of propaganda for a change in stock-raising practices.

The budget provided for some small allocations to stock raising. In 1937, 4.3 million tugriks were expended; in 1938, 5.5 million; and in 1939, 2.8 million.[24] Some credit was also extended (as we have remarked earlier), but details do not seem to be available. This help enabled nomads to sink some wells, improve some hay pastures, and build some primitive corrals and windbreaks for their stock. The budgetary allocations also enabled the government to provide some veterinary assistance. Nevertheless, as in range stock raising generally, losses remained high (see table 11).

Generally, then, the government, apart from its program of assisting the nomads insofar as its means allowed, decided to "let sleeping nomads lie." Perhaps one consequence of this approach was the large increase in livestock between 1932 and 1941, when herds reached the highest recorded point in Mongolian history (see table 12).

[20] I. F. Shul'zhenko, "Zhivotnovodstvo MNR," *Trudy Mongol'skoi Komissii,* no. 61 (Moscow and Leningrad, 1954), p. 31. Maslennikov, p. 56, shows that 79 percent of the households in cooperatives were poor or middle-income ones.

[21] Maslennikov, p. 85.

[22] M. Stepanov, "Ekonomicheskoe razvitie MNR," *Vneshniaia Torgovlia,* no. 6 (1949), p. 3.

[23] Shul'zhenko, p. 33.

[24] Holzman, in *MPR,* III, Ec. 29.

TABLE 11

Nomads' Stock Losses in Outer Mongolia, 1936–1938

Year	Percentage loss of total herd	Percentage loss by cause		
		Lack of fodder	Epizootic disease	Wolves
1936	13.5	a	a	a
1937	7.1	50.0	34.0	16.0
1938	8.8	35.1	47.3	17.6

a Data unavailable.
Source: I. Ia. Zlatkin, *Mongol'skaia Narodnaia Respublika: Strana novoi demokratii* (Moscow, 1950), p. 235.

Private stock raising must have posed a serious problem for the Outer Mongolian government. Apparently, obligatory deliveries were not in force during this period. The regime thus had no established mechanisms for extracting agricultural products from the nomad and for maintaining high rates of forced savings. It also lacked a concrete method for monetizing the nomadic sector and integrating the average nomad into a *national* division of labor. The available sources are noticeably silent on these problems. Three methods were used to ensure government control of resources: (1) inflation, for tax receipts did not reach planned levels, whereas expenditures did; (2) some direct taxation of nomads; and (3) emphasis on the growth of consumer cooperatives. As in the Soviet Union, the nomads could obtain highly preferred commodities—such as sugar, tea, and silks—only by selling livestock products. The trade cooperatives' share of all goods circulated

TABLE 12

Growth in Outer Mongolia's
Livestock Herds, 1932–1941

Year	Million head
1932	16.0
1933	17.6
1934	21.1
1935	22.4
1936	22.5
1937	23.3
1938	25.1
1939	26.1
1940	27.4
1941	27.5

Source: George G. S. Murphy, "Planning in the Mongolian People's Republic," *Journal of Asian Studies*, XVIII (1959), 256.

reached 68 percent in 1941, the remainder being handled largely by state trading agencies like Gosmedsnab and Gostorg.[25] As the state could manipulate both the prices of consumer goods (and did so by means of the turnover tax) and the purchase price of livestock products (for the state was a monopsonist), it had control over the terms of trade. Essentially, however, its control must have been weak. The government could not drive too hard a bargain, for fear the nomads would reduce buying to the very minimum.

A similar problem must have confronted the state in extracting agricultural products, but it was much less severe because agriculture remained of minimal importance. In 1928, 17,390 hectares were under cultivation, but by 1939 the figure had advanced only to 19,240.[26] For that matter, in each year between these dates, a smaller amount of land than the 1928 average was under cultivation. One-quarter of this area was under the control of state farms (*goskhoz*, analogous to the Soviet *sovkhoz*). Private farming had thus recovered to neither the 1911 nor the 1921 level. Furthermore, many farms were very small and were inefficiently run.[27]

Besides the few state farms and the small number of modified artels, the MPR also introduced mechanized hay-mowing stations (MHS), an adaptation of the Soviet machine and tractor station (MTS). Initiated in 1937 with Soviet aid, the MHS numbered twenty-four by 1938. Their political function was to supervise the few stock-raising collectives that were formed voluntarily by Mongols after large-scale collectivization had been abandoned. The major technical role of the MHS was to crop hay for winterfeed, but they also helped in digging wells, constructing cattle shelters, and the like. These stations employed 326 tractor drivers, 194 chauffeurs, 50 mechanics, and more than 100 tractors.[28] In the early 1940's, reputedly because they did not suit the low-productivity conditions of the MPR,[29] the MHS were disbanded and their equipment was transferred to state farms to provide forage for the horses used by the Mongolian Army. After that, nonmechanized hay-mowing stations (*konno-senokosnye stantsiia*) came into vogue.

---

[25] Maslennikov, p. 124.

[26] B. Perlin, *MNR* (Moscow, 1941), p. 45.

[27] The number of Mongols who were working small plots in 1938 was 17,800. If state farms and the area cultivated by Chinese farmers are subtracted from the total cultivated area, the area worked by Mongols averages out to approximately 1 acre per capita.

[28] Zlatkin, *MNR: Strana novoi*, p. 234.

[29] *Ibid.*, p. 235; Shul'zhenko, p. 34.

Educational and Antireligious Policies

The ill effects of the policy of gradualism, which show up most markedly in education, may be illustrated by a few salient facts. In 1941, 90 percent of the population was illiterate. In that year the middle schools produced their first graduates—thirteen in all.[30] In 1940 the total number of students in middle schools (11 to 17 years old) had been only fifty. The campaign against illiteracy was not started until 1947, and only the Second Five-Year Plan (1953–1957) aimed at compulsory elementary education from the age of 8 to 11 years in the countryside and at a seven-year education, from the age of 8 to 14, in the towns. A university was established in Ulan Bator in 1942 to receive the graduates of the middle schools (a negligible number at that time) and other "qualified" persons, but its student body remained small for a number of years. In fact, the extension of general education to the Mongols did not take place until the late 1940's and the 1950's. A partly offsetting factor was the spread of literacy and skills among army personnel, though to what extent is not known.

Throughout this period, while little positive action was being taken except in defense, the campaign against Lamaism continued slowly but relentlessly. In general, the policy was to split the lower ranks of lamas from their leaders. Legal prohibitions and restrictions placed on the monasteries prevented their growth and made life in them largely undesirable; at the same time, lower-ranking lamas were given inducements to take up secular occupations.

In 1933 the government placed agents in monasteries to ensure that all anti-Buddhist laws were being obeyed. The construction of new monasteries was banned; the search for reincarnations was forbidden; enrollment of minors was outlawed; and lower-ranking lamas were told they did not have to submit to the authority of their superiors [31] and were given the right to join craft artels (see table 13), engage in private trade, and accept minor jobs in state enterprises.[32]

Beginning in 1935, higher-ranking lamas were tried publicly. In 1936 families with less than three male children were forbidden to devote even one son to religion, and all lamas were made liable to military service.[33] At the same time a medical center was set up in

---

[30] John R. Krueger, N. N. Poppe, and Martin Kilcoyne, "Education," in *MPR,* Human Relations Area Files (New Haven, 1956), I, 294.

[31] Zlatkin, *MNR: Strana novoi,* p. 220 ff.

[32] *Ibid.,* p. 221.

[33] *Ibid.,* p. 221 ff.

TABLE 13

INCORPORATION OF LAMAS INTO OUTER MONGOLIAN ARTELS IN
SELECTED YEARS BETWEEN 1931 AND 1939

Year	Total number of artels	Number of artels composed of lamas only	Composition of artels	
			Workers	Lamas [a]
1931	14	b	734	b
1934	33	b	1,091	b
1938	47	21	2,353	912
1939	145	118	7,337	5,543

[a] The number of lamas is included in the number of workers.
[b] Data unavailable.
SOURCE: I. G. Iur'ev, "Gosudarstvennaia i kooperativnaia promyshlennost'," in I.
Ia. Zlatkin (ed.), *Mongol'skaia Narodnaia Respublika: Sbornik statei* (Moscow, 1952),
p. 158.

Ulan Bator to give treatment to lower-ranking lamas, treatment that was liberally interspersed with propaganda for the new regime. A final piece of legislation in 1936 gave lower-ranking lamas five-year credits at 2 percent interest for the purchase of equipment that would enable them to enter agriculture and stock raising.[34]

In 1937 and 1938, 2,000 lamas of higher rank were shot.[35] In 1938 and 1939 the monasteries were gradually closed; this task was easily accomplished, as they had been economically crippled much earlier.[36] By 1935 monastic treasuries owned only 1 percent of the total stock of the country.[37]

As the power of the lamas steadily declined, the number of supporters of the regime increased. By 1940 MNRP membership had grown from the original 160 of 1921 to 13,385, and the number of Revsomols had reached 17,000.[38] As in the past, a large percentage of both organizations comprised current or former members of the army.

The 1940 Constitution

The changes in the authority structure of the MPR were recognized by the 1940 Constitution: "The Mongolian People's Republic is an independent state of workers . . . who have annihilated the imperialistic and feudal yoke." The new constitution also stressed that

---

[34] *Ibid.*, p. 223 ff.
[35] *Ibid.*, p. 227.
[36] *Ibid.*, p. 231.
[37] A. Rish, "Mongoliia na strazhe svoie nezavistimosti," *Tikhii Okean*, no. 4(6) (1935), p. 101.
[38] Zlatkin, *MNR: Strana novoi*, p. 243.

this organization of the state ensured "a noncapitalistic approach to the development of the country to pave the way to socialism in the future." This statement recapitulates Lenin's basic revision.

The preceding constitution (1924) had set up a government that was closely modeled on the pre-1936 government of the Soviet Union. The 1940 Constitution added a bill of rights, stipulated that the MPR was to be subject to an economic and educational plan, and provided more details on organs of government. Essentially, however, as a Western political theorist has described it, the "basic pattern of the government was similar to that outlined in 1924." [39] Moreover, despite its emphasis on planning, the 1940 Constitution did not herald a fundamental change in the policy of gradualism.

---

[39] William B. Ballis, "The Political Evolution of a Soviet Satellite: The MPR," *Western Political Quarterly*, IX (1956), 314.

7

THE TRANSITION TO PLANNING,
1940 TO 1960

Although Outer Mongolia's 1940 Constitution had made provisions for planning, neither full-scale planning nor a basic change in the policy of gradualism emerged. As late as 1956, Damba, the secretary-general of the MNRP, spoke of the "gradual transition of agricultural collectives to a sedentary situation." He felt that collectives should "become model, high-income farms and should show the individual Mongol household the advantages of the socialist system of farming." [1] The fact that collectivization was voluntary did not make it more attractive to the Mongols. In 1956 it was pointed out that

The herdsmen [of the MPR] are at once the pride and frustration of the leaders. Despite the impact of the Buddhist Lamaist religion, which was introduced from Tibet and taught inactivity and virtual indolence, the people acquitted themselves like true Mongols—which means "brave men," against the Japanese in World War II. They just as stubbornly resist socialization.[2]

That such resistance was tolerated needs explanation, as does the abrupt termination of the policy of gradualism in 1958. In that year most households were collectivized.

Unfortunately, as we come closer to the present, it is more difficult to find adequate clues to the shifts in Mongolian policy. Provisionally, matters may be explained in the following way. Until the death of Stalin in 1953, Soviet domestic economic policy

---

[1] *Pravda,* March 1, 1956.
[2] Jack Raymond, "Mongols Resist Collectivization," *New York Times,* Aug. 30, 1956.

showed a basic conservatism. It is possible that the policy of gradualism in Outer Mongolia persisted because of a similar inertia. A tranquil MPR under the trustworthy Choibalsan was a firm bulwark in the Soviet Union's eastern position; it could be forgotten.

SOVIET POLICY TOWARD THE MPR

In 1954 Khrushchev and his supporters had to reappraise all political solutions and reshape many policies. The record suggests that the new Soviet leaders also considered the political and economic situation in the MPR. The policy shifts occurring in the MPR in the same year closely resembled those of the USSR; they did not appear to be tailor-made for the Mongols.

After 1954 three factors assumed growing importance. First, thanks to the expansion of education, a Mongolian educated elite had emerged whose members became increasingly interested in the social, economic, and cultural development of their country. Without drastic purging, some consideration had to be given to the aspirations of this elite, lest it become disaffected. Second, with the rise of Communist China and thus of competition for spheres of influence over satellites, the Soviet government had to reappraise the international status of the MPR. The evidence is plain that the leaders of Communist China attempted to woo the Mongols by gifts of capital and labor; they also attempted to plant a Chinese population (with formal Mongolian citizenship) in the MPR. Clearly, China's competition must have impelled the Soviet leaders to match gift for gift, as a result of which the MPR moved into a climate of liberality in foreign aid. Had the Soviet Union not given some favors to the Mongols, she could not have called for an end to the influx of Chinese labor, as she apparently did.

Molotov's presence in Ulan Bator as Soviet minister may also have played an important part in this period. We do not know how, or to what extent. Korostovetz, Maiskii, and Borodin had all left some impact on this small country. It is hard to believe that a man of Molotov's abilities would not do likewise.

The final factor was obviously the dismal failure of Outer Mongolia's two five-year plans of 1948–1952 and 1953–1957. Both were aimed at increasing output without collectivization, which had proved costly in the 1930's. When, however, planning without collectivization also failed, it seemed almost inevitable that the solution of planning with collectivization be tried.

Enforcement of the Soviet Solution to Nomadism

Unquestionably, the MPR was expected to implement policies of nomadic collectivization similar to those carried out in the USSR.[3] The external political situation had to be ripe, however, before such changes could be set in motion. When that time had come, the Mongols paid mere lip service to collectivization in their economic plans of 1948–1952 and 1953–1957. Apparently not until 1958 was the Soviet government able to bring sufficient pressure to bear to force the Mongols to do as was expected of them.

Since the catastrophic failure of her first attempt to deal with the nomadic problem in 1929 and the early thirties (see chap. 5), a failure that was duplicated in the MPR, the USSR had gained experience in handling her own nomadic populations within a framework of collectivization. Subsequent to the collapse and reversal of her initial policy, the Soviet Union saved face by insisting that the surviving nomads, with their drastically reduced herds, set up permanent winter quarters. She took steps, however, to prevent any resurgence of the traditional aristocracy of the nomads. The 1932 Soviet decree on the liberalization of private ownership and the Model Statute of the Agricultural Artel (1935) allowed the nomads sufficient livestock for following their customary pattern of life. This tolerance did not last long, however. By 1936 and 1937, permanent winter quarters had been established and collectivization had been imposed on all Central Asian Turkic nomads. It is of interest that private ownership among the nomads of the arctic—for instance, among the Chuckchi—continued beyond World War II. That tribe, however, was small, had adapted to a severe climate, and was something of an anthropological curiosity.

At first the Soviet authorities had difficulty in evolving a system that could exploit thin pasture lands as efficiently as pastoral nomadism does. By World War II, however, the Soviet Union had settled on a system known as *otgonnyi* stock raising.[4] Under this system, stock-raising families lived in sedentary villages while the

---

[3] F. S. Tsaplin, "Sel'skoe khoziaistvo," in I. Ia. Zlatkin (ed.), *MNR: Sbornik statei* (Moscow, 1952), p. 126, takes it for granted that Mongolian stock raising will change to the *otgonnyi* system. See also *Bol'shaia Sovetskaia Entsiklopediia* (2d ed.), XXIII, 171.

[4] *Bol'shaia Sovetskaia Entsiklopediia*, XXXI, 375; G. Badir'ian and I. Kurov, "Otgonno-pastbishchnoe soderzhanie skota v kolkhozakh Zakavkaz'ia," *Sotsialisti-cheskoe Sel'skoe Khoziaistvo*, no. 4 (1947), pp. 44–50; and G. Badir'ian, "Otgonnoe zhivotnovodstvo," *Sel'skokhoziaistvennaia Entsiklopediia*, III, 515.

household heads and unmarried persons above school age left their quarters to drive the collectively owned herds to the best pastures for the particular season, often a long distance from the village. The otgonnyi system combined the manifest political and cultural advantages (to the Soviet government) of having stock raisers concentrated in villages while enjoying also the technical advantages of pastoral nomadism. In addition, the village could become a center for veterinary aid, stockpiling of feed, and the like. Inasmuch as under the otgonnyi system officials could be appointed to operate collectives, the patriarchal authority of the nomadic group could be supplanted by one more favorable to the state. Later, in 1949–50, the Soviet Union introduced mechanized livestock stations (MLS) (*mashinno-zhivotnovodcheskaia stantsiia*) in areas using the otgonnyi system. The MLS was roughly comparable to the Soviet MTS, and presumably was instituted with similar objectives in mind.

One great disadvantage of the otgonnyi system is that the herder is deprived of family life, a factor that makes alternative sedentary occupations much more attractive than they are under the nomadic pastoral system. For a developing country, this problem is short-term rather than long-term, in that the normal movement of labor is out of agriculture. Hence, wage differentials favoring this movement are not disadvantageous in the long run, although they may cause serious short-term problems.

Although the Soviet government lost some influence over the Mongols on the death of Stalin, it soon reasserted itself and pressed for changes consonant with Soviet policies; introduction of the otgonnyi system was one such change. How the Mongols reacted to the Soviet attitude can be seen in broad outline, but the details of their specific response are far from clear. Part of the problem is lack of information. Mongolian domestic politics, despite the reports of visitors to the country, are hard to interpret. Tsedenbal, who enjoyed considerable power under Choibalsan as deputy commander in chief and later as secretary-general of the MNRP, became both prime minister and leader of the party on Choibalsan's death in January, 1952. Tsedenbal's rise to power was a matter of normal succession. He lost control of the party to Damba (not the Damba of earlier chapters, of course) in 1954, but not the premiership. Damba himself was dismissed by the party and became director of a state farm in 1958; the lack of speed in economic development was held to his account. Tsedenbal then reassumed the position of secretary-general of the MNRP. Whether these changes in his career reflect fluctuations in Soviet-Mongol relationships is not known.

It is difficult to discern sharp divisions in modern Mongolian politics. Educated Mongols know that they must live under Soviet influence because of the geographic location of their country. At the same time they seem to have no liking for the Chinese. Whether there was, or is, a genuinely pro-Communist Chinese party contesting for power in the country is a moot question. Perhaps we can best interpret domestic Mongolian political changes purely on the basis of a power struggle within an organization whose warring factions are divided by mere day-to-day, rather than fundamental, ideological differences. The impression one gains, and it is only an impression, is that the Mongols have learned, for the moment, to accept Soviet influence and to concern themselves only with the implementation of policies laid down for them. Administratively, however, they can to some small degree temper to their own liking the policies evolved for them.

A stronger show of independence is hardly to be expected from a small country fated to deal with the USSR and lying next to Communist China. The balance of advantages over disadvantages to the USSR in having the MPR as a satellite, rather than as a union republic, cannot be substantial. Any move toward real independence on the part of the Mongols would again bring Soviet military forces to Ulan Bator, especially now that Communist China views the MPR as "lost territory" and would be quick to seize upon any such move in order to increase her influence in the MPR. To have Chinese settlers on the northern rivers of the MPR, as in the 1880's, would be intolerable. The Soviet Union is in a position to wield extreme coercive power over the Mongols—she did not hesitate to so treat Hungary when the costs to herself were far greater—and the Mongols have no choice but to accept the tenuous status of "independence" which is theirs. At the moment they have no better alternative, and any move to force an alternative would only worsen the situation.

The Soviet Presence

In all fairness, it must be admitted that the restraint the Soviet Union has displayed toward Outer Mongolia has not been without disadvantage to herself. Thanks to Soviet action in 1944, Tannu-Tuva is no longer an open question; any threat to it now is a threat to the USSR proper. Yet the Soviet Union neglected the opportunity

TABLE 14

PERCENTAGE COMPOSITION OF THE OUTER MONGOLIAN WORK
FORCE BY NATIONALITY, 1934–1939

Date	Nationality		
	Mongol	Soviet Russian	Chinese
April 1, 1934	50.6	39.2	10.2
January 1, 1935	64.6	26.6	8.8
January 1, 1936 ª	76.0	19.0	4.5
January 1, 1937	82.1	12.9	5.0
January 1, 1938	85.4	8.7	5.9
January 1, 1939	87.7	5.7	6.6

ª For the year 1936 the three percentages do not add up to 100 percent in the
source table.
SOURCE: V. Tudev, "Formirovanie rabochego klassa Mongol'skoi Narodnoi
Respubliki," in A. T. Iakimov (ed.), *Mongol'skii sbornik, ekonomika, istoriia, arkheologiia* (Moscow, 1959), p. 67.

in 1944 to annex the MPR. In addition, the Soviet government has
shown continuing concern to keep its advisers and workers in the
background and to train as rapidly as possible a Mongol work force
to run Outer Mongolia's industry (see tables 14 and 15). The
decision of 1934 to mute the Soviet presence in the MPR has never
been revoked. Census data show that in 1956 only 1.6 percent of
the population were Soviet citizens, and that only 1.9 percent were
Chinese.

WARTIME TRANSITION TO PLANNING

Within this rather imperfectly defined political framework, we can
describe how the Mongols made haste in planning rather slowly. To

TABLE 15

PERCENTAGE OF MONGOLS
ENGAGED IN INDUSTRY, IN VARIOUS YEARS
BETWEEN 1939 AND 1949

Industry	Year	Percentage
Total industry	1939	79.0
State industry	1939	70.0
Choibalsan combine	1941	87.6
Transportation	1940	73.2
Mongolbank	1949	90.0 +
Coal	1940	90.0

SOURCES: I. G. Iur'ev, "Gosudarstvennaia i kooperativnaia promysh-
lennost'," in I. Ia. Zlatkin (ed.), *Mongol'skaia Narodnaia Respublika:
Sbornik statei* (Moscow, 1952), pp. 154-160; I. Ia. Zlatkin, *Mongol'skaia
Narodnaia Respublika: Strana novoi demokratii* (Moscow, 1950), p. 237.

do so, it is necessary to retrace our steps to the period immediately after promulgation of the Constitution of 1940.

The policy of the Soviet Union toward the MPR underwent no basic change during the war years, but the struggle with Germany did influence Soviet-Mongol economic relations. Although the MPR did not enter the war against Germany, her economy was nonetheless put on a war footing, insofar as possible, in order to aid the Soviet Union. Soon after the German attack on the USSR, her exports to the MPR had to be cut drastically. By 1942 all vegetable and forage exports ceased, as well as exports of agricultural tools, spare parts, plant equipment, automobiles, salt, soap, and butter; exports of cereals were considerably diminished.[5] To counteract that unilateral, but unavoidable, Soviet action, the Mongolian government gave high priority to the replacement of imported materials by domestic production. At least one formerly imported commodity, butter, the Mongols started to export.[6] In addition, 83 million tugriks, a sizable sum for the MPR, was dispatched during the war to aid the Soviet armies.[7]

MPR Economic Strategy

The war years had mixed effects on the Mongolian economy, but wartime exigencies did permit the introduction of yearly planning and of an interesting variant of the basic Soviet capital-accumulation mechanism. Heavy governmental defense expenditures continued, mounting in total but occupying a reasonably stable percentage share of total government expenditures.[8] In addition, there must have been loss of manpower to the army and to industries servicing the army. The introduction of yearly plans in 1941 must have been designed partly to meet the problem of wartime scarcities.

The Mongolian economic strategy followed the classic Soviet pattern. In 1939 the government commenced mass sales of bonds. In 1940 the following taxes were introduced: a new income tax; a cultural and housing tax, levied as a markup on the income tax; [9]

---

[5] N. T. Vargin, "Torgovlia," in Zlatkin (ed.), MNR: Sbornik statei, p. 214; I. Ia. Zlatkin, MNR: Strana novoi demokratii (Moscow, 1950), p. 263.

[6] V. A. Maslennikov, MNR na puti k sotsializmu (Moscow, 1951), p. 103.

[7] William Mandel, "Outer Mongolia's Five Year Plan," Far Eastern Survey, XVIII (1949); L. M. Gataullina, "Ekonomicheskoe i kul'turnoe sotrudnichestvo MNR so stranami sotsialisticheskogo lageria," in A. T. Iakimov (ed.), Mongol'skii sbornik, ekonomika, istoriia arkheologiia (Moscow, 1959), p. 33, instances 60,000 horses as gifts and 40,000 cattle as aid to reoccupied areas in the USSR.

[8] F. D. Holzman, "The Financial System of the MPR," in MPR, Human Relations Area Files (New Haven, 1956), III, 32 ff.

[9] N. T. Vargin, "Finansy," in Zlatkin (ed.), MNR: Sbornik statei, p. 232.

and a profits tax for state and cooperative enterprises. In 1941 the income tax on individuals was modified by being based on total income instead of on income from stock raising only.[10] Between 1940 and 1941 revenue from direct taxes doubled, and thereafter a money-goods lottery, war loans, and increased commodity taxes helped defray the cost of the wartime burden. There was undoubtedly also some inflation.[11]

In order to gain command over resources, the government introduced physical procurements.[12] Each person owning more than 100 sheep (or their equivalent in other stock) had to deliver 1 kilogram of wool per sheep per year.[13] In addition, the stock raisers had to perform transport duties at fixed state prices. Each individual owning transport beasts had to carry 500 ton-kilometers per camel per year and 320 ton-kilometers per yak per year at a fixed price of 20 mung a ton.[14] Obligatory deliveries for live cattle were introduced in February, 1944.[15] It is possible that procurements were introduced on other commodities.[16] The state thus acquired forced deliveries from stock raising *without* collectivization.

Given forced deliveries, the state than followed the Soviet strategy of turning the terms of trade more strongly against agriculture. After the outbreak of war, shops were closed, differential rationing was introduced, and retail prices of goods were increased. While these measures were being enacted, wages also were increased, but Vargin claims that the real wages of urban workers remained the same.[17] If he is correct, we must infer a drop in real wages for agriculturists; the nomad at this time did not earn a wage. As the commodities whose prices had been increased were goods such as flour, tea, and matches, it seems obvious that the move was intended to favor the urban working class at the expense of the stock raiser.[18] Despite wartime scarcities, there was a small

---

[10] *Ibid.*, p. 233.

[11] Holzman, in *MPR*, III, 74 ff.

[12] Zlatkin, *MNR: Strana novoi*, p. 275; I. G. Iur'ev, "Gosudarstvennaia i kooperativnaia promyshlennost'," in Zlatkin (ed.), *MNR: Sbornik statei*, p. 166; Holzman, in *MPR*, III, 92 ff.; G. S. Matveeva, *Sotsialisticheskie preobrazovaniia v sel'skom khoziaistve MNR* (Moscow, 1960), p. 38.

[13] Zlatkin, *MNR: Strana novoi*, p. 271.

[14] *Ibid.*, p. 256.

[15] *Ibid.*, p. 263.

[16] I. F. Shul'zhenko, "Zhivotnovodstvo MNR," *Trudy Mongol'skoi Komissii*, no. 61 (Moscow and Leningrad, 1954), p. 44 ff., speaks of a range of commodities as being under procurement in 1951. It is not possible to find records of the dates when many commodities first were made liable to procurement.

[17] Vargin, "Torgovlia," p. 214.

[18] Wages were raised for "workers and servants," i.e., the urban work force (*ibid.*).

increase in industrial output. The output of light engineering products, gold, and construction materials was expanded, as was the production of warm clothing for the Soviet armies.[19]

These gains were small, however; the major changes of the war came in the food industry. In 1940 there had been only 24 food enterprises in the MPR, but by 1942 the number had increased to 252.[20] By 1950, 44.8 percent of all industrial output was food products, and in fact practically all the growth in gross industrial output between 1940 and 1950 was due to this expansion.

The labor problems that inevitably arose were solved by typical Soviet legislation. In November, 1942, labor conscription was introduced. In January, 1943, penalties for low-grade work were being imposed. In July of the same year measures designed to reduce labor turnover, progressive piece rates, and obligatory technical instruction were initiated. A month later a law against "plundering of national property" was passed.[21]

It would be incorrect to exaggerate the scope of these changes; though giving some experience to Mongolian planners, they hardly created the prerequisites for planning. To all intents and purposes, the MPR continued to have no industry.

A few small advances were recorded in agriculture. In 1942 the state farms were reorganized into a trust to meet the need for cereals.[22] In the same year land-tenure laws were altered to encourage private agriculturalists. Land was granted in perpetuity, regardless of nationality, and gratis, no renting or purchase being involved.[23] As a result, state farms expanded their hectarage from 5,364 to 38,710, and private Mongol and Chinese farmers (many were smallholders or owners of urban allotments) expanded their hectarage from 20,763 to 41,290.[24]

Stock raising failed to show progress, for it was bearing the major burden of the war. In addition to discriminatory taxes and prices, stock raisers still had to supply horse-relay service and provide obligatory deliveries of transport, and probably were subject to strong social pressure to donate stock to both their own government and the Soviet Union. In 1941 livestock herds totaled

---

[19] George G. S. Murphy, "Industrial Potential," in *MPR*, Human Relations Area Files (New Haven, 1956), II, 833.

[20] M. Stepanov, "Ekonomicheskoe razvitie MNR," *Vneshniaia Torgovlia*, no. 6 (1949), p. 4.

[21] Iur'ev, p. 164 ff.

[22] V. F. Shubin, "Zemledelie MNR," *Trudy Mongol'skoi Komissii*, no. 52 (Moscow, 1953), p. 50.

[23] Tsaplin, p. 130.

[24] Stepanov, p. 3; Shubin, p. 90.

27.5 million head; by 1945 the number had dropped to 20.9 million.[25]

PLANNING BASED ON THE SOVIET STRATEGY FOR DEVELOPMENT

After the end of World War II, the Mongols waited until 1948 to introduce their first five-year plan. Before we turn to a fairly detailed discussion of that plan, it is useful to set it within the broader framework of Soviet development strategy.

The Soviet Union, in the years of her first development plans, secured foodstuffs from agriculture by the network of collectives policed by the MTS and other special procurement agencies. Through these devices the government was able to feed the workers who were attracted to the cities or were forced there by collectivization. Throughout the first Soviet plans, manpower flowed from a low-production agriculture to a more highly producing industry. In the industrial sector, the heavy branches, especially machine tools, were emphasized. The planners of the Soviet Union had worked out a method whose essence was the supply of foodstuffs to the increasing number of industrial workers without a concomitant increase in demand for industrial goods by the peasants who raised the foodstuffs. The Soviet planners also were able to generate funds for capital formation in the growth process itself: the imposition of high taxes, largely on the urban population, and of discriminatory procurement prices on the agricultural population, combined with inflation, enabled the state to gain control of the resources it needed for investment. Over time, agricultural taxation, whether by formal taxes or by the procurement system, yielded a declining proportion of all taxation.

World War II had seen the introduction in the MPR of most of the Soviet Union's broad solutions for industrialization, except for collectivization. The state, nonetheless, had considerable power to turn the terms of trade against the nomads. So long as the war demanded that the MPR keep a large standing army and send unrequited exports to the Soviet Union, however, there was no likelihood of considerable formation of capital in the MPR. The end of World War II and the emergence of Communist China, which relieved the Mongols of the necessity of defending a long border, created the final conditions necessary for growth on the Soviet model.

---

[25] George G. S. Murphy, "Planning in the MPR," *Journal of Asian Studies*, XVIII (1959), 256.

The First Five-Year Plan

Background.—It is well to be aware of the conditions the Mongols faced in this enterprise. Above all else the plans for growth on the Soviet pattern were based on an economy highly dependent on an uncollectivized agriculture, and an economy that showed the effects of the policy of gradualism.

The Mongolian government had to transform a nomadic pastoral economy, based on private ownership of herds, into a Soviet-type

TABLE 16

GROWTH OF COLLECTIVES DURING OUTER MONGOLIA'S FIVE-YEAR PLANS, 1948–1959

Plan and year	Number of collectives	Number of members	Head of live-stock owned	Collective livestock as percentage of total
First plan				
1948	110	7,725	60,742	
1951	139			
1952	167	10,000 a	280,000	
Second plan				
1953	167		427,000	
1954	198	15,400	979,500	
1955 (March)	198	25,000		
1955 (October)	240		1,900,000	
1956 (July)	509	15 b		
1956 (end of year)	565	84,000	3,893,344	16.3
1957		20 b		22.4
1958 (January 1)	658	35 b	5,200,000	
1958	694	75 b		62.0
1959 (March)	389	99.3 b		73.3

a Approximate figure.

b As percentage of nomad households.

SOURCE: George G. S. Murphy, "Planning in the Mongolian People's Republic," *Journal of Asian Studies*, XVIII (1959), 254.

planned economy. By 1948, out of some 600,000 nomads, the government had persuaded only 7,725 to enter 110 stock-raising collectives of the kind established by the Soviet Union in Central Asia (see table 16).[26] The vast majority of stock raisers continued to own their own herds, had inheritance rights, and could hire labor and pay wages in kind.[27]

The output of stock raisers was essential to the economy of the MPR. In 1952, for instance, 60 to 70 percent of all goods produced

[26] V. Trubenkov, "30 let denezhno-kreditnoi sistemy MNR," *Den'gi i Kredit*, no. 10 (1954), p. 39, states that four-fifths of the population were engaged in stockbreeding. The population in 1947 was 759,200.

[27] S. S. Demidov (ed.), *Konstitutsiia i osnovnye zakonodatel'nye akty MNR* (Moscow, 1952), *passim*. See especially Article 6 of the 1940 Constitution and Article 124 of the Law on Labor (Feb. 14, 1941).

for market (i.e., excluding goods the stock raisers themselves consumed) came from stock raising. As much as 50 percent of all raw materials used by the Ministry of Industry and 30 to 35 percent of those used by the Ministry of Food came from livestock.[28] In 1954 more than 80 percent of all Mongolian exports were composed of livestock and its by-products.[29]

The reports of the Soviet Academy of Sciences' Agricultural Expedition to the MPR (1947–1952) suggest the backwardness of Mongolian stock raising.[30] The expedition found the breeds of livestock to be primitive and unspecialized (i.e., consisting of range animals not bred for beef or dairy purposes). The Mongols still continued to use their centuries-old techniques. Investments in wells, cattle shelters, improved pastures, fencing, and stocks of winterfeed were almost nonexistent. According to Shul'zhenko, the major expert on stock raising in the MPR, "the techniques of livestock raising in the country continue to remain at a low level, and the breed of livestock has not been improved," and "the breed of sheep and the technique of sheep raising have not changed in the past eighteen years."[31] Shul'zhenko had, in fact, as we have noted earlier, made a study some eighteen years before, and at that time had concluded that the Mongolian techniques still were those of the twelfth and thirteenth centuries. His comments on sheep raising are fully corroborated by an expert on sheep breeding.[32] Another student, B. A. Nichik, after concluding a study of the Gobi area, was convinced that the "system of maintenance and feeding of stock in the Mongol households of the Gobi steppe region needs fundamental change."[33] After a quarter of a century of Soviet tutelage, the nomads still drew a large part of their subsistence from their own output, and had not yet been completely drawn into a market economy. They continued to maintain large herds of horses, choosing to store their wealth in livestock rather than in money or commodities, despite the fact that the state did not favor

---

[28] Tsaplin, p. 101.

[29] A. P. Borisenko, "Vneshniaia torgovlia MNR," in M. F. Kovrizhnykh, A. B. Frumkina, and V. S. Pozdniakova (eds.), *Vneshniaia torgovlia stran narodnoi demokratii* (Moscow, 1955), p. 315.

[30] See especially Shul'zhenko, which, with other pertinent works, is reviewed in George G. S. Murphy, "Recent Publications of the Mongolian Commission," *Far Eastern Survey*, XXV (1956), 91–95.

[31] Shul'zhenko, pp. 15, 83.

[32] G. R. Litovchenko, "Voprosy ovtsevodstva MNR," *Trudy Mongol'skoi Komissii*, no. 43 (Moscow, 1953), p. 190.

[33] Nichik's remarks are in "Produktivnost mongolskikh porod zhivotnykh: Sbornik eksperimentalnykh rabot," *Trudy Mongol'skoi Komissii*, no. 66 (Moscow, 1954), p. 95.

this traditional practice because it led to a lower output of exportable beasts, such as sheep or cattle. Neither had the nomadic herding camp, the hoton, despite pressures, made real technical advances since Maiskii's visit.[34]

In view of the nomads' backwardness, it should come as no surprise that old cultural mandates still had some influence over them.[35] True, the growing Communist party gave the government a firmer grip over the MPR than it had had in 1931. The government had created a small class of bureaucrats and technicians. Compulsory military service had given the government the opportunity to indoctrinate large numbers of its younger citizens. The nomads had long been deprived of their traditional sources of leadership, the Mongol princes and the lamaist hierarchy. Their herds were subject both to inspection by the state veterinary service and to the fiscal demands of the state. The nomads depended on state stores for the consumer goods they could not produce themselves. Nonetheless, so long as they relied on their own production for part of their consumption, the nomads retained a measure of economic independence. Furthermore, the customary sources of authority in nomadic groups based on kinship must have retained some vitality, and the nomads must have remained strongly attached to their customary ways, unchallenged by formal attempts at reeducation. Nomads who were not liable to military service could not have been subjected to any educational influence outside the nomadic herding group. Unfortunately, there are no sociological studies that would permit a more precise definition of the situation.

It is relevant at this point to recapitulate the statistics on education cited in chapter 6. In 1940, 90 percent of the population of the MPR was illiterate. Only 50 persons were in middle schools established for the 11-to-17-year age group.[36] In 1942, when the first state university was opened in Ulan Bator, the authorities

---

[34] For descriptions of herding camps made on field trips, see Shul'zhenko; M. Navan-Chimid, in "Produktivnost mongolskikh porod zhivotnykh"; and Litovchenko. Shul'zhenko's monograph, with its map of itineraries (*marshruty*) of the Soviet "expeditions" to the MPR in 1930, 1931, and 1947–1952, almost gives the impression that these were concerned with basic exploration.

[35] On resistance to social change, see Raymond, p. 13. Jean Chesneaux, "Du Féodalisme pastoral à la planification socialiste," *Economique et Politique*, XIX (1956), 48–54, remarks: "Même vingt-cinq ans après la disparition du joug féodal, les habitudes ancestrales restent encore fortement ancrées chez de nombreux arats." Brief mention of this fact is also made by Prime Minister Iu. Tsedenbal, "O piatiletnem plane razvitiia narodnogo khoziaistvo i kul'tury MNR na 1948–1952 g.," in N. T. Vargin (ed.), *Planirovanie narodnogo khoziaistvo Mongolii* (Moscow, 1951), pp. 20, 34, 51.

[36] V. A. Maslennikov, *MNR* (Moscow, 1955), p. 47.

found it difficult to make up an entering class of 150 persons, so few were qualified.[37] The fact that the campaign against illiteracy was not launched until 1947 suggests that it had to wait upon the beginning of a flow of trained persons from the school system. It was only the Second Five-Year Plan that finally aimed at introducing compulsory elementary education for the age group 8 to 11 in the countryside and a seven-year education for the age group 8 to 14 in the towns.[38]

Somehow or other the Mongolian government, in addition to transforming the social structure of the nomads as it existed in 1947, also had to achieve a sufficient yearly rate of capital investment to ensure economic growth. In short, the government would have to hold down, if not actually depress, the consumption levels of its citizens to acquire command over resources for investment. The goal might be achieved, so far as stock raisers were concerned, by forcing them—in the familiar Soviet way—to surrender their output at very unfavorable terms. But if the terms of trade were turned too drastically against the nomads, and if they were subjected to too high levels of taxation in kind, they might use their livestock for their own consumption rather than surrender their animals to the state for a bad bargain in manufactured commodities. If the state's demands were too pressing, the nomads might even revolt and destroy their herds, as they had done in 1931, thus embarrassing the government's economic plans for a long time to come. One bad year in stock raising (in contrast with agriculture) has a lasting effect; a drop in the total number of stock takes some time to make good.

A failure to obtain high and stable levels of obligatory deliveries would create other difficulties for the government. The small industrial sector of the MPR would suffer as a consequence, because such a failure (1) would lead to raw-material shortages and (2) might damage the country's capacity to import. Export of livestock was, after all, the major means by which the MPR could finance her imports, unless she were extended Soviet credits. Faced with exporting difficulties, the government would have a difficult choice to make between cutting imports of capital goods and cutting imports of consumption goods. The MPR has always been heavily dependent on imports of many basic consumption goods,

---

[37] See John R. Krueger, N. N. Poppe, and Martin Kilcoyne, "Education," in *MPR*, Human Relations Area Files (New Haven, 1956), I, 294. The law instituting the university mentions that the first class that had undergone education from 8 to 17 years of age was graduated in 1941 (Demidov, p. 249).

[38] Maslennikov, *MNR*, p. 55; T. A. Iakimova, *MNR: Ekonomika i vneshniaia torgovlia* (Moscow, 1956), p. 51.

for under the Manchus the nomads had come to concentrate heavily on stock raising to the exclusion of agriculture and the crafts. The following figures illustrate the Mongols' high dependence on foreign trade. In 1927, when the Mongolian national income was estimated at 51 million tugriks, Outer Mongolia's total foreign-trade circulation was 49.9 million tugriks; in 1930, when her national income was estimated at 85.5 million tugriks, the total foreign-trade circulation was 57.9 million tugriks.[39] Few households would not feel the pinch if imports of cereals, tea, cloth, and small manufactured goods were cut. As well as causing popular dissatisfaction, such a policy might damage the incentives of the nomads to produce livestock for sale, because fewer trade goods would be available to them. In view of the foregoing, the Mongolian planners had to devise some method that would ensure stable deliveries of livestock products. Otherwise the whole foundation of the First Five-Year Plan would be shaky indeed.

Even if it had had a good solution to the tactical problems of introducing otgonnyi stockraising, the measure required by the Russians, the Mongolian government in 1947 still was faced with the problem of deciding how to allocate the country's investment resources among the different branches of the national economy and society. The Soviet Union, in her economic development, had stressed industry at the expense of agriculture and transport. The industrial prospects of the MPR, on the eve of the First Five-Year Plan, could hardly have appeared promising to her planners. Their country had a small population of a low, although rising, level of skill; a small absolute capacity to invest, owing to the low level of national income; no easily accessible mineral deposits or high-grade coal deposits on which to base industry; only a restricted area of arable land; and a rudimentary transportation system, the bulk of goods still being carried by camel caravan.

As a sparsely populated country, the MPR faced an additional problem. The mistaken belief has gained ground that underdeveloped countries in general employ too many persons in agriculture and, therefore, that such surplus workers (1) can be forced into industry in large numbers, without a serious drop in agricultural output, and (2) will produce industrial goods that will be a clear gain to their country's output. Thinly populated areas, however, have little of even low-productivity labor to draw upon, not to

[39] For national income data for 1927, see E. G. Botvinnik, "Opyt ishchislennia narodnogo dokhoda MNR," *Khoziaistvo Mongolii*, no. 3(10) (1928), p. 19; for 1930, see *Sibirskaia Sovetskaia Entsiklopediia*, III, 535. For trade data, see Vargin, "Torgovlia," p. 206. Until 1950, when the tugrik was set at parity with the ruble, the exchange rate was 1.314 tugriks to the ruble.

speak of zero-productivity labor. Had the government of the MPR decided to divert labor from stock raising to industry, it would certainly have had to face a drop in the production of livestock unless stock-raising techniques were changed or investments were increased. Thus, when the Mongolian government decided to stress stock raising despite Soviet precedent, the question still remained as to how best to improve stock-raising productivity. The government either could invest in improvement of breeds, or it could invest more money in wells, cattle shelters, and stockpiles of winterfeed. The need for the last-mentioned type of expenditure was crucial. About every four years the MPR suffers serious stock losses owing to the severity and variability of the climate; the winters of 1940, 1944, and 1954 and the springs of 1945, 1951, and 1955 are recent examples.[40]

It may be that investment in stock raising was quite uneconomic. It has been suggested that the Mongols have already overreached the capacity of their rangeland, and that it is being damaged permanently, even without having to bear an increased load.[41] If so, it would be fruitless to expend capital on range stock raising without basic changes in techniques. The major Soviet expert on Mongolian stockraising does not, however, share this view; he believes that the rangeland of the MPR can bear heavier loads.[42]

The critical problem in the MPR, when all is summed up, was the capital intensification of the agricultural sector when capital was least likely to increase productivity in that sector without a basic transformation of agricultural institutions. The way the problem was tackled, however, revealed no firm grasp of the situation.

The role of the Eleventh Party Congress.—The Eleventh Party Congress, when debating the First Five-Year Plan in December, 1947, called for a speeding up of socialization of Mongolian stock raising.[43] This approach seems to have been nothing more than a pious recognition of desirable ends. The data in table 16 indicate that few additional persons were incorporated in collectives during the period 1948–1952. Although this might be taken as proof of failure to accomplish the directives of the Eleventh Congress, the emphasis the First Five-Year Plan placed on assistance to private

[40] Shul'zhenko, p. 65.
[41] Herold J. Wiens, "Geographical Limitations of Food Production in the MPR," *Annals of the Association of American Geographers*, XLI (1951), 361.
[42] Shul'zhenko, pp. 54–73.
[43] G. A. von Stackelberg, "Mongolia and the XIIth Congress of the MNRP," *Bulletin of the Institute for the Study of the History and Culture of the USSR*, no. 2(4) (1955), pp. 11–17.

stock raising suggests that large-scale collectivization had not really been contemplated at all.

Stress was placed, however, on the need to induce private stock owners to construct wells and corrals and on teaching them to harvest hay and stockpile it as a winter reserve. Such measures were designed to help safeguard stock, ranged on open pastures the year round, against weather and seasonal fluctuations in the availability of water and pasture. The plan also placed strong emphasis on the expansion of veterinary services. In the absence of collectivization, the Mongols were to be encouraged, as in the past, to help one another in the work of herding, in improving pastures, and in constructing wells and corrals (*vzaimopomoshch'*).

Targets.—It was planned that Mongolian livestock herds should grow to 31 million animals. In as much as the highest level of herds ever recorded in Mongolia was 27.5 million animals in 1941 (table 17), this was an ambitious target. It was the more so because a severe winter and spring in 1944–45, coupled with slaughterings and gifts of livestock made during World War II to help the Soviet Union, had brought down the level of herds to less than 21 million animals on the eve of the plan. The plan also called for stepped-up production of sheep and cattle in preference to horses, camels, and goats.

Plans for industrial expansion were also ambitious, in view of the problems the country faced. By 1947 the MPR's state industries included a large meat-packing plant, a number of plants producing commodities from livestock raw materials, a small coal-mining industry, and various other minor industries. There was also a small group of producers' cooperatives engaged in handicraft production. The combined gross output of these industries was to grow by 97 percent over the plan period. The output of state industry was to grow by 99 percent and that of cooperative industry, by 90 percent. Manufactured-food output, based largely on meat and milk products, was particularly stressed by the plan and was to be increased by 116 percent. Coal output was to be increased by 85 percent.[44] It was also planned to raise the proportion of goods manufactured domestically to between 58 and 63 percent of goods in retail trade [45] in order to make the MPR less dependent on imported consumer goods. Agriculture as opposed to stock raising was not emphasized strongly in the plan, for it had never been of importance to the Mongolian economy, contributing

[44] The First Five-Year Plan is described in Vargin (ed.), *Planirovanie*, pp. 20–99. N. V. Tsapkin, *MNR* (Moscow, 1948), p. 96 ff.; and Mandel, p. 140 ff.

[45] Zlatkin, *MNR: Strana novoi*, p. 272.

TABLE 17

COMPOSITION OF LIVESTOCK HERDS IN THE MONGOLIAN PEOPLE'S REPUBLIC, 1931–1941
AND 1945–1960

Year	Camels	Horses	Cattle	Sheep	Goats	Total
1931	493,680	1,588,270	2,003,740	16,739,730	4,379,710	25,205,130
1932						16,032,000
1933						17,600,000
1934	531,900	1,638,000	2,068,000	12,984,000	3,884,100	21,107,000 [sic]
1935	550,000	1,770,000	2,350,000	13,700,000	4,000,000	22,370,000
1936						22,500,000
1937	575,000	1,909,400	2,410,600	14,165,500	4,205,000	23,266,400
1938						25,115,376
1939						26,095,800
1940	660,600	2,387,900	2,874,700	16,135,800	5,311,600	27,370,600
1941	700,000	2,600,000	2,800,000	15,900,000	5,500,000	27,500,000
1945	665,000	2,125,000	1,105,000	12,140,000	3,865,000	20,900,000
1946						20,670,000
1947	723,200	2,036,800	1,979,500	11,722,000	4,315,900	20,777,400
1948						21,000,000 ᵃ
1949						22,040,000
1950	865,000	2,345,000	2,100,000	13,190,000	5,195,000	23,695,000
1951	680,000	2,235,000	2,010,000	13,165,000	5,335,000	23,740,000
1952						22,780,000
1953						22,994,000
1954						22,716,500
1955						23,085,000
1956						24,448,000
1957						24,185,000
1958	864,400	2,449,300	1,954,800	12,579,900	5,594,200	23,442,600
1959	850,100	2,460,300	1,949,900	12,787,600	5,847,200	23,895,100
1960	859,000	2,502,700	1,905,600	12,101,900	5,631,300	23,000,500 ᵇ

ᵃ Approximate figure.
ᵇ The total for 1960 in the original plan was 25 million; in the revised plan, 24.3 million.
SOURCES: For 1931–1957: George G. S. Murphy, "Planning in the Mongolian People's Republic,"
Journal of Asian Studies, XVIII (1959), 256; for 1958–1960: *Statistical Handbook* (Ulan Bator, 1961), p. 57.

only some 6 percent of national income. Some expansion of private agriculture was, however, envisaged.[46] The plan also placed considerable stress on the development of the health and educational systems of the country.

It is possible to get some idea of the relative emphasis the government placed on its various objectives from its planned capital investments. A total of 253 million tugriks was to be expended on capital construction over the five years of the plan, 10.3 percent of which was to be spent on agriculture and stock raising, 13.8 percent on industrial construction, and 11.0 percent on other branches of the economy. Fully 64.9 percent was to be devoted to social and cultural ends such as the provision of schools,

---
[46] Tsaplin, p. 127.

hospitals, cinemas, libraries, clinics, administrative buildings, and the like.[47] In addition, it was planned to extend to private stock raisers over the plan period long-term loans of a total value of 26.4 million tugriks, as well as short-term loans, to be limited each year to 0.9 million tugriks. The loans were to be used for capital improvements such as wells and shelters for cattle, and for purchases of tools.[48]

Actual expenditures fill out the picture. The data in table 18 (which shows both planned and actual expenditures) indicate above all a redirection of governmental expenditures from defense to peacetime needs. Expenditures over the plan period on stock

TABLE 18

BUDGETARY EXPENDITURES OF THE MONGOLIAN PEOPLE'S REPUBLIC FOR THE FIRST FIVE-YEAR PLAN, 1948–1952

(In millions of tugriks)

Expenditure	Year				
	1948	1949	1950	1951	1952
Total	329.2	290.1	337.3	364.4 [a]	364.1
National economy	47.7 [a]	[b]	[b]	[b]	98.7
Stock raising	[c]	[c]	[c]	[c]	[c]
Sociocultural services	84.3 [a]	90.9	100.4	103.9	112.2
Defense	110.1 [a]	[d]	[d]	[d]	53.4

[a] Not actual expenditures, but projected plan figures.
[b] A total of 261.4 million tugriks was spread over the years 1949–1951.
[c] A total of 97.7 million tugriks was spread over the years 1948–1952.
[d] Data unavailable.
SOURCE: F. D. Holzman, "The Financial System of the Mongolian People's Republic," in *The Mongolian People's Republic*, Human Relations Area Files (New Haven, 1956), III, Ec. 34.

raising ran at about 25 percent of those on the national economy as a whole. Expenditures for sociocultural purposes increased gradually between 1948 and 1952. The impression conveyed by the capital investment plan and the budgets is that the government chose to stress the development of both stock raising and industry, despite the fact that it gave the former "leading-link" status. Yet the need to establish and operate health and educational facilities (which constitute the major part of sociocultural expenditures) made heavier demands on the country than any other type of expenditure.

A comparison of the MPR's budgets for her First Five-Year Plan with the Soviet budgets for the years 1948 to 1952 yields the

[47] Vargin (ed.), *Planirovanie*, p. 76.
[48] *Ibid.*, p. 85.

interesting observation that the Mongols spent a larger percentage on defense in 1948 than did the Soviet Union. By the end of the Mongolian plan period, however, the MPR's defense expenditures had fallen below those of the Soviet Union. From 1948 to 1952 the Mongols spent a considerably smaller percentage on their national economy and a slightly larger percentage for sociocultural purposes than did the USSR.[49]

The Mongolian government already had a fiscal policy, modeled on that of the Soviet system, to raise the funds to finance its budgetary expenditures and capital investments. The nomads were subjected to taxes in kind (obligatory deliveries), and the manufactured goods they bought were priced to include healthy turnover taxes in typical Soviet style; they also had to pay a livestock ownership tax. Workers in sectors of the economy other than stock raising were to contribute their share mainly by way of the turnover tax.[50] It is possible that this tax policy was intended to favor workers in industry over those in stock raising in order to promote expansion of the industrial work force. During World War II goods had been rationed in the MPR according to the occupation of the consumer, stores being reopened for privileged persons only; both wage and price policies seem to have been manipulated to the disadvantage of the nomads.[51] Inasmuch as rationing continued in the MPR until 1950, it is possible that the system designed to promote wartime industrial growth continued into the period of the First Plan. But this is mere conjecture.

In short, the government had instituted a fiscal system that taxed the nomads heavily and turned the terms of trade against them. But the government had no infallible method of inducing the nomads to produce goods in the first place. Its solution to this problem was to use taxes and obligatory deliveries in such a way as to guarantee a stable flow of raw materials for industry and export, without completely destroying the nomad's incentive to produce. This system, which seems to have taken some time to evolve, may have resulted from trial and error during the first years of the plan. It was not until February 19, 1949, that each stock-raising household was assigned an individual target. At that time it was also stipulated that livestock produced by a household in excess of its

[49] F. D. Holzman, "The Soviet Budget, 1928–1952," *National Tax Journal*, VI (1953), 244; and "The Budget Expenditures of Outer Mongolia," *Finances Publiques*, XII (1957), 41.

[50] Holzman, in *MPR*, III, Ec. 38–104.

[51] Vargin, "Torgovlia," p. 214.

planned targets be excluded from obligatory deliveries, an obvious attempt to stimulate production.

In 1949 the level of obligatory deliveries was increased.[52] In that year the government also abolished the traditional urton duties, which required stock raisers to provide labor and livestock both to individuals and to the state transportation and communication systems.[53] Creating a transportation system manned by a permanent work force and freeing stock raisers from such duties were obviously expected to bring gains by permitting greater specialization in the economy. In 1950 the livestock tax of the country was revised. Thenceforward the tax was to be levied on each head of stock, but animals produced in excess of the target set for each household were subjected to smaller taxes according to a specified schedule (see table 19). The system of tax reliefs, besides being

TABLE 19

TAX RELIEFS PERMITTED IN MONGOLIAN PEOPLE'S REPUBLIC BY 1950
LAW ON LIVESTOCK TAX

Percentage increase in size of herds after August 1, 1949	Percentage of tax reduction				
	Goats	Sheep	Cattle	Horses	Camels
15 to 20	15	25	25	10	15
21 to 30	25	50	50	15	25
31 and above	50	100	100	25	50

SOURCE: *Konstitutsiia i osnovnye zakonodatel'nye akty* (Moscow, 1952), pp. 137–143.

intended to stimulate livestock production in general, was also designed to promote sheep and cattle production.[54]

When the system had finally assumed concrete shape, obligatory deliveries and the livestock tax were based on the planned size of a nomad's herd. This procedure gave the government a known amount of livestock (or its by-products) each year as the raw-material intake for industry or export. The state had thus shifted to the nomad the burden of loss of livestock by drought, windstorm, or the like. In good years the stock raiser would gain from such a system, but the bad years would hurt him, not the state. Hence the nomad's income rather than the state's share of livestock produc-

---

[52] Stackelberg, pp. 11–17.
[53] Tsaplin, p. 124.
[54] Demidov, pp. 137–143. There is an odd anomaly in the 1950 tax law; whereas tax reliefs for herds produced in excess of plan are clearly intended to encourage sheep and cattle raising, the regular tax schedule may actually encourage cattle, horse, and camel raising (see F. D. Holzman, "Equity of the Livestock Tax of Outer Mongolia," *American Slavic and East European Review*, XV [1957], 506–510).

tion would fluctuate, as had the income of the Soviet collective farmer.

In summary, the First Five-Year Plan aimed at (1) a substantial increase in private stock-raising output, (2) a doubling of the modest industrial output of the country, and (3) considerable expenditures designed to make the Mongols "Soviet men" and to supply them with the perquisites of "Soviet men." As the government, in order to achieve its ends, had to rely heavily on the private stock raiser, it attempted to devise its tax and procurement systems in such a way as to get a stable flow of goods for itself while maintaining the stock raiser's incentive to continue to produce stock for the state.

Results.—Livestock production failed rather dismally to meet the targets the First Five-Year Plan had set for it.[55] By 1952 herds had reached some 23 million head of stock (table 17), 8 million below the planned figure. This failure must have made a strong impression on the Mongolian planners, for the Second Five-Year Plan target was set at only 27.5 million head of stock, a figure well below the target of the First Five-Year Plan and equal only to the size of the herds in 1941. The severity of the winter and spring of 1950–51 had contributed to this failure, but, as is shown below, it was largely due to problems connected with the methods used in taxing the nomads.

Given the failure in stock raising, it is not surprising that the target for industrial expansion was not met either. Whereas gross industrial output had been planned to rise to 370.0 million tugriks annually by 1952, it reached only 189.6 million.[56] Not all the blame

---

[55] Totals of livestock output are misleading indicators of success or failure in stock raising. As Mongolian herds are composed of five types of animals, not all of equal value, data on the value of the total herd would be a better indicator. But there is not enough information on Mongolian prices to prepare an index of changes in the value of the total number of livestock in the MPR. It is possible, however, to make a rough approximation. Shul'zhenko, p. 43, expresses the value of other animals in terms of sheep: 1 goat equals .75 sheep equivalents; 1 head of cattle, 6; 1 horse, 6; and 1 camel, 12. An index of changes in the total number of Mongolian livestock expressed in sheep equivalents would run as follows:

1930	100.0	1940	128.2
1931	102.1	1941	130.7
1934	95.7	1945	104.0
1935	103.2	1950	116.3
1937	107.8	1951	115.8

Such a scheme does not allow for changes in the value of the total number of livestock resulting from a larger percentage of young animals (or rams, bulls, etc.) in one year as against another year. Furthermore, Shul'zhenko's equivalents are probably based on the amount of pasture taken to support different animals, rather than on relative price values.

[56] E. Bavrin and G. Prokhorov, "Uspekhi ekonomicheskogo razvitiia MNR," *Voprosy Ekonomiki,* no. 7 (1956), p. 74. Target outputs and actual outputs are in constant 1940 prices.

can be laid at the door of stock raising, of course. The Mongols complained, for instance, of high turnover rates in industry, and state industry did not achieve planned levels of output.[57] Coal output also fell short of the goals set for it.[58] The Ministry of Food actually produced only 81.7 million tugriks worth of food in 1952 as against the 162.9 million planned.[59] It does not seem unreasonable to conclude that this failure was connected with shortages in raw-material intake from stock raising. In any event, the Second Five-Year Plan set for industrial output a target that was below that of the First Five-Year Plan, that is, 271.6 million tugriks (see table 16).

The Second Five-Year Plan

The Second Five-Year Plan of the MPR seems to show some response to the difficulties that had appeared during the period of the First Plan. It called for an end to seasonal industrial production by building up stockpiles of industrial raw materials. Total capital investment in agriculture and stock raising was to be seven times that made during the First Plan, a decision that suggests a change in investment patterns, for capital investment as a whole was to be increased only 2.7 times.[60] Most of the planned investment in 1955 was for development of roads, mining, and oil wells,[61] implying attempts at diversification.

For the most part, however, the Second Five-Year Plan continued the policies of the first. Livestock herds were to reach 27.5 million head, an increase of 20.7 percent over the period. Nomadic households were expected to increase their output by only 10 percent, suggesting a growing realism in planning. The plan again called for more sheep and cattle relative to other animals. It projected breed improvement by artificial insemination and suitable crossing, and called for more haymaking stations, wells, cattle shelters, and veterinary facilities. Industrial output was to be increased by 46 percent, although few new plants were planned, existing facilities being expanded instead. For example, the Ulan Bator power station was to be enlarged, a shaft was to be con-

---

[57] Maslennikov, MNR na puti, p. 99.

[58] The coal target is given in Vargin (ed.), Planirovanie, p. 63, as 542,000 metric tons. In 1952 production was 238,700 metric tons (see A. I. Denisov, D. I. Ignat'ev, and N. G. Pal'gunov (eds.), Zarubezhnye strany [Moscow, 1957], p. 472).

[59] T. A. Iakimova, "Vneshneekonomicheskie sviazi MNR," Vneshniaia Torgovlia, no. 8 (1957), p. 3. See also Vargin (ed.), Planirovanie, p. 61.

[60] The Second Five-Year Plan is described by Ivor Montague, Land of Blue Sky (London, 1956), p. 169 ff.

[61] Iakimova, MNR, p. 47.

structed at the Nalaikha coal mines with a planned 1957 output of
0.5 million metric tons, and the facilities of the meat-packing plant
were to be expanded to handle 8,000 tons of chilled meat per year.
Coal production was to be organized in some of the outlying areas
of the Republic, and flour-milling and fishing industries were to be
built up. To attain these goals, the output of cooperative industry
was scheduled to increase by 6 percent a year, a rate somewhat
slower than that of state industry, which was to grow 8 percent a
year. Health and educational facilities again were stressed heavily.
As already mentioned, the foundations of a universal compulsory
educational system were to be laid during the years of the plan. By
September 1, 1957, all children from eight to twelve were to be
under instruction.[62] It is well to remember that date: it was
precisely thirty-six years after the Red march into Urga.

The government of the MPR does not seem to have envisaged a
rapid transformation of existing institutions. Private stock raising
was to continue, although 2.5 million head of stock were to be
incorporated in collectives, which indicates some stepping up in the
rate of collectivization. As little was done to meet this target until
late 1955 (see table 16), the first years of the Second Five-Year
Plan give the impression of the same leisurely approach to collectivization which had characterized the First Plan.

Difficulties.—The Second Five-Year Plan ran into difficulties in
its first year. The Mongolian government was able to make neither
its planned expenditures (see table 20) nor its planned capital
investment in 1953. Whereas the planned amount of capital
investment was 90 million tugriks, the actual amount of investment was only 58.1 million tugriks.[63] A similar inability to fulfill
planned expenditures and capital investment might have been
typical of the First Five-Year Plan, were data available to analyze it.
It seems that the relatively full publication of data for 1953 was
permitted in order to show cause for the policy changes made in
1954.

In 1954 Prime Minister Tsedenbal admitted that the government
had "failed to stimulate the personal economic interests of the
Mongols," the blame being laid squarely on the procurement
system.[64] The Twelfth Party Congress in November, 1954, wrote off
arrears of deliveries of livestock and produce to the government
valued at 33 million tugriks. The general tax on livestock was

---

[62] A. Kh. Makhnenko, *Gosudarstvennyi stroi MNR* (Moscow, 1955), p. 55.
[63] Holzman, in *MPR*, III, Ec. 35; Iakimova, *MNR*, p. 47.
[64] A. T. Iakimov, "Uspekhi mongol'skogo naroda na puti k sotsializmu," *Voprosy Ekonomiki*, no. 12 (1954), p. 55. See also Iakimova, *MNR*, p. 16.

TABLE 20

PLANNED AND ACTUAL BUDGETARY EXPENDITURES IN THE MONGOLIAN PEOPLE'S REPUBLIC FOR THE SECOND FIVE-YEAR PLAN, 1953–1957

(In millions of tugriks)

Category	1953 Planned	1953 Actual	1954 Planned	1954 Actual	1955 Planned	1955 Actual	1956 Planned	1956 Actual	1957 Planned	1957 Actual
National economy	123.5	100.2		147.4	150.8	150.8				240.2
Livestock raising and agriculture				21.9		29.1				
Industry				22.9		30.8				
Transport and communications				46.9						
Trade				16.6		50.6				
Sociocultural	136.1	124.5		139.7	160.3	160.3				228.1
Education	72.3			69.5		77.3				57.3
Health	36.5			36.5		44.2				41.1
Administration	33.6				47.0					
Defense	50.0									
Other	89.0									33.6
Total	432.2	369.9	434.8	412.2	507.6	462.1	592.7	510.3	587.4	600.3

SOURCES: George G. S. Murphy, "Planning in the Mongolian People's Republic," *Journal of Asian Studies*, XVIII (1959), 252; *Statistical Handbook* (Ulan Bator, 1961), p. 50. Individual items do not always add to subtotals or totals owing to unavailability of data.

lowered to an average of 23 percent. Government procurement
prices (i.e., on goods subject to obligatory deliveries) were raised
substantially. In addition, a series of price cuts on goods sold to the
nomads gained them 100 million tugriks.[65] In 1955 the procurement prices for wool and goat hair were raised and the level of
meat procurements was cut.[66]

The method of assessing liability to taxation and obligatory
deliveries was also changed. Whereas before 1954 liability had
been calculated on the basis of the plan-projected number of
livestock each stock raiser was to produce, from 1954 on it was to
be calculated on the basis of the livestock actually owned by each
nomad. Indeed, any stock produced in excess of 1953 ownership as
established by the census of that year was looked upon as in excess
of plan in all subsequent years and was exempted from taxation.[67]
This change was fundamental; although the government might
secure more livestock by stimulating the nomads' incentives, it
could no longer count on a definite planned intake for industry and
export.

The new legislation was not addressed entirely to economic
problems; it aimed also at crippling the richer Mongols. Whereas
the taxes of poor and middle-income Mongols were lowered, those
of more prosperous Mongols were substantially increased. In
addition, poor households were exempted from procurements, but
deliveries from the wealthier ones were increased.[68] This in itself
was a noticeable change for the Mongolian government to make in
its policies, for, since the debacle of the 1930's, it had recognized its
dependence on the wealthier households, frequently the most
efficient stock producers, and had not actively discouraged them.
But it is obvious that during 1954 the government had decided to
press for more radical social change. While concessions were being
made to all but the more prosperous nomads, the rate of collectivization was somewhat increased. It may be inferred that this was
looked upon as a major political objective, for during 1954 and
1955 members of both the MNRP and the administration were
ordered to take up posts as directors of collectives. Furthermore, the
Central Committee of the MNRP took over the direction of the
schools that trained presidents and other high administrative
personnel of the collectives. Graduates of these schools were given

[65] Iakimova, *MNR*, p. 55.
[66] Maslennikov, *MNR*, p. 45; B. Bal'zhinniam, "Zhivotnovodstvo, bogatstvo nashei
strany," *Sovremennaia Mongoliia*, no. 1 (1956), p. 5.
[67] Iakimov, "Uspekhi mongol'skogo," p. 55 ff.; Bavrin and Prokhorov, p. 76.
[68] Makhnenko, p. 28; V. A. Maslennikov, *Stroitel'stvo osnov sotsializma v MNR*
(Moscow, 1955), p. 15.

a three-year supplement to their income on taking up a post in a collective, an expense charged against the state budget.[69]

In March, 1955, a congress of "outstanding" workers in stock-raising collectives was held to discuss a "model statute" for their collectives. As noted in chapter 6, the Mongolian collectives, when originated in 1935, had charged new members only a small entrance fee, payable in livestock which became part of the capital of the collective, other livestock remaining private property. The model statute that was eventually introduced placed limits on the size of the privately owned herds of members of the collectives. In addition, the statute raised the entrance fees, setting them at from 25 to 50 percent of the livestock owned by those entering the collectives; fees were levied on a progressive scale, wealthier Mongols being required to surrender higher percentages of their herds. Furthermore, shares in the income that accrued from the fees that had become the capital of the collective were based, not on initial fee contributions, but on labor days performed in tending the collectivized herds.[70] The entrance fee, thus nothing more than a progressive capital levy, fitted in with the government's general policy of moving against the richer Mongols.

The hand of the Soviet Union can be clearly seen in the policy changes of 1954. In the first place, the tax reforms were modeled quite closely on those Khrushchev had introduced after September, 1953. Second, a Soviet delegation attended the conference on the model statute. Finally, in 1954 the Soviet Union concluded a trade agreement with the MPR calling for exports of livestock and its by-products at an increased rate. At the same time the Soviet Union raised Mongolian export prices and depressed her own export prices to the MPR, a concession costing 29 million tugriks in 1954–55 alone.[71] It is interesting at this point to observe how little control the Mongolian government seems to have had over its own foreign-trade prices. In any event, the concessions must have helped it to make its domestic price cuts in 1954.

In that year more energetic steps were also taken to introduce the otgonnyi system. Collectives were encouraged to engage in land cultivation as a subsidiary occupation, and the state gave free timber for the construction of homes and farm buildings.[72] Some collectives already had schools, Red Corners (rooms reserved for

---

[69] Iakimova, *MNR*, p. 19 ff.

[70] *Ibid.*

[71] Iakimov, "Uspekhi mongol'skogo," p. 55; Iakimova, *MNR*, p. 10; Borisenko, p. 315.

[72] Maslennikov, *Stroitel'stvo osnov*, p. 15.

educational needs), reading rooms, dining rooms, radio rooms, hospitals, veterinary centers, and state shops.[73] The Soviet Union also equipped the MPR with the six mechanized livestock stations mentioned earlier in this chapter. In 1956 eighty Mongolians were sent to the Soviet Union to learn how to run the MLS.[74]

Apparently even the first wave of reforms did not bear fruit, for in 1955–56 the level of obligatory deliveries was reduced "to permit accumulation of herds in the private sector." [75] We may trace this policy to the persistent failure to stimulate incentives. It is true that natural conditions of range stock raising do pose difficulties. Shul'zhenko estimated that hay supplies in the MPR in 1954 would support the livestock for only ten days; [76] Bavrin and Prokhorov speak of only 60 kilograms having been available for each animal.[77] But a dairy cow, if stalled, eats 1,000 pounds of hay a month. The standard American authority calculates that 400 to 600 pounds of hay are required to carry a full-grown breeding ewe over the winter period of five to six months.[78] Thus the winterfeed situation was critical. A recent study put average winter weight losses due to severities of climate at 14.2 kilograms for sheep and 46.7 kilograms for cattle,[79] and these data do not account for actual losses of animals in bad winters. The 1954–55 winter was hard, and might have led to loss of stock, but range stock raising faces recurrent climatic problems. In any event, the Second Five-Year Plan failed to achieve its livestock target by a substantial amount. There can be little doubt that such collectivization as did take place influenced this outcome negatively.

The MPR had much more success in fulfilling her industrial goals during the Second Five-Year Plan; most targets were met, if not exceeded. In fact, during the Second Plan the Mongolian government actually complained of labor shortages. This seeming contradiction is easily explained. The Mongols did not have to rely on domestic sources of capital for economic expansion, as they were being literally showered with Chinese and Soviet capital. It is not surprising, therefore, that they were able to achieve their planned industrial targets during the Second Five-Year Plan and that, at the levels of techniques and capital investment used, they

---

[73] Maslennikov, *MNR*, p. 31.
[74] U.S. State Department, *Foreign Broadcast Information Services*, Far East, Daily Report, Jan. 16, 1956.
[75] Matveeva, p. 17.
[76] Shul'zhenko, p. 57.
[77] Bavrin and Prokhorov, p. 75.
[78] F. B. Morrison, *Feeds and Feeding* (20th ed.; New York, 1945), p. 790.
[79] "Produktivnost mongolskikh porod zhivotnykh," p. 91.

faced industrial-labor shortages. Although the MPR had not solved the basic problem of stimulating stock-raising output, the whole climate of the Second Five-Year Plan was better than that of the first.

Benefit from foreign aid.—It is important to review the abundance of aid that was flowing to the Mongols at this time. From 1951 on, the MPR entered into treaties of trade with China and other countries of the Sino-Soviet bloc, whereas before that date the Soviet Union had jealously guarded her monopoly over Mongolian trade. In October, 1952, the MPR concluded a ten-year agreement with Communist China specifying reciprocal economic and cultural assistance.[80] On February 7, 1956, a new trade protocol signed in Ulan Bator scheduled a doubling of Sino-Mongol trade in 1956 relative to 1955. Since then Sino-Mongol trade has been conducted on a regular basis. Trade with China and other countries of the Communist bloc has accounted for some 20 to 25 percent of Outer Mongolia's total trade circulation.[81] The bulk of this trade is probably exports to and imports from China. Although the break in the Soviet monopoly came before 1953, it is likely that the major changes occurred at a later date, for reasons that will soon become apparent.

Both the USSR and China began to be extremely generous with assistance to the MPR. From 1946 to 1957, but especially during the Second Five-Year Plan, the Soviet Union supplied the MPR with aid to the amount of 900 million rubles and made her an outright gift of property to the value of 100 million rubles.[82] For example, Soviet technicians and capital constructed the large shaft in the Nalaikha coal mines, which reputedly has a capacity of 600,000 metric tons of coal.[83] The Soviet Union also constructed a dairy plant and four rolling mills for felt, and furnished a water supply, heating plants, and 40,000 square meters of living space in Ulan Bator. In addition, she provided the six mechanized livestock stations [84] and blueprints for homes, schools, kindergartens, hospitals and equipment.[85] Moreover, in 1956 the Moscow-Peking line

---

[80] Iakimova, *MNR*, p. 42; M. V. Meshcheriakov, "Ekonomicheskoe sotrudnichestvo MNR s sotsialisticheskimi stranami," *Vneshniaia Torgovlia*, no. 2 (1959), p. 12.

[81] N. Samsonov, untitled article in *Vneshniaia Torgovlia*, no. 11 (1959), p. 10; Meshcheriakov, p. 11. Jack Raymond, "Mongolia Favors Trade with West," *New York Times*, Aug. 29, 1956, shows that trade with the Soviet Union constituted 50 to 60 percent of Outer Mongolia's total trade.

[82] Meshcheriakov, p. 11; Gataullina, p. 40 ff.

[83] M. V. Meshcheriakov, *Ocherk ekonomicheskogo sotrudnichestva Sovetskogo soiuza i MNR* (Moscow, 1959), p. 100.

[84] *Ibid.*, p. 99.

[85] Bavrin and Prokhorov, p. 78.

began to bear freight across the MPR.[86] Undoubtedly, a great deal of the 900 million rubles mentioned above was exhausted by cash put up by the Soviet Union to finance the Mongols' share in the railroad company.

In 1957 the Soviet Union also transferred to the MPR her share in the joint company Mongolneft (an oil company), worth 300 million rubles, and her interest in Sovmongmetal (a mining company); however, the Mongols were expected to start paying interest on this acquisition in 1962.[87]

From 1958 to 1960 the Soviet Union provided a credit of 200 million rubles to pay for equipment, materials, and technical assistance she had guaranteed in connection with Outer Mongolia's Third Economic Plan. The Soviet Union also bore 50 percent of the cost of developing public health facilities during the Third Plan.[88]

On February 10, 1959, an agreement was signed to send an agricultural mission and technicians to develop virgin lands to the MPR. The Soviet Union also provided the MPR with 550 tractors and additional needed equipment, and Soviet technicians were to aid the Mongols in investigating the hydroelectric possibilities of Outer Mongolia's rivers adjoining the Soviet border. Credit on easy terms was extended to cover these items of expense.[89] For that matter, an agreement on virgin lands had been signed earlier (1957), and aid in geological surveying had been extended.[90]

The Third Economic Plan

On September 9, 1960, Tsedenbal and Khrushchev signed an agreement guaranteeing Soviet aid to the MPR during the projected Third Five-Year Plan (1961–1965), including delivery of tractors, combine harvesters, and other agricultural machinery, and of motor vehicles, pedigreed livestock, and building materials. In addition, there was a promise of technical assistance that would enable the MPR to build fifteen industrial enterprises and electrical transmission lines, of Soviet technicians, and of practical training for Mongols in Soviet firms. But, most important of all, the Soviet Union granted the MPR a 615-million-ruble long-term loan and deferred, at the MPR's request, the repayment of 245 million rubles lent previously which was due in the period 1961–1965.

The Mongols thus were finally benefiting after their many

---

[86] Meshcheriakov, Ocherk, p. 101 ff.
[87] Meshcheriakov, "Ekonomicheskoe sotrudnichestvo MNR," p. 11; Gataullina, p. 43.
[88] Gataullina, p. 43.
[89] Vneshniaia Torgovlia, no. 3 (1959); Gataullina, p. 44.
[90] Meshcheriakov, "Ekonomicheskoe sotrudnichestvo MNR," p. 11.

slender years under Soviet influence. The reason is not difficult to find. Since May, 1955, Outer Mongolia had had to import Chinese workers.[91] By the end of 1956, some 10,000 Chinese had been admitted, a number that reached some 15,000 by 1960.[92] Originally, it was claimed, Chinese workers had contracted to stay five years and were to be eligible for Mongolian citizenship if required.[93] Later, under the plan started in 1961, Mongol labor was to replace the Chinese.[94]

In 1956 an agreement with China provided the MPR with 160 million trugriks for construction of a textile mill, a paper mill, a plywood factory, and a glass works and for the building of roads and bridges. Between 1959 and 1961 China extended to the MPR a 100-million-ruble credit, repayable in goods from 1962 on.[95] In May, 1960, China provided another loan, 200 million tugriks—presumably for the forthcoming development plan—to be used in industry, irrigation, and the construction of public utilities.[96] It needs to be stressed that none of these sums is trivial compared with the MPR's national income; quite the reverse.

Collectivization.—Foreign aid to the MPR naturally carried a price tag. Chinese assistance was instrumental in establishing a small Chinese population in the country.[97] After 1958, when Chinese influence was purposely reduced, the privilege of exacting a price for aid could be confined to the Soviet Union. Undoubtedly one such price was the introduction of collectivization on a broad scale during 1958–59. The basic features of that change were implemented by the Third Economic Plan.

Although at first the aims of the Third Plan did not include extensive collectivization, the targets were later revised upward. The Third Plan, when it was introduced, covered only three years instead of the originally scheduled five. Whether this change was made in order to keep in step with the USSR, or whether the Mongols could not make long-term projections until they knew Soviet plans, is a matter for speculation. The Thirteenth Party Congress called for livestock herds to reach 25 million head by 1960, some 6 million less than the number planned for 1952 and some 2.5 million less than the number planned for 1957.[98] If the livestock herds at the

[91] *Soviet News*, Sept. 13, 1960; Maslennikov, *MNR*, p. 62.
[92] I was so informed in a meeting with a number of Mongolian economists.
[93] Jack Raymond, "Mongolia Imports Chinese Workers," *New York Times*, Aug. 28, 1956.
[94] See n. 92.
[95] Gataullina, p. 46 ff.
[96] *Keesing's Contemporary Archives*, no. 174760 (1960).
[97] Maslennikov, *MNR*, p. 62; Raymond, "Mongolia Imports Chinese Workers."
[98] For details of the Third Plan see *Pravda*, March 20, 21, 23, 1958.

end of the Third Plan were of better quality and heavier in weight, and were biased in favor of sheep and cattle, then what at first sight appears to be a record of failure might, indeed, not be one. There is, however, little evidence of such qualitative improvement in Mongolian livestock herds; even on some of the state farms the livestock was still unimproved. It was planned, however, to continue with collectivization at a fairly rapid rate, with 50 percent of the nomads of the country in collectives by 1960.[99] One hundred and fifty collectives were to be converted to sedentary life during the three years of the plan. Forty-five HHS were to be converted into MLS. Furthermore, the rate of collectivization was hastened to such a degree that by March, 1959, the country was completely collectivized. As expected, the goal of the plan later was lowered; a target of 24.3 million head of livestock was set for 1960, but it was not reached.

Administrative reorganization.—Simultaneously with collectivization, reorganization of the administrative apparatus took place. The new system was tried out in selected localities in 1957, and by 1959 it had been installed throughout the country. The Mongols themselves liken their system to the Communist Chinese and Korean systems of administration. Each region (*somon*) is directly responsible to its aimak, or subprovince, which in turn is responsible to Ulan Bator. The somon is the lowest administrative unit. The director of a state farm or the chairman of a collective farm is the administrative, political, and economic head of a somon. He also holds police powers and assembles the people's courts to try offenses that are committed within his jurisdiction. As he is similarly responsible for livestock and human censuses, it may well be that he is empowered to handle matters connected with the militia.

This administrative arrangement bears striking resemblances to the system that obtained in the period when the old ruling nobility wielded considerable power over prerevolutionary Mongolia. As a result of the policy of gradualism and of neglect of education, the managerial class tends to be young and small at a time when the problems it has to face are constantly expanding. Hence the merging of party, economic, and governmental functions in the person of one man ensured firm control over the countryside and helped to minimize the difficulties created by long distances in a sparsely populated country.

---

[99] D. Tumur Ochir, "Ot Mongolii feodal'noi k Mongolii sotsialisticheskoi," *Sovetskoe Vostokovedenie*. no. 5 (1957), p. 67.

Agricultural and industrial growth.—Agriculture was emphasized by the Third Economic Plan; the cultivated area was to be
enlarged to 2.3 times its former size. In part, the increase was to be
achieved by the cultivation of land by new sedentary cooperatives,
but in the main it reflected the planned expansion of state farms in
the MPR. The Soviet Agricultural Expedition of 1947–1952 to the
MPR had recommended that future agricultural expansion take
place not so much by use of collective farms as by development of
state farms.[100] This recommendation seems to have been implemented recently.

Over the plan period, industrial output was to be increased by 52
percent; oil output, by 170 percent; and mining, by 100 percent. A
billion tugriks was to be invested in industry, a sizable portion of
the funds being foreign assistance.[101] The plan emphasized expansion of the state sector rather than of the cooperative sector to
ensure that, as in agriculture, cooperative enterprises would gradually become less important. The Third Plan also stressed the
creation of a compulsory universal educational system. Finally,
long-term plans (for five- and even ten-year periods) were to be
prepared for the MPR, analogous to the longer-range plans of the
USSR.

Whatever strains showed up during implementation of the Third
Plan were owing primarily to the abundance of capital relative to
labor and to bottlenecks in certain areas; building materials, for
instance, were in acutely short supply in 1960. In part the strains
were also caused by unevenness in planning, though they reflected
essentially the new condition of capital abundance. Planning is not
a difficult task in a small country with so uncomplicated an
industrial structure.

In any event, in reviewing the introduction of both planning and
collectivization, it is difficult to resist the conclusion that the desires
of the Soviet leaders rather than those of the Mongols themselves
were the most important ones. The changed political climate within
the Soviet Union, however, and the diplomatic and other maneu-
vers of the Chinese, demanded that the Russians use a new set of
instrumentalities to move matters along in the direction they
wished. We may be quite sure that, had the Mongols themselves
been able to discuss openly and to decide their future policies for
themselves, the course of change would have been different.

---

[100] Shubin, p. 120.
[101] Iakimov, *Mongol'skii sbornik*, p. 5.

8

THE COSTS AND BENEFITS
OF SATELLITESHIP

Socioeconomic and Cultural Conditions in 1960

The year 1960 witnessed an Outer Mongolia that had been transformed by broad changes since Maiskii's visit in 1919–20. Our account suggests that this statement would not be equally valid for 1950, is hardly true of 1940, and is inapplicable to 1930. We can gauge the extent of the changes that have occurred, largely in the decade of the 1950's, by thumbing through the *Statistical Handbook* published in Ulan Bator in 1961.

Population Characteristics

The *Statistical Handbook* records a population growth from 647,-500 in 1918 to 936,900 in 1960. Although the 1918 figure may be somewhat too low, there can be no doubt of the real population growth, which now continues at a very fast rate compared with world gross population growth rates. Since 1955 the annual gross population growth rate in Outer Mongolia has steadily increased from 1.8 to 3.3 percent. No longer do inadequate data leave us in doubt whether the Outer Mongolian population is stable, declining, or advancing. The country's crude birthrate in 1960 was 41.2 per thousand, a high figure, and the death rate was 10.0 per thousand, a low figure, compared with world patterns of fertility and mortality. The recently accelerated population growth rate is directly attributable to the youthfulness of the current Outer Mongolian population (see table 21).

Viewed in a broader framework, the population picture (i.e., the distribution of the population by age) reflects also the benefits of improved overall policy. Modern health practices and modern medicine have had beneficial effects on both birthrate and death rate. The availability of better and less hazardous employment opportunities, combined with a sense of change and progressive purpose, may also have contributed to faster population growth. The population picture, however, also mirrors the costs of Soviet control. High mortality rates in the earlier period, the result partly of lack of socioeconomic change under the policy of gradualism and partly of the loss of life brought about by outbursts of political

TABLE 21

AGE DISTRIBUTION IN THE MONGOLIAN
PEOPLE'S REPUBLIC, 1956[a]

Age group [b]	Number of persons (in thousands)	Percentage of total population
2	62.1	7.3
7	162.9	19.3
13	242.5	28.7
17	302.0	35.7
24	401.6	47.5
39	580.6	68.7
59	760.3	89.9
All	845.5	100.0

[a] Based on census of February 5, 1956.
[b] Each age group includes all persons of that age and below.

opposition and social disorder, obviously must have reduced the number of persons now in the older age groups. One striking, positive feature of Outer Mongolia's contemporary population is the even balance between males and females in certain age groups, attributable to the fact that the MPR did not enter World War II. The opposite situation prevails in the Soviet Union, where the war caused substantial losses in the number of younger men.

The population of the MPR is now basically Mongol, with representation of such tribes as Khalkhas, Kazakhs, Durbets, Baiats, Buriats, Ulets, Torguts, Tuvinians, and others. The Chinese population is small and no longer constitutes a real threat to the regime. And the Soviet Union, as we have learned, has been careful not to build up the number of her citizens in the MPR.

Occupational, educational, and cultural changes.—The occupational composition of Outer Mongolia's population has also changed

sharply since 1918, again largely in the last decade. In 1960, 36
percent of the population consisted of civil servants, industrial
workers, and other nonagricultural employees and their families.
The other 64 percent were engaged in agriculture, either on state
farms or in collectives. (Incidentally, as a result of state policy,
private traders and their families, nomads working for themselves
and their families, and lamas now account for only 0.3 percent of
the population.) Although all these figures indicate a significant
improvement, they also show that the MPR still has an underdeveloped economy.

According to the *Statistical Handbook,* 72 percent of the population above eight years of age is literate; however, given the late
development of the educational system, the standard of literacy is
bound to be generally low. The majority of the country's inhabitants continue to live in the countryside and remain basically
nomadic; only about 200,000 persons live in towns. Ulan Bator,
with a population of 164,000, is the only fairly large town, but, except for the state offices located there, it presents much the same
pattern as a small provincial administrative center in the Soviet Union. The countryside at large as yet gives little evidence of
capital investment. There is the railroad linking the MPR with
China and the Soviet Union, and the administrative centers of
collective farms have offices, restaurants, sleeping quarters, and
meeting places. In general, however, the Mongol of the countryside
still uses his yurt and has not to any great extent been converted to
the otgonnyi system of stock raising. The preference for some
vestige of nomadic life remains strong even among urban dwellers.
For example, many cabinet ministers and civil servants have
retained their yurts as quarters for the summer months.

Although the population has preserved some of its traditional
ways, the crafts have virtually disappeared. Only in the state-
fostered athletic games, in opera, in the theater, and in art do the
people try to work out a Mongolian style of life. Needless to say,
such artistic endeavor takes place within the framework of a
culture that is, in the words of the Soviet slogan, "nationalist in
form but socialist in content."

The Economy

Production and budget structures.—The conclusion to be drawn
from the occupational structure prevailing in 1960 is that the MPR
was then still heavily oriented toward primary production; the
amount of fabrication of products remained small. Of the 1960

nonagricultural work force of 121,000, only 35,000 were directly engaged in industry. Education, culture, and health accounted for almost as many employees, 27,100 in all. The only other important groups of nonagricultural workers were distributed in the following types of enterprise: construction, 17,300; transportation, 14,500; and trade, 15,400.

TABLE 22

STRUCTURE OF BUDGET OF MONGOLIAN PEOPLE'S REPUBLIC IN SELECTED
YEARS BETWEEN 1940 AND 1960

(In percentages)

Income							
Source	1940	1947	1952	1957	1958	1959	1960
Turnover tax	10.9	21.8	16.1	20.8	19.4	60.0	60.0
Profits tax	7.8	10.6	13.0	26.5	33.5	20.5	17.6
Customs duties	17.6	12.5	15.7	12.6	11.5	a	a
Loans and lotteries	10.1	4.2	3.0	0.7	0.1	a	a
State and social insurance	a	3.0	3.3	4.3	4.7	4.9	4.1
Local taxes and duties	a	1.6	2.6	1.5	1.4	1.6	1.5
Income tax	16.7	14.3	16.5	13.0	9.5	6.4	5.6
Surcharge on turnover tax	23.7	17.3	18.6	17.1	16.6	a	a
Other	13.2	14.7	11.2	3.5	3.3	6.6	11.2

Expenditures							
Purpose	1940	1947	1952	1957	1958	1959	1960
National economy	21.9	15.6	25.6	40.0	43.8	44.6	49.1
Sociocultural services	19.7	26.7	29.0	38.1	36.6	34.1	32.9
Administration	6.3	13.0	14.2	9.5	9.0	7.7	7.2
Defense	46.6	36.7	19.0	6.8	5.7	2.6	6.4
Repayment of loans and lotteries	1.6	6.1	6.8	1.7	1.8	6.4	2.9
Other	3.9	1.9	5.4	3.9	3.1	4.6	1.5

a Data unavailable.
SOURCE: *Statistical Handbook* (Ulan Bator, 1961), pp. 51–52.

Major items of industrial output in 1960 were minerals (coal and fluorspar), fuels (crude oil, diesel fuel, and gasoline, all in small quantities), building materials (bricks, lime, timber, and felt and frames for yurts), and cloth and dressed skins. Apart from mining and mineral installations, the bulk of capital facilities were concentrated in Ulan Bator, primarily in two factory complexes.

In chapter 7 we discussed the introduction in the MPR of the Soviet system of financing capital investment. No set of statistics can illustrate the application of this system in Outer Mongolia more graphically than the budgetary data given in table 22. Compared with the budget of autonomous Mongolia (see table 1, chap. 1), the change to a Soviet-type budget is indeed historic, if we consider what items made the largest revenue contribution to the MPR budget during the decades 1940–1960. Under this Soviet-type budget, the twin instruments of turnover and profits taxes were being used to assure the state command over the country's economic resources. That command was being used positively for investment in the national economy and for raising the levels of education and health (although defense, of course, consumed the largest share of the budget). The following figures on capital formation (in millions of tugriks at prices current in those years) from domestic sources, taken from the 1961 *Statistical Handbook*, demonstrate the efficacy of the Soviet system of resource mobilization, even though that system did not begin to produce major gains until the late 1950's.

1930	0.7
1940	39.8
1945	41.1
1952	49.5
1953	60.2
1954	88.5
1955	113.9
1956	145.3
1957	190.8
1958	233.8
1959	299.7
1960	427.6

Inasmuch as domestic price inflation prevailed in the MPR until the end of World War II, no striking change in capital formation took place between 1930 and 1945; the great increase came only in 1955. Given the rise in the Mongolian population, it is hard to believe that a substantial increase in the per capita income could have occurred prior to 1955. Nor is it known to what extent the post-1955 increases in investment were taking place at the expense of personal consumption. Regardless of the answer to this question, it seems likely that per capita consumption increased substantially from 1955 on.

The MPR's comparative economic position.—Although the statistics available do not permit precise estimation, all the indirect evidence suggests that the MPR's per capita output was below that of the Soviet work force, and probably was even lower than that of the most backward union republic of the USSR.

Despite the adoption of Soviet growth policies, the overall orientation of the MPR economy has not changed greatly. Basically, the economy of the 1960's still rests on the importation of consumer goods financed by the export of primary products. Although capital goods are a growing item in the import bill, they still are not the most important item. Nomadism persists, even though within the framework of collectives, and the primary sector of the economy retains its dominance for the time being.

This broad picture, sketched on the basis of data provided by the *Statistical Handbook,* gives a rough idea of the current state of Outer Mongolia's economic development. The most valid comparison one can make of the MPR economy is with the economies of New Zealand and Denmark, both of which have developed on the basis of primary exports. These two countries have become largely manufacture- and service-producing, even though their sectors of specialization and diversification are largely dependent on primary production. Whereas the MPR continues to employ two-thirds of her population in agriculture and stock raising, the corresponding figures for Denmark and New Zealand are one-quarter and one-fifth, respectively. Compared with these models, and despite the considerable improvements she has accomplished in the last decade, the MPR still has a long way to travel on the road to comparable status.

FORTY YEARS OF SATELLITESHIP: THE PROS AND CONS

The Political and Economic Balance Sheet

In this and the five preceding chapters we have learned what have been the consequences, both proximate and remote, of the Soviet invasion of Outer Mongolia in 1921. Viewed from the broader perspective of history, this event brought mixed benefits and costs in both the political and economic spheres. Thanks to the Bolshevik take-over in that year, Outer Mongolia was spared both the evils of Chinese warlordism and the losses her forced participation in the Sino-Japanese conflict of that period would have entailed. It would be foolish in the extreme to ignore the fact that Outer Mongolia in 1921 was inevitably destined to be under either Russian or Chinese influence. This study has perhaps demonstrated that the events that tipped the scales in favor of the Soviet Union do not themselves seem to have carried the flavor of inevitability. Minor departures from the historic events that did occur might easily have produced a very different outcome. For example, a determined reaction to the Soviet probes of 1921 and a speedy and effective answer to the invasion of Chinese territory by remnants of the White Russian troops might have removed any cause for Soviet intervention in what were, essentially, domestic Chinese affairs. Once within the Soviet sphere of influence, Outer Mongolia's defense did become a matter of Soviet policy, and the continued sensitivity of Eastern affairs spared the Outer Mongolian people from the losses of World War II. Had Chinese troops vanquished those of Ungern-Sternberg, the story would probably be quite different. Given the current Communist Chinese policy in adjacent Tibet, the Outer Mongolians might by now have ceased to exist as a people, or at the least would be swamped by Chinese military colonists. This is but one side of the coin.

For those who consider the expansion of political freedom as one of the most prized social ends, evaluation of Outer Mongolia's progress will always be colored by the nature of the Soviet political system. None of the colonies of the West, or at least of the enlightened West, ever had to pay the price of initial submission to a party dictatorship in return for the right to embark on the road to economic development. Moreover, no small satellite within easy reach of Soviet ground forces can advance toward political freedom at its own speed; each must keep in step with the Soviet bloc as a whole, although some may be leaders and others laggards. Should there be a regression toward autocratic rule within the bloc as a whole, small satellites would inevitably suffer the most.

In addition to enduring external constraints of this nature, the Outer Mongolians have found their aspirations for a wider Pan-Mongol polity consistently frustrated by the Soviet Union. To all intents and purposes the Pan-Mongol question no longer exists, because those areas where Mongols formerly predominated outside Outer Mongolia are now peopled by Chinese and Soviet citizens. In the foreseeable future, Pan-Mongolism cannot be considered a realistic political possibility.

Outer Mongolian aspirations have thus been channeled toward ends acceptable to alien Soviet planners. The country's traditional leaders have been replaced or liquidated, and the traditional religion has been systematically destroyed, without being given an opportunity to free itself of corruption. The customary secular and religious law of the Outer Mongolians has been supplanted by the more complex code of modern Soviet law, a law that, despite its apparent modernity, devotes little attention to individual rights and interests.

The typical Westerner will conclude that the Outer Mongolians have paid a heavy political price for the economic development they have enjoyed in the past decade. And a measure of genuine economic development has been achieved, including assurance of health and education to the population at large. Yet, it is equally important in this connection to realize that, under Soviet control, a number of alternative, more favorable policies might easily have been applied in the MPR before 1950. Because of the country's small population, marginal changes in Soviet policy could have had far-reaching beneficial effects on the national economy of the MPR. This observation is borne out by Outer Mongolia's history since the death of Stalin.

THE PRICE OF "ECONOMIC DUALISM"

To record a certain measure of economic gain in the MPR is not to say that the transplanted Soviet mechanism of economic growth has flourished vigorously in Outer Mongolian soil. There is a striking similarity between the pattern of economic growth in satellite Outer Mongolia and the pattern that evolved in underdeveloped countries under Western colonial rule, where "dual economies" were characteristic.

Definition of economic dualism.—The dual economy is so called because it has two economic sectors that operate side by side, with few interconnections. The two sectors are a small, capital-using but labor-conserving industrial one (often referred to as the enclave sector) and a large, labor-using but capital-conserving agricultural one. The size of the sectors refers to the work force employed rather than to the levels of output. Thus, the small industrial sector may contribute more to the national product than the large agricultural one.[1]

The Growth and Operation of Dualism

Historically, dual economies emerged in the following way. Toward the end of the nineteenth century, as the Western industrial

---

[1] The term "dual" economy or society was used by Dutch economists prior to its adoption by Americans. For example, J. H. Boeke, *The Structure of Netherlands Indian Economy* (New York, 1942), asserts that a dualism appears in colonial countries. There is, however, a sharp distinction between Boeke's use of the term and the meaning American economists later ascribed to it. Essentially, Boeke defines the dualism in colonial countries as one between capitalist and precapitalist values and the habits and ways of life that evolve from such values. He sees the inhabitants of the urban capitalistic sector of a society as having values and goals that are distinctly different from those of the inhabitants of the rural precapitalistic sector.

The economist who uses dualism as an analytical concept assumes that all individuals have similar values and objectives in economic matters: they are, essentially, wealth maximizers. The specific constellation of factor endowment and factor use in the precapitalist and capitalist sectors of the economy (using Boeke's distinction) leads, however, to very different economic outcomes. Economic growth and change take place in the capitalist sector, whereas economic stagnation or even decline, with little change, is typical of the other. This sharp difference in the assumptions used should not obscure the substantial agreement on descriptive matters displayed by both types of users of the term.

economies had surplus capital at their disposal, private investors sought outlets for profitable investments abroad. Moreover, the new industrial systems needed raw materials as inputs. At the same time, the level of effective demand for industrial goods in the non-Western areas of the world was so low that capital investment in colonial markets was unprofitable. Yet, if the raw materials of the colonial areas were processed and exported to the West, where levels of effective demand were high, capital-using projects became warranted. Thus, rubber, coal, oil, ores, wool, meat, and cotton became valuable as inputs for production of goods to be sold to Western populations. As a result, "oil" economies, "rubber-plantation" economies, and "mineral" economies emerged as sectors in underdeveloped economies. This phenomenon, which has attracted a good deal of attention,[2] has also appeared in Outer Mongolia, partly as a result of the Soviet-imposed strategy for economic development.

To recapitulate: Private investors wishing to exploit the resources of newly discovered, non-Western areas found that, owing to low levels of domestic income and low effective internal demand, it was not worthwhile to build capital facilities for the production of goods for the native populations. In contrast, investments devoted to extraction of raw materials useful to the industrial machines of the Western economies were profitable. Such investments failed, however, to trigger economic growth in the receiving areas. It is indisputable that the underdeveloped countries themselves, prior to the start of their trade with the West, were not making substantial contributions to their own capital formation. Foreign investment, however, tended to move toward projects that used a great deal of capital relative to labor and provided little new employment. Wages thus had little effect on raising effective demand in an underdeveloped society, because the total wage bill in industry remained small. The gains of such foreign investment to the underdeveloped society in the form of rental incomes to those owning land were dissipated by the income-demonstration effect, in the sense that the rentier group indulged in luxury consumption such as attendance at horse races, absorption of Riviera sunshine, or purchase of gold-plated Cadillacs, instead of devoting its wealth to investment purposes at home. Neither did the social overhead investment (roads, harbors, and similar facilities), made to facilitate the working of mines, oil wells, and plantations, generate external

---

[2] For a discussion of the dual economy see Benjamin Higgins, *Economic Development, Principles, Problems and Policies* (New York, 1959), chap. xiv. See also Brinley Thomas, "The Alleged Exploitation of Underdeveloped Countries: A Review of the Evidence," *Proceedings of the Western Economic Association* (1958).

economies. Railroads and ports funneled out resources and did not generate economic growth. One cause of this failure is probably that such facilities do not create a dense concentration of population, a feature that is fairly common in industrial societies and perhaps provides one explanation of why certain investments promote so-called external economies. Thus, after the usual types of foreign investment had been made, the economy of an underdeveloped country showed little improvement in economic growth and domestic capital formation.

Capital projects to be financed by foreigners in underdeveloped countries naturally had to compete in regard to profitability with the investment needs of the more developed economies. As a result, the supply of capital to an underdeveloped area, as soon as all its natural resources were undergoing use, became restricted. Once the basic industry of a colonial country had been shaped to the purpose of channeling out raw materials to the West, further investments were contingent upon the increased demand for raw materials in industrial economies. It is a historical fact that modern economies tend to become raw-material conserving. Hence, shifts in demand for raw materials tended to move less than proportionately to the growth of the national products of the developed countries. The capital supply thus became limited—a supply shortage often intensified by the riskiness of investment owing to political instability in the underdeveloped countries.

Although it is true that employment in the industrial sector of a dual economy is contingent on the supply of foreign capital, it is incorrect to say that a dual economy by its very nature prevents economic growth. The seeming illogic of locating heavily capital-using facilities in an underdeveloped economy with an overabundance of labor is easily explained. Local trained labor may have been in short supply and too expensive to train. Management and production costs may have been too high with use of local labor, necessitating operational economizing. Or, for purely technological reasons, the construction of facilities that relied heavily on industrial techniques instead of on labor may have been the only rational choice, or at least the entrepreneurs may have thought so.[3] More-

---

[3] That is, it is necessary that technical coefficients are fixed, or, to put it another way, that the isoquants of the production function are ∟-shaped, and that the capital-labor ratio favors capital inputs. We may view trained labor as extremely expensive, and the costs of research and development as prohibiting the innovation of more labor-using techniques. As Western managers in underdeveloped areas command high salaries, management-conserving technical processes are more economic than techniques that use a great deal of both labor and management. These analytical assumptions may not seem too realistic, as they entail zero marginal physical productivities of factors for given techniques. Some technical processes, however, do in fact permit little variation of labor input.

over, it is implicit in the use of some technical processes that the quantity of labor used in production does not vary a great deal, regardless of whether the price of labor drops or rises. Oil technology, for example, requires substantial investments in research and development if the use of labor is to be intensified. In short, private investors had many price variables to consider besides the cost of labor.

Why did the relationship between the underdeveloped and the developed sector of dual economies generally prevent economic development? Some domestic sources of capital formation did, after all, exist. Moreover, it is now generally held that the initial conditions of a growth process are less important that the parametric changes that take place in the economic variables during the very process of growth. Hence, why has a higher rate of domestic capital formation usually not been achieved in dual economies? The answer to that question is that the institutions that grew up around the underdeveloped sector were, by their very nature, resistant to economic growth.

For a period of indefinite duration the dual economy seemed to be self-preserving. Foreign investors, in order to protect the profitability of their enterprises, generally brought pressure to bear on domestic governments (whose members usually belonged to the rentier class) to limit competition, to provide privileges such as extraterritoriality, to discipline labor, and so forth. As the foreign industries were frequently monopsonists in the labor market, and as they faced a virtually elastic supply of labor, the general level of wages could be held down. Furthermore, the governments of underdeveloped countries were likely to assist the foreign investor by preventing the emergence of labor unions, which were likely to have brought about a rise in wages. Work populations were usually unstable, preventing any general advance in the level of skills. Or —and this feature is more consistent with the picture of a dual economy we are drawing—a small labor aristocracy emerged, jealous of its distinctiveness and isolated from the population at large. Generally, the interests of the private foreign investor and of the domestic government involved in a given sphere of influence coincided: both wanted political stabilization of the area. Hence, no attempt was made to displace the traditional rentier group as the social elite; social reformers tended to get short shrift. For that matter, the rentier group, itself firmly loyal to both the foreign investor and the foreign controlling power, helped them in disciplining labor. Thus, no demand-induced domestic investment could take place.

The members of the rentier group, wealthy themselves—in some instances extremely so—saw no reason for change in the social order. They tended to view society as it existed as good, to display a conservatism reinforced by nationalism. In general, groups outside the elite, the non-Establishment as it were, such as junior army officers and radical political groups, were the only ones who called for change. But, as political change threatened the interests of both the elite and the investing companies, there was every reason to maintain the status quo. Western governments, confronted with many immediate political problems demanding solution, also appreciated areas free from trouble. Thus, lack of social change was considered desirable by the social elements that profited from it. In many areas the foreign investing firm had virtual sovereign power, had the privilege of extraterritoriality for its own national employees, and could manipulate the elite into disciplining labor and granting additional legal rights and privileges.

Analyzed from this perspective, Western imperialism was an economic arrangement in which the governments of the larger imperialist powers played a passive role, gratefully accepting the neutralization of conflicts in colonial areas through the agency of Western investing firms. This does not mean, however, that an imperial power did not at times override the rights of its overseas firms if its own national interest argued for different arrangements in one of its imperial dependencies.

There is a good deal of statistical evidence that a typical dual economy tended to be closely associated with only one major Western power. The inflow of currency, of capital, of civil servants where they were needed, and of army advisers tended to come from one country. Trade relationships might be reinforced by special bilateral agreements or other forms of trade control. As investment tended to come from the country that had political control over the underdeveloped economy, and as the elite group of the underdeveloped country tended to accept the consumption patterns of the developed, controlling economy, export and import flows were overwhelmingly concentrated both by bill of goods and by major supplier-purchaser.[4] It has been argued that within this framework of concentration a subtle form of exploitation took place, in that the terms of trade tended to shift over the course of time against

---

[4] Geographic concentration of foreign trade has been measured by Albert O. Hirschman, *National Power and the Structure of Foreign Trade* (Berkeley and Los Angeles, 1945), chap. vi. M. Michaely, "Concentration of Exports and Imports: An International Comparison," *Economic Journal*, LXVIII (1958), 722–736, established measures for both geographic and commodity concentration.

the underdeveloped economy. In addition, the very investors and managers who brought industry to new areas also brought medical techniques that prolonged life expectancy and lowered mortality rates. The small though heavily capital-using industrial sector, however, could not absorb rising populations, for further capital investments that would employ more labor depended on demand shifts for resources in foreign countries. Thus, overcrowding appeared in the agricultural sectors of colonial countries, where variable proportions between capital and labor were possible.[5] On balance, taking both sectors together, the standard of living remained stationary or even fell.

These, then, are the significant features of a dual economy. On the one hand, the supply of foreign capital is limited; on the other, domestic capital formation is inhibited by a set of institutional relationships that have formed around the foreign-trade sector. Although no formal constraints prevent the domestic elite from changing the prevailing state of affairs, that elite is easily manipulated because its economic interests coincide with those of the foreign investors. The general per capita income is very low, but the elite groups and the labor aristocracy that has sprung up usually enjoy high incomes. In other words, income distribution is highly unequal. Net capital formation relative to new national product may be quite high in the period when investments are made in the exporting sector. But such investment sets up claims by foreigners on the domestic product by way of exports. In fact, such exports may not even be considered a legitimate part of the net national product, inasmuch as the exporting sector might well be considered part of the industry of the larger power. Furthermore, as capital formation is tied to exports, a larger net national product may be achieved, but it will not lead to rising per capita domestic consumption, as the level of domestic sales is always lower than that of domestic production. Thus it is possible to have high rates of investment, as measured by the net capital formation–net national product ratio (NCF/NNP), without a corresponding rise in consumption. If the population increases in the agricultural sector, there may even be falling per capita consumption levels. In the developed sector Western manners, Western medical standards, and Western levels of literacy are typical. In contrast, the agricultural sector is characterized by traditional customs, deep illiteracy, and high mortality and disease rates. The

---

[5] This phenomenon occurred when the trend of technology was toward resource saving per unit of product.

consumption-goods component of imports will be high and heavily biased in favor of commodities that satisfy the style of life of the elite. Whatever the general applicability of this analysis of economic dualism,[6] on the basis of the MPR's recent historical experience the economy of that country fits the picture of dualism.[7]

The MPR Economy as an Example of Dualism

Oleg Hoeffding has questioned whether what we might call the rules of thumb for economic development which have evolved from the Soviet experience necessarily export well to countries where the initial conditions of the development process are radically dissimilar to those that had prevailed in the USSR prior to the period of planning.[8] For example, the blend of production factors which is characteristic of the Soviet Union—the relative neglect of transport and housing and the complete economic neglect of agriculture—is likely to be unsuitable for developing an economy heavily dependent on natural-resource exploitation. The problem of factor proportion, however, is not specific to Soviet methods, but is one that applies to underdeveloped economies in general.

According to Eckaus, imbalance of production factors in underdeveloped countries occurs because they must make major, not marginal, changes in their factor balance.[9] Other causes of the

---

[6] For example, Charles P. Kindleberger, *The Terms of Trade: A European Case Study* (New York, 1956), shows that the terms of trade may have moved in favor of developed countries relative to underdeveloped countries. He also shows, however, that the terms of trade did not move in favor of countries exporting industrial commodities relative to those that exported primary products. Inasmuch as industrial commodities are changed over the course of time with quality improving, whereas primary products remain unchanged in quality and form, the terms of trade may have favored primary exporters when quality of the product is included as a variable.

[7] The term "dual economy" clearly applies to what we normally think of as sparsely populated countries. An "oil" economy would be an appropriate example. Such an economy might display large differences in output per capita by sector of the economy. There are, however, differences from the less sparsely populated country. In the latter we may view the marginal physical product of labor as approaching zero. This trend is not characteristic of sparsely populated countries, and it certainly is not characteristic of Outer Mongolia. Taking workers from the agricultural sector thus implies that agricultural output will be lost. Such countries encounter special development problems in addition. They face extremely high per capita expenditures for an adequate social capital structure, for example, in transportation facilities. Moreover, relocation of population to exploit a natural resource that has physical limits, in addition to making an economy vulnerable to world shifts in demand for the resource, poses the problem of a population based on what is essentially a declining industry.

[8] Oleg Hoeffding, *Soviet State Planning and Forced Industrialization as a Model for Aisa,* Rand Corporation Publication P-1450 (Santa Monica, Calif., 1958).

[9] Richard S. Eckaus, "Factor Proportions in Underdeveloped Areas," *American Economic Review,* XLV (1955), 539–565.

TABLE 23

OUTER MONGOLIA'S VISIBLE FOREIGN TRADE, 1924–25 to 1957 [a]

(In millions of rubles)

Date [b]	Exports			Imports		
	Total	To the Soviet Union	To other countries [c]	Total	From the Soviet Union	From other countries [c]
1924–25		12.5			9.7	
1925	52.4	12.6	39.8	52.2	10.1	42.1
1925–26		13.1			12.8	
1926	68.0	25.9	40.1	58.7	13.2	45.6
1926–27		26.5			16.1	
1927	67.0	33.5	33.5	65.4	14.7	50.7
1927–28		42.2			26.7	
1929	62.4	53.3	9.0	72.6	35.1	37.5
1930	76.4	68.9	7.5	79.8	62.2	17.6
1931	101.4	100.6	0.8	143.7	130.3	13.4
1932 [d]		67.3			144.5	
1933		60.3			134.6	
1934		71.8			156.4	
1935 [e]		27.6			40.6	
1936		25.6			40.2	
1937		25.4			49.7	
1938		29.1			52.7	
1939		37.3			56.9	
1940		52.3			118.3	
1941		92.2			117.9	
1942		118.5			53.4	
1943		122.5			84.2	
1944		139.5			86.2	
1945		117.0			110.5	
1946		113.1			167.8	
1947		149.1			180.8	
1948		134.8			157.7	
1949		144.1			171.0	
1950		156.8			172.9	
1951		224.9			317.5	
1952		202.4			264.3	
1953		200.4			349.5	
1954		220.4			530.0	
1955		215.1			486.8	
1956		217.2			413.6	
1957	270.0	200.5	70.0	340.0	270.7	70.0

[a] All data are current prices adjusted to the 1950 ruble exchange rate. It is standard Soviet practice to re-value trade data when they devalue. This table conforms to Soviet usage because most of the entries are Soviet in origin.

[b] Until 1929 the data are for the period from September of one year to October of the next. Figures for the standard year are estimates. From 1929 on, the basic trade series are for the calendar year.

[c] Mainly China.

[d] From 1932 through 1949 Outer Mongolia traded only with the Soviet Union.

[e] The series show an odd break in 1935, resulting not from a sharp change in the physical structure of exports and imports, nor from a change in the ruble exchange rate. Harriet L. Moore, *Soviet Far Eastern Policy, 1931–1945* (Princeton, 1945), p. 264, suggests that the cause of the break is the fact that Mongolian transactions were valued in "goods rubles or chervonets" before 1934.

SOURCE: George G. S. Murphy, "The Mongolian People's Republic: Dual Economy?" in *Trudy dvadtsat' piatogo mezhdunarodnogo kongressa vostokovedov*, V (Moscow, 1963), 345.

difficulty are that factor endowments are radically different in the underdeveloped economy, and that technological change becomes a matter of conscious government policy in the underdeveloped country.[10] So far as the MPR is concerned, the Soviet emphasis on capital-intensive projects, which has become something of a doctrine for the other economies in the ruble area, has meant that the Outer Mongolians have invested heavily in a few capital facilities that have absorbed only a few members of the agricultural work force. The budget's heavy emphases on defense and educational and welfare measures imply that domestic sources of capital formation are rather meager. Consequently, an important source of domestic capital formation had to be Soviet (and later Communist

TABLE 24

EXPORTS FROM THE MONGOLIAN PEOPLE'S REPUBLIC TO THE
SOVIET UNION AS PERCENTAGE OF TOTAL EXPORTS IN 1934–1936
AND 1955–1957

Commodity group	1934	1935	1936	1955	1956	1957
Minerals	None	None	None	4.4	4.3	4.1
Gasoline and oil	None	None	None	a	a	a
Livestock	31.1	38.7	39.4	34.4	35.2	30.9
Animal by-products	66.3	58.6	55.2	60.6	58.7	64.1
Wool	13.2	18.4	21.8	39.5	37.4	43.1
Other	2.6	2.7	5.4	0.6	1.8	0.9

a Less than 0.05 percent.
SOURCE: George G. S. Murphy, "The Mongolian People's Republic: Dual Economy?" in *Trudy dvadtsat' piatago mezhdunarodnogo kongressa vostokovedov,* V (Moscow, 1963), 347.

Chinese) lending, which until recently was severely limited. This situation clearly has features that are analogous to those of a dual economy, and the analogy could be pushed much further.

Outer Mongolia came under Soviet influence in mid-1921. Until 1929 the leaders of the country used a range of fiscal and administrative devices to drive out Chinese traders and to reorient the whole of Mongolian trade toward the USSR. In 1929 a Soviet foreign-trade monopoly was established, and by 1931 Outer Mongolia had virtually ceased to trade with any country but the Soviet Union (see tables 23 and 24). This state of affairs continued until 1951, when Outer Mongolia started to trade with Communist China, although in very small amounts. By 1957, perhaps 25 percent of all foreign trade was with various countries of the Soviet bloc and mainly with China (see table 23).

---

[10] *Ibid.*, L (1960), 642.

Thus, trade is heavily concentrated not only in one major supplier-demander, but also by type of product. In order to justify establishment of this pattern of trade dependence, both Soviet and Outer Mongolian sources assert that Soviet exports to Outer Mongolia during this period were below world prices and that imports were above world prices.[11] The terms of trade did shift in the Mongols' favor in the period 1925–1929 (see table 25). But one authority, Violet Conolly, points out that much more favorable

TABLE 25

OUTER MONGOLIA'S NET BARTER TERMS OF TRADE, 1925–26 TO 1934

Year	Import unit values [a]		Export unit values [a]		Net barter terms of trade	
	1925–26 weights	1934 weights	1925–26 weights	1934 weights	1925–26 weights	1934 weights
1925–26	100.0	100.0	100.0	100.0	100.0	100.0
1926–27	106.5	97.9	115.2	96.8	108.2	98.9
1927–28	113.3	103.0	131.4	118.5	116.0	115.0
1929	122.5	103.0	156.9	149.5	128.1	145.1
1930	147.7	106.7	138.7	125.7	93.9	117.8
1931	177.9	138.6	129.4	114.6	72.7	82.7
1932	187.8	144.1	128.0	113.7	68.2	78.9
1933	201.0	143.0	154.5	135.3	76.9	94.6
1934	141.0	107.7	206.5	171.0	146.5	158.8

[a] Fairly large commodity groups were used to establish the unit value indexes. As Outer Mongolia's imports and exports were fairly homogeneous in commodity groups, and were stable over time, the indexes are not too unreliable. Table 26, which uses smaller commodity classes and is thus somewhat more reliable, corroborates the indexes above.

SOURCE: S. N. Bakulin and D. D. Mishustin, *Vneshniaia torgovliia SSSR za 20 let, 1918–1937: Statisticheskii spravochnik* (Moscow, 1939), p. 7. Computations are my own. For definition of terms used in table see Charles P. Kindleberger, *The Terms of Trade: A European Case Study* (New York, 1956), pp. xix–xx.

terms were extended to areas like Sinkiang, Turkey, and Persia, where Soviet political influence was weaker.[12] Be that as it may, Outer Mongolia was given special tariff privileges and apparently was a preferred, if not the most preferred, trading partner of the Soviet Union.[13]

With the declaration of the foreign-trade monopoly in 1929, conditions changed noticeably. Not only did the terms of trade shift rather heavily against the Mongols, but this shift occurred at a time when their first (and abortive) economic and social development

[11] I. Ia. Zlatkin, *MNR: Strana novoi demokratii* (Moscow, 1950), p. 196; Bazaryn Shirendyb, *Narodnaia revoliutsiia v Mongolii i obrazovanie MNR* (Moscow, 1956), p. 76.
[12] Violet Conolly, *Soviet Economic Policy in the East: Turkey, Persia, Afghanistan, Mongolia and Tana Tuva, Sin Kiang* (London, 1933), p. 13.
[13] Anatolii D. Kallinikov, *Revoliutsionnaia Mongoliia* (Moscow, n.d.), p. 57.

plan of 1931–1935 called for a steeply increased level of exports to the Soviet Union (see table 26). This unfavorable change may reflect the general shift in the world terms of trade against agricultural exporting countries. But the shift seems to have been unique to Outer Mongolia at that time. The trading position of Sinkiang, Tuva, Persia, Afghanistan, and Turkey, which as a group traded under arrangements similar to those Outer Mongolia had made (and some of which had comparable problems of transport

TABLE 26

COMPARISON OF OUTER MONGOLIA'S INDEXES OF UNIT VALUE AND NET BARTER TERMS OF TRADE WITH SOVIET DATA, 1929–1932 AND 1934

Year	Soviet export prices (1)	Outer Mongolian import unit values (2)	Soviet import prices (3)	Outer Mongolian export unit values (4)	Outer Mongolian net barter terms of trade (4/2) (5)	Soviet net barter terms of trade (3/1) [a] (6)
1929	100.0	100.0	100.0	100.0	100.0	100.0
1930	82.7	87.0	85.1	81.1	93.2	102.9
1931	60.1	97.9	77.7	77.5	79.2	129.3
1932	48.7	93.6	68.0	78.6	84.0	139.6
1934	44.0	75.9	56.0	123.5	162.7	127.3

[a] The method here used to calculate the Soviet net barter terms of trade is not the usual one. It does, however, permit a comparison of what Outer Mongolia's trading experience would have been at general Soviet world prices.

SOURCES: Base-year weights used for the Outer Mongolian indexes have been computed from commodity classes in A. Voznesenskii and A. Voloshinskii, *Vneshniaia torgovlia Soiuza Sovetskikh Sotsialisticheskikh respublik za pervuiu piatiletku* (Moscow and Leningrad, 1933). Soviet indexes have been derived from S. N. Bakulin and D. D. Mishustin, *Statistika vneshnei torgovli* (Moscow, 1939). Alexander Gershchenkron, *Economic Relations with the USSR* (New York, 1945), p. 51, uses a terms-of-trade index based on S. N. Prokopovicz, *Russlands Volkswirtschaft unter den Sowjets* (Zurich and New York, 1944), p. 342, which is almost identical with the Bakulin and Mishustin index.

costs), does not seem to reflect the same negative features either in unit-value indexes or in net barter terms of trade.

Horst Mendershausen has suggested that the dynamics of big power–small power trade bargaining can put the small country in the ruble area in a disadvantaged position, in the absence of formal policy decisions from the top level.[14] Furthermore, trade relationships and trade bargaining involve more than mere import and export commodity flows; that is, there is the question of capital and technical assistance at favorable terms, both part of a general trading bargain. Unfortunately, in regard to both types of assistance to Outer Mongolia, no statistical data are available to throw light on this matter. As the shift in the Mongolian terms of trade

[14] "Terms of Trade between the Soviet Union and Smaller Communist Countries, 1955–1957," *Review of Economics and Statistics*, XLI (1959), 118.

was halted in 1933, it seems reasonable to assume that this was a matter of policy decision at the highest level. The failure of Outer Mongolia's first economic and social plan had involved the country in severe difficulties, had placed both the Soviet Union and the MPR in a troublesome situation vis-à-vis the Far Eastern political situation, and had called for drastic action.[15] From 1933 onward, the terms of trade unambiguously shifted in Outer Mongolia's favor. This ability to tackle problems created by trade relations with speed is clearly one of the strengths of the Soviet system and coexists with the weakness and disadvantage the smaller power always derives from big power–small power bilateral bargaining.

Because no data are available from the 1930's until 1955, we cannot specify exactly the nature of Outer Mongolia's trade experience with the Soviet Union. The Mongols did, however, make substantial transfers of commodities and capital to the Soviet Union during World War II, as an important part of their contribution to the joint war effort.[16] Since 1955 export and import prices have been quite stable, and the MPR has had a heavy import surplus with the Soviet Union, thanks to unusually large capital loans after 1954.[17]

During the past two decades the volume of Outer Mongolia's foreign trade has increased because of more efficient extraction of raw materials. The value of exports to the USSR in current prices increased eightfold between 1936 and 1955–1957. This gain must, however, reflect a good deal of price inflation, for, if the basic exports of the MPR to the Soviet Union are weighted in 1936 prices, they show only a threefold growth.[18] Interestingly, the degree of domestic fabrication of export commodities seems to have remained fairly stable. Gross industrial output in constant prices were only 3.6 times larger in 1955 than in 1940. In 1955 the annual gross industrial output was about 300 rubles per capita in 1940 prices. As some of this amount represents a shift from domestic fabrication or processing, it seems reasonable to conclude

---

[15] Prime Minister Gendun, "Iz doklada prem'er ministra MNR Genduna, VII Velikomu Khuralu," *Tikhii Okean*, no. 1(3) (1935), p. 260, remarked: "Exports of cattle and raw material from our country to the USSR were curtailed because the exports of earlier years were clearly at exaggerated levels and did not correspond to our potential."

[16] M. V. Meshcheriakov, *Ocherk ekonomicheskogo sotrudnichestva Sovetskogo soiuza i MNR* (Moscow, 1959), pp. 73–82.

[17] An index of Mongolian exports to the USSR based on 1955 and using 1955 price weights shows no significant change in the level of exports: 1955, 100; 1956, 101.8; 1957, 101.8; and 1958, 99.7.

[18] Exports in current unit values with 1936 as base year for the index were: 1936, 100; 1955, 840.2; 1956, 848.4; and 1957, 783.2. Exports in 1936 unit values were: 1936, 100; 1955, 343.6; 1956, 338.7; and 1957, 287.5.

that processing of raw materials has done little more than keep up with the increase in raw-material extraction. There has, however, been a shift in Outer Mongolia's import patterns, intermediate commodities taking the place of consumption goods as the most important category (see table 27).

These data, like others on the MPR, pose a statistical problem in that much of the output was by joint companies. Mineral output, for instance, is not included in gross industrial-output data, and it is likely that the export figures are also understated.[19] Joint companies played an important role in the exploitation of the Mongolian raw-material base. The first joint company was the Mongolian Trade and Industrial Bank set up in 1924.[20] The directors of the bank were Soviet officials who were instrumental in reforming the Outer

TABLE 27

IMPORTS INTO THE MONGOLIAN PEOPLE'S REPUBLIC FROM THE SOVIET UNION AS
PERCENTAGE OF TOTAL IMPORTS, 1934–1936 AND 1955–1957

Commodity group	1934	1935	1936	1955	1956	1957
Consumption goods	53.4	70.3	74.4	46.4	40.4	48.5
Intermediate goods	37.7	21.4	20.2	52.7	56.9	47.1
Unallocable	8.9	8.3	5.4	0.9	2.7	4.4

SOURCE: George G. S. Murphy, "The Mongolian People's Republic: Dual Economy?" in *Trudy dvadtsat' piatogo mezhdunarodnogo kongressa vostokovedov*, V (Moscow, 1963), 349.

Mongolian currency system and played a not unimportant role in driving Chinese trade from Outer Mongolia. Prior to the introduction of joint companies, individual Soviet companies had operated in the USSR, Sibgostorg, and Nephtesyndicat).
country, purchasing raw materials from the population largely on a barter basis (e.g., Tsentrosoiuz, Dal'gostorg, Sherst', Torgpredstvo
After the national bank had been instituted, Mongolstroi (1925), a construction company, Mongoltrans (1929), and Sovmontorg (1932), a company that handled all Soviet-Mongolian trade, became important. Other joint companies of the period until roughly the end of World War II were Mongolsherst', Mongsovbuner, and Avtokontor. Apart from those that had a paramilitary purpose (such as Mongoltrans), these companies were largely devoted to handling livestock and its by-products.[21] Additional facilities set up during this period were an industrial combine (also a joint

---

[19] S. K. Roshchin, *Sotsialisticheskii uklad i ekonomike MNR* (Moscow, 1958), p. 77.
[20] Meshcheriakov, p. 46.
[21] *Ibid.*, p. 55 ff.

company) for processing of livestock by-products [22] and a meat-packing plant, the latter in 1946 with Soviet assistance.[23]

During these years the supply of capital to the area was obviously limited by both political and economic considerations. Soviet policy was to neutralize Outer Mongolia as a buffer zone and to make no investments that might be captured in the event of enemy attack. Assistance probably was largely military, devoted to building up the Mongolian Army. Until 1949, for instance, no railroads were built in the country except for a narrow-gauge spur from the Trans-Siberian Railroad to Choibalsan, constructed in 1939, probably for the purpose of supplying the troops who later fought off the Japanese at Khalkhin-gol.

A noticeable shift in Soviet policy which began in 1949 was reflected in the type of joint companies that were established. In 1949 a railroad line was built from the frontier to Ulan Bator, and in the same year Sovmongolmetall and Mongolneft' were formed. Because of the success of the Chinese Communists it was possible to devote more Soviet resources to Outer Mongolia, but this aid was clearly based on a more intensive utilization of the country's raw materials with a view to exporting oil and minerals to the USSR.

In 1954 another shift in Soviet policy took place. The joint bank was handed over to the Mongols, as well as Soviet steamships plying on Mongolian rivers. In addition, sixteen meteorological stations, all telephone communications, and two airports (one in Ulan Bator and the other in Sain Shanda) were transferred.[24] In 1957 the mining and oil corporations passed into Mongolian hands.[25] When the Ulan Bator Railroad was extended to China, the existing joint company was presumably expanded, and the Soviet Union extended cheap credit to the Mongols to pay their share in the cost of constructing the line. As the MPR received transit charges, she could meet yearly interest payments of unknown extent.

So long as a substantial portion of Outer Mongolia's output was administered by joint companies, the Mongols had limited control over their own economy, and their plan of development was obviously linked to the needs of the Soviet export market. It would, however, be wrong to suggest that joint facilities in general were of no use to the MPR. Furthermore, the Soviet Union was actively engaged in rapidly training a Mongolian work force to take over

[22] V. A. Maslennikov, *MNR na puti k sotsializmu* (Moscow, 1951), p. 94.
[23] E. M. Murzaev, *MNR: Strana, liudi, khoziaistvo* (Leningrad, 1947), p. 75.
[24] Meshcheriakov, p. 100.
[25] *Ibid.*, pp. 98–100.

operation of the plants and installations she had set up in the MPR. These workers have been under general Soviet direction, and capital allocation has been in terms of Soviet economic interest, but Soviet and Outer Mongolian interests need not necessarily diverge. The analogy to the raw-material–exporting sector of a dual economy is strong. No detailed cost information on Soviet investments in Outer Mongolia seems available. From data on industrial production, however, it is clear that until 1954 Soviet capital was confined to the joint companies, except for minor gifts of agricultural equipment. This is not to ignore a substantial but unknown Soviet investment in the Mongolian Army.

Thus, for a considerable time the supply of capital was limited by political considerations and thereafter was focused on raw-material extraction. Generally, the facilities were capital-intensive, for there has been a continual emphasis on the use of advanced techniques. In essence, acceptance of Soviet technology implied fixed proportions between capital and labor and undoubtedly contributed to the slow growth of the industrial work force. In 1939 there had been only 5,500 workers in state industrial employment out of a population of close to 1 million. By 1947, some 7,300 were so employed, and by 1955 27,500.[26] It was in this sector of the economy that the joint companies functioned. The Mongols, however, did have a small industrial-cooperative work force of some 10,000 during this period.

Meanwhile Outer Mongolian agriculture (mainly stock raising) persisted in a state not greatly different from that of earlier centuries. Partially commercialized but using age-old techniques, it was still nomadic. Not until 1956 was there substantial collectivization or promotion of sedentary life among the nomads. Institution of an adequate educational system, except for instruction provided during military service, was tardy.

It is not easy to make productivity comparisons between the two main sectors, but data on the small cooperative industry, which lies between them, suggest that yearly output per worker has been 2.5 to 4 times as much in state as in cooperative industry.

It may be objected that the Soviet system of financing economic development ensures a good supply of domestic capital. There are no rentiers in Outer Mongolia, and hence there is no income-demonstration effect in upper-class spending. Nevertheless, there was a demonstration effect in Outer Mongolia, one that plagues

---

[26] I. G. Iur'ev, "Gosudarstvennaia i kooperativnaia promyshlennost'," in I. Ia. Zlatkin (ed.), *MNR: Sbornik statei* (Moscow, 1952), p. 172; V. A. Maslennikov, *Stroitel'stvo osnov sotsializma v MNR* (Moscow, 1955), p. 44.

underdeveloped countries in general: it was due to budgetary emphasis on social and cultural expenditures. Badly underdeveloped though their country was, the Outer Mongolians attempted to emulate the standards of the Soviet Union in health, art, monument building, and the like. Until World War II defense expenditures had consumed the bulk of funds, but after 1949 the consumption of social goods took on considerable importance. Since 1954 the MPR has had the advantage of substantial loans from both the Soviet Union and Communist China. The capital shortage thus has been eased, although investment still seems oriented toward export of raw materials.

The dualistic economy is a relatively recent phenomenon. The world quantum index of exports and the world record of capital flows would place the origin of economic dualism largely in the third quarter of the nineteenth century. But the phenomenon has not been a persistent one. In the period between World Wars I and II, countries like Mexico were already beginning to break out of the traps dualism presented. Rostov would assert that this tendency was attributable to "negative demonstration effects." The intercourse between a colony and the Western nation to which it was attached led to the formation of a domestic elite dedicated to breaking the mother country's economic hold over the colonial nation.

Outer Mongolia's period of economic dualism lasted about thirty years, a duration that may well be modal for all dualistic economies. Be that as it may, the country's breakout from this economic harness was largely an externally imposed solution. The buildup of Soviet trade and such Soviet capital investment as there has been in the MPR have not had the salutary effects that Western trade and Western capital investment have had on the colonial countries, the most significant of these effects being undoubtedly the colonies' reactive nationalism.

In summing up, we may say that Soviet investments in the MPR served primarily the interests of the USSR; at least, this was completely true in Stalin's time. The MPR budget of that period reflected the preferences of the Soviet leaders instead of those of the Outer Mongolian people at large. The style of life and the culture that evolved in the cities bore a Soviet flavor, as did the goals and values of the urban dwellers. The countryside remained nomadic, illiterate, and poor, but its abler representatives were brought to the cities by the selective educational system. This policy, combined with the Communist apparatus of power, assured the country peace. Outer Mongolia's leaders, tamed by purges and commanding only the weak bargaining power that any small country has vis-à-vis a dominant one to whose sphere of influence it is securely attached, became obedient servants of their Soviet masters. As if to hide this colonial sore on their body politic, the Soviet leaders brought down a curtain of secrecy on Outer Mongolia; even Soviet citizens were not permitted to visit the area, save by special and rare permission. By comparison, no Western nation in recent years has had a comparable power to hide its mistakes.

If we wish to assess the phenomenon of dualism in a wider perspective, we might consider Stalin's attempt to establish a similar pattern in what became the Eastern European satellites after World War II. Had full-blown Stalinism continued, it is not unlikely that other satellites of the Soviet Union would also have displayed the features of dualism to a marked extent.

It is too early to assume with confidence that the changes that have taken place in the Soviet bloc are so fundamental as to preclude the reappearance of "colonial" features in the satellites. It may well be that the essence of a future "colonialism" will result from the autocratic enforcement in a satellite nation of the wishes of the dominant country's planners.[27] This picture certainly pertains to the MPR in the period 1928–1953. Stalin's policy preferences of forced planning in, and economic neutralization of, Outer Mongolia netted her costs and burdens aplenty; conversely, her neutrality during World War II gained her obvious advantages. At no time, however, did conformance to Stalin's wishes lead to amelioration of the dualistic character of the economy.

It is not inconceivable that autocracy will reemerge in the USSR. In this event, it is likely that the leaders of her satellites, cowed by renewed purges inspired from Moscow, will once again have to bow to the personal policy preferences of a Soviet autocrat and thus may be forced to introduce "colonial" features in their economic systems. As each year passes, and as each Soviet satellite is treading its own path to a fully developed economy, the preconditions of dualism are disappearing. Until full economic development is assured, however, each satellite runs the risk of backsliding, owing to potential regressive changes in the Soviet Union.

At this point a fundamental distinction must be made. We may call a satellite any country that persistently votes with the Soviet bloc in the United Nations; this is the common use of the term today. Owen Lattimore, however, has defined the essence of

---

[27] I have developed this theme more fully in "On Satelliteship," *Journal of Economic History*, XXI (1961).

satelliteship as the great institutional conformity within the entire Soviet bloc. According to that definition, satelliteship, at least as we have known it, is dying a natural death, a view that seems to have much merit. A key element of the satellite relationship used to be the system of power which enforced the preferences of the highest Soviet leader, Stalin, in the bloc countries. Stalin's successors have not managed to wield that system in such a way as to ensure the obedience of the leaders of the countries in the Soviet sphere of influence. Stalin insisted on institutional conformity by the MPR, but not to an extent that might injure the Soviet self-interest. Gradually, the attachment of the Soviet leaders to a static ideology has been declining, and current Soviet policy reflects the normal pressures of the country's national interest to a much greater degree. But, whereas the exercise of personal autocratic rule has diminished in the USSR, the system of power itself, which lends itself to autocratic exploitation, has not changed in substance. Hence, until more fundamental changes appear in the Soviet body politic, a small adjacent country like the MPR faces a future fraught with hazard. As a return to autocracy in one form or other is possible in the Soviet Union, the future may once more present us with surprises.

CONCLUSIONS

The principles of "socialist" trading which Lenin had originally formulated and which were implemented in the MPR, together with the subsequent modifications made by Stalin, did not lead to the emergence of a strikingly novel set of historical relationships; quite the contrary. Recent Soviet propaganda has been emphasizing the special nature of foreign trade among countries of the Soviet bloc. For Outer Mongolia, there are no hard facts to back up this propaganda for at least the first thirty-three years (1921–1954) of that country's history. The invasion of 1921, which ushered in the possibility that a new set of relationships might evolve for the Mongols' benefit, bestowed mixed blessings on them; it brought them neither an ideal state of affairs nor a costless road to plenty.

It is true that the increased extent of foreign assistance the MPR now enjoys will undoubtedly help to raise the country's economic standard of living. Yet, if we offset against the gains of the present generation the costs that had to be borne by the preceding generation of Outer Mongolians, we must conclude that the country did not have the opportunity to select the cheapest and most efficient way of achieving economic development. The record of Outer Mongolia's history suggests that considerations of Soviet foreign policy continually influenced the choice of policies the Mongolian government actually used. In addition, the solutions for economic development were those that had been worked out in the Soviet Union and were mechanically transposed to the Mongolian People's Republic, regardless of whether they were optimal solutions for a small economy whose basic problems were quite different from those of the large economy of the USSR. The generosity currently being displayed by the Soviet Union toward her formerly neglected dependency has won her the support of the present Outer Mongolian regime. But, in no way can current benefits be considered adequate compensation to those who were the losers under the policies of the past. This is tantamount to saying that a high price has been paid for the benefits of modern medicine, the introduction of universal education, the enjoyment of a moderate per capita income, and the "blessing" of pervasive conformity to the Soviet style of life.

What made the Outer Mongolians accept this bargain? In 1921 the absence of a national political life, the sense of loyalty to a family group, a hereditary prince, or a religious leader rather than to a nation, meant that the group that could control Urga could occupy Outer Mongolia. After the Soviet invasion, the steady purging of all those whose opinions diverged from the Bolshevik party line ended the possibility that a genuine national life would evolve in Outer Mongolia until after the death of Stalin. The building of a political apparatus staffed by Mongols who were benefiting from the favors of the new regime gradually supplied the administrative structure necessary for turning occupation into national control of the country. On October 20, 1945, a plebiscite was taken in the MPR to determine the people's desire for "independence" from China. Chiang Kai-shek's China had never recognized the MPR, despite the fact that there was not the slightest shred of Chinese control over the area. As is usual with voting in Communist countries, the majority was overwhelmingly in favor of the proposal, that is, "independence." Thus, by the end of World War II, the outer Mongolians had learned who their new masters were. Able persons likely to contest the authority of the regime either were absorbed into administration or party activity, were purged, or were intimidated. The population at large, deprived of its traditional leadership on the part of the nobility and the religious authorities and unable to produce its own leaders, had no choice but to accept the situation.

Since the end of Stalinist autocracy, and once their country had been admitted to the United Nations, the Outer Mongolians have not had to pay quite so much attention to the wishes of their Soviet masters. Nonetheless, their freedom of action is still much more limited than that of the average small nation outside the Sino-Soviet bloc. The Outer Mongolians, lying between Communist China and the Soviet Union, are in an unenviable situation: however much they may reappraise their past, they can do but little to mold their future.

Bibliography

MONGOLIAN SOURCES AVAILABLE IN TRANSLATION

Public Laws

China Year Book, 1926–27. Tientsin, n.d. Contains the Mongolian Constitution of 1924.
Demidov, S. S. (ed.). *Konstitutsiia i osnovnye zakonodatel'nye akty MNR.* Moscow, 1952. Contains the 1940 Constitution and amendments to it.
Mongol'skoi Zakonodatel'stvo. Number 1. Osnovnoi Zakon i Prilozheniia. Ulan Bator, 1928.
Ugolovnoe zakonodatel'stvo zarbeshnykh sotsialisticheskikh gosudarstv. Moscow, 1951.

Official Minutes, Transcripts, and Reports of Party, Political, and Economic Organs

Chetvertyi s'ezd MNRSP. Ulan Bator, 1925.
Mongol'skii tsentral'nyi narodnyi kooperativ sed'moe sobranie upolnomochennykh. Ulan Bator, 1929.
Novaia Mongoliia: Ekonomiko-politecheskoe i kul'turnoe sostoianie strany. Protokoly pervogo Velikogo Khuraldana MNR. Ulan Bator, 1925.
Protokoly zasedanii 4-go s'ezda upolnomochennykh paishchikov Mongol'skogo narodnogo kooperativa. Ulan Bator, 1925.
Tretii s'ezd MNP. Urga, 1924.
Trudy i materiali 5-go s'ezda upolnomochennykh mongol'skogo tsentral'nogo narodnogo kooperativa. Ulan Bator, 1929.

Speeches and Writings of Political Leaders

Amor and Doksom. "Istoricheskie uroki 15 let revoliutsii," *Tikhii Okean,* no. 3(9) (1936).
Choibalsan, Khorloin. "Mongol'skaia naroda na puti k sotsializmu," *Pravda,* Nov. 26, 1949.
———. "Velikii prazdnik mongol'skogo naroda," *Bolshevik,* no. 13 (1951).
———. *Kratkii ocherk istorii mongol'skoi narodnoi revoliutsii.* Moscow, 1952.
Damba. "Vse sily i energiiu po vypolnenie i perevypolnenie narodno khoziaistvennogo plana 1951 g.," in N. T. Vargin (ed.), *Planirovanie narodnogo khoziaistvo Mongolii.* Moscow, 1951.
———. "Doklad tovarishcha D. Damba," *Pravda,* March 20, 1958.
———. "Rukovodiashchaia sila mongol'skogo naroda," *Pravda,* March 1, 1965.
Gendun. "Iz doklada prem'er ministra MNR Genduna, VII Velikomu Khuralu," *Tikhii Okean,* no. 1(3) (1935).
Tsedenbal, Iu. "O piatiletnem plane razvitiia narodnogo khoziaistvo i kul'tury

MNR na 1948–1952 g.," in N. T. Vargin (ed.), *Planirovanie narodnogo khoziaistvo Mongolii.* Moscow, 1951.

———. *O zhizni i deiatel'nosti Marshala Choibalsana.* Moscow, 1952.

———. Untitled article in *Pravda,* Nov. 23, 1954.

Articles by Mongols

Balzhid, G. Untitled article in *Den'gi i kredit,* no. 8 (1956).

Bal'zhinniam, B. "Zhivotnovodstvo, bogatstvo nashei strany," *Sovremennaia Mongoliia,* no. 1 (1956).

Demchig, D. "Promyslovaia kooperatsiia MNR," in *Promyslovaia kooperatsiia stran narodnoi demokratii.* Moscow, 1957.

Dugardzhap. "Zadachi narodnogo prosveshcheniia MNR," *Khoziaistvo Mongolii,* no. 4(17) (1929).

Erdeni-Ochir. "Na puti k sotsialisticheskomu stroitel'stvu (VIII s'ezd MNRP)," *Khoziaistvo Mongolii,* no. 3(21) (1930).

Luvsandamba, Maninibu. "Lenin's Advice," *Novoe Vremia,* no. 44 (1957).

Ochir, D. Tumur. "Ot Mongolii feodal'noi k mongolii sotsialistcheskoi," *Sovetskoe Vostokovedenie,* no. 5 (1957).

Otorchi, Ulan. "Ozero Tolbi," *Khoziaistvo Mongolii,* nos. 1–6 (1928).

Books by Mongols

Banzaragchi, B. *MNR: Geograficheskii i politiko-ekonomicheskii ocherk.* Ulan Bator, 1951.

Nachukdorji, Shagdarjavin. *Life of Sukhe Bator.* Trans. Owen Lattimore and Urgungge Onon. In Owen Lattimore, *Nationalism and Revolution in Mongolia.* New York, 1955.

Shirendyb, Bazaryn. *Narodnaia revoliutsiia v Mongolii i obrazovanie MNR.* Moscow, 1956.

Zhagvaral, N. *MNR.* Ulan Bator, 1956.

Soviet Sources
Books

Blagoveshchenskii, M. N. *MNR.* Moscow, 1950.

Bogdanov, M. N. (ed.). *Ocherki istorii Buriat-mongol'skogo naroda.* Verkhneudinsk, 1926.

Demidov, S. S. (ed.). *Konstitutsiia i osnovnye zakonodatel'nye akty MNR.* Moscow, 1952.

Dylykov, S. K. *Demokraticheskoe dvizhenie mongol'skogo naroda v Kitae, ocherk istorii.* Moscow, 1953.

Gorbunova, M. N., and D. N. Konstantskii. *Koreia—Mongoliia: Strany Azii.* Moscow, 1956.

Iakimov, A. T. (ed.). *Mongol'skii sbornik, ekonomika, istoriia, arkheologiia.* Akademiia Nauk SSSR, Institut vostokovedeniia. Moscow, 1959.

Iakimova, T. A. *MNR: Ekonomika i vneshniaia torgovlia.* Moscow, 1956.

Kallinikov, Anatolii D. *Revoliutsionnaia Mongoliia.* Moscow, n.d.

Maiskii, I. M. *Sovremennaia Mongoliia.* Irkutsk, 1921.

———. *Mongoliia nakanune revoliutsii.* Moscow, 1959.

Makhnenko, A. Kh. *Gosudarstvennyi stroi MNR.* Moscow, 1955.

Maslennikov, V. A. *MNR na puti k sotsializmu.* Moscow, 1951.

———. *MNR.* Moscow, 1955.

————. *Stroitel'stvo osnov sotsializma v MNR.* Moscow, 1955.

————. *Bor'ba mongol'skogo naroda za postroenie sotsializma.* Moscow, 1956.

Matveeva, G. S. *Sotsialisticheskie preobrazovaniia v sel'skom khoziaistve MNR.* Moscow, 1960.

Meshcheriakov, M. V. *Ocherk ekonomicheskogo sotrudnichestva Sovetskogo soiuza i MNR.* Moscow, 1959.

Mikhailov, G. I. *Kul'turnoe stroitel'stvo v MNR.* Moscow and Leningrad, 1948.

Moskovskii gosudarstvennyi universitet. *Noveishaia istoriia stran zarubezhnogo vostoke.* Moscow, 1955. 2 vols.

Murzaev, E. M. *MNR: Strana, liudi, khoziaistvo.* Leningrad, 1947.

————. *Geograficheskie issledovaniia MNR.* Moscow and Leningrad, 1948.

————. *MNR: Fisiko-geograficheskie opisanie.* 1st ed. Moscow, 1948. 2d ed. Moscow, 1952.

Ogin, P. *MNR.* Moscow, 1939.

Perlin, B. *MNR.* Moscow, 1941.

Pomus, M. I. *Buriat-Mongol'skaia ASSR.* Moscow, 1937.

Roshchin, S. K. *Sotsialisticheskii uklad v ekonomike MNR.* Moscow, 1958.

Sanzheev, Garma D. *Dharkati.* Leningrad, 1930.

Shishkin, S. N. *Khalkhin-gol.* 2d ed. Moscow, 1954.

Tsapkin, N. V. *MNR.* Moscow, 1948.

Vargin, N. T. *MNR: Politicheskaia geograficheskaia.* Moscow, 1949.

Viktorov, S., and N. Khalkhin. *MNR.* Moscow, 1936.

Vilenskii, V. D. *Sovremennaia Mongoliia.* Moscow, 1925.

Vladimirtsov, B. Ia. *Obshchestvennyi stroi Mongolov, Mongol'skii kochevoi feodalizm.* Leningrad, 1934.

Zlatkin, I. Ia. *MNR: Strana novoi demokratii.* Moscow, 1950.

————. *Ocherki novoi i noveishei istorii Mongolii.* Moscow, 1957.

Zlatkin, I. Ia. (ed.). *MNR: Sbornik statei.* Moscow, 1952.

Articles

Anon. "Imushchestvennoe rassloenie skotovodcheskogo naseleniia MNR," *Khoziaistvo Mongolii,* no. 5(28) (1929).

————. "Khoziaistvennoe i kul'turnoe stroitel'stvo MNR," *Planovoe Khoziaistvo,* no. 6 (1936).

————. "MNR," *Bol'shaia Sovetskaia Entsiklopediia.* 1st and 2d eds.; yearbooks.

————. "MNR," *Sibirskaia Sovetskaia Entsiklopediia.* Vol. III.

Badir'ian, G. "Otgonnoe zhivotnovodstvo," *Sel'skokhoziaistvennaia Entsiklopediia,* III, 515.

Badir'ian, G., and I. Kurov. "Otgonno-pastbishchnoe soderzhanie skota v kolkhozakh Zakavkaz'ia," *Sotsialisticheskoe Sel'skoe Khoziaistvo,* no. 4 (1947).

Bakulin, I. "Uspeshnoe razvitie MNR," *Vneshniaia Torgovlia,* no. 6 (1952).

Baradin, B. B. "Buddiiskie monastyri," in M. N. Bogdanov (ed.), *Ocherki istorii Buriat-mongol'skogo naroda.* Verkhneudinsk, 1926.

Bavrin, E., and G. Prokhorov. "Uspekhi ekonomicheskogo razvitiia MNR," *Voprosy Ekonomiki,* no. 7 (1956).

Belen'kii, B. M. "Voprosy kolkhoznogo stroitel'stva," *Khoziaistvo Mongolii,* no. 2(20) (1930).

Bespalov, N. D. "Pochvy MNR," *Trudy Mongol'skoi Komissii,* Akademiia Nauk SSSR, Komitet Nauk MNR, no. 14. Moscow, 1951.

Borisenko, A. P. "Vneshniaia torgovlia MNR," in M. F. Kovrizhnykh, A. B. Frumkina, and V. S. Pozdniakova (eds.), *Vneshniaia torgovlia stran narodnoi demokratii.* Moscow, 1955.

Botvinnik, E. G. "Opyt ishchisleniia narodnogo dokhoda MNR," *Khoziaistvo Mongolii,* no. 3(10) (1928).

————. "K voprosu o kontrol'nykh tsifrakh na 1931 god," *Khoziaistvo Mongolii,* no. 1(25) (1931).

Breiter, E. "Denezhnaia reforma i narodnoe khoziaistvo Mongolii," *Novyi Vostok,* no. 25 (1929).

Daurskii, V. "Lamaism, the Family and Sex Morals," *Sovremennaia Mongoliia,* no. 1(26) (1938).

F. T. "Mestnye organy vlasti Tsetserlik aimaka," *Revoliutsionnyi Vostok,* no. 4–5 (1928).

Gataullina, L. M. "Ekonomicheskoe i kul'turnoe sotrudnichestvo MNR so stranami sotsialisticheskogo lageria," in A. T. Iakimov (ed.), *Mongol'skii sbornik, ekonomika, istoriia, arkheologiia.* Moscow, 1959.

Genkin, I. I. "Dva s'ezda MNP," *Novyi Vostok,* no. 12 (1926).

————. "Konets Ungerna i nachalo novoi Mongolii," *Severnaia Azii,* no. 2 (1928).

G. P. "Uspeshnoe razvitie MNR," *Vneshniaia torgovlia,* no. 6 (1953).

Iakimov, A. T. "MNR na puti k sotsializmu," *Voprosy Ekonomiki,* no. 6 (1951).

————. "Uspekhi mongol'skogo naroda na puti k sotsializmu," *Voprosy Ekonomiki,* no. 12 (1954).

Iakimova, T. A. "MNRP v bor'be za likvidatsiiu klass feodalov i postroenie osnov nekapitalisticheskogo puti razvitiia, 1932–1940 gg.," *Kratkie soobshcheniia instituta vostokovedeniia,* Akademiia Nauk SSSR, Institut vostokovedeniia, no. 9 (1954).

————. "MNR," in M. I. Sladkovskii and Iu. N. Kapelinskii (eds.), *Razvitie ekonomiki stran narodnoi demokratii Azii.* Moscow, 1957.

————. Vneshneekonomicheskie sviazi MNR," *Vneshniaia Torgovlia,* no. 8 (1957).

Iudin, V. I. "U istokov mongol'skoi narodnoi revoliutsii," in A. T. Iakimov (ed.), *Mongol'skii sbornik, ekonomika, istoriia, arkheologiia.* Akademiia Nauk SSSR, Institut vostokovedeniia. Moscow, 1959.

Iunatov, A. A. "Kormovye rasteniia pastbishch i senokosov MNR," *Trudy Mongol'skoi Komissii,* Akademiia Nauk SSSR, Komitet Nauk MNR, no. 56. Moscow and Leningrad, 1954.

Iur'ev, I. G. "K voprosu ob inostrannom kapitale vo Vneshnei Mongolii do narodno-demokraticheskoi revoliutsii 1921 g. i v pervye ee gody," *Kratkie soobshcheniia instituta vostokovedeniia,* Akademiia Nauk SSSR, Institut vostokovedeniia, no. 6 (1952).

————. "Gosudarstvennaia i kooperativnaia promyshlennost'," in I. Ia. Zlatkin (ed.), *MNR: Sbornik statei.* Moscow, 1952.

Ivanov, N. "Khoziaistvennoe razvitie stran narodnoi demokratii," *Voprosy Ekonomiki,* no. 7 (1955).

Kallinikov, Anatolii D. "U istokov mongol'skoi revoliutsii," *Khoziaistvo Mongolii,* no. 3(10) (1928).

————. "Aratskoe revoliutsionnoe dvizheniia v doavtomnoi Mongolii," *Revoliutsionnyi Vostok,* no. 5–6 (1934).

Kashintsev, D. "Chuiskii trakt v Mongolii," *Novyi Vostok*, no. 8–9 (1925).

Kiubyshev, A. "Ekonomicheskoe razvitie MNR," *Vneshniaia Torgovlia*, no. 11 (1950).

Linda, M. I. "Pervaia konstitutsiia MNR," *Vestnik Leningrad'skogo Universiteta*, Seriia ekonomiki, filosofii i prava, no. 4 (1957).

Litovchenko, G. R. "Voprosy ovtsevodstva MNR," *Trudy Mongol'skoi Komissii*, Akademiia Nauk SSSR, Komitet Nauk MNR, no. 43. Moscow, 1953.

Lus, Ia. Ia., N. N. Kolesnik, I. F. Shul'zhcnko, *et al.*, "Domashnie Zhivotnye Mongolii," *Trudy Mongol'skoi Komissii*, Akademiia Nauk SSSR, Komitet Nauk MNR, no. 22. Moscow and Leningrad, 1936.

Maiskii, I. M. "Present Day China," *International Press Correspondence*, no. 76 (Sept. 5, 1922).

Meshcheriakov, M. V. "Ekonomicheskoe sotrudnichestvo MNR s sotsialisticheskimi stranami," *Vneshniaia Torgovlia*, no. 2 (1959).

N. K. "Ekonomicheskoe razvitie MNR," *Vneshniaia Torgovlia*, no. 11 (1950).

Penskii, N. E. "Ekonomicheskie vzaimo-otnosheniia SSSR s Mongoliei," *Novyi Vostok*, no. 10–11 (1925).

Petrishchev, I. "K tridtsatoi godovshchine narodnoi revoliutsii v Mongolii," *Vneshniaia Torgovlia*, no. 7 (1951).

Rinchino. "K voprosy o natsional'nom samoopredelenii Mongolii v sviazi z zadachami kitaiskoi revoliutsii," *Revoliutsionnyi Vostok*, no. 2 (1927).

Rish, A. "Mongoliia na strazhe svoie nezavistimosti," *Tikhii Okean*, no. 4(6) (1935).

Ryskulov, T. "Velikii Khuraldan Mongolii," *Novyi Vostok*, no. 8–9 (1925).

Ryzhik, Ia. "Khoziaistvennoe i kul'turnoe stroitel'stvo MNR," *Planovoe Khoziaistvo*, no. 6 (1936).

Samsonov, N. Article in *Vneshniaia Torgovlia*, no. 11 (1959).

Shleifer, I. O. "Osnovnye problemy piatiletnego plana khoziaistvennogo i kul'turnogo stroitel'stva MNR," *Khoziaistvo Mongolii*, no. 2(20) (1930); no. 3(21) (1930).

Shoizhelov, Siren. "Zapadnaia Mongoliia," *Novyi Vostok*, no. 4 (1923).

———. "Natsional'no-osvoboditel'noe dvizhenie v Mongolii," *Novyi Vostok*, no. 6 (1924).

———. "Perelomnyi moment v istorii natsional'nogo-osvoboditel'nogo dvizheniia v Mongolii," *Novyi Vostok*, no. 10–11 (1925).

———. "Mongoliia i iaponskii imperializm," *Novyi Vostok*, no. 8–9 (1925).

———. "Mongoliia i tarskaia Rossiia," *Novyi Vostok*, no. 13–14 (1926).

Shubin, V. F. "Zemledelie MNR," *Trudy Mongol'skoi Komissii*, Akademiia Nauk SSSR, Komitet Nauk MNR, no. 61. Moscow, 1954.

Shul'zhenko, I. F. "Miasnoe khoziaistvo MNR," *Trudy Mongol'skoi Komissii*, Akademiia Nauk SSSR, Komitet Nauk MNR, no. 8. Leningrad, 1933.

———. "Zhivotnovodstvo MNR," *Trudy Mongol'skoi Komissii*, Akademiia Nauk SSSR, Komitet Nauk MNR, no 61. Moscow, 1954.

Shumiatskii, B. "Na zare osvobozhdeniia Mongolii," *Pravda*, July 12, 1936.

Simukov, A. D. "Rol' SSSR v dele issledovaniia Mongolii," *Khoziaistvo Mongolii*, no. 5(28) (1929).

———. "Skotovodstvo MNR v sviazi s geograficheskimi landshaftami," *Khoziaistvo Mongolii*, no. 1(25) (1931).

Staritsina, P. P. "Marshal Choibalsan (iz zhizni i deiatel'nosti)," *Kratkie soobshcheniia instituta vostokovedeniia*, Akademiia Nauk SSSR, Institut vostokovedeniia, no. 6 (1952).

———. "O narodnykh khuralakh MNR," *Kratkie soobshcheniia instituta vostokovedeniia,* Akademiia Nauk SSSR, Institut vostokovedeniia, no. 5 (1952).

Stepanov, M. "Ekonomicheskoe razvitie MNR," *Vneshniaia Torgovlia,* no. 6 (1949).

Trubenkov, V. "30 let denezhno-kreditnoi sistemy MNR," *Den'gi i Kredit,* no. 10 (1954).

Tsapkin, N. V. "Gosudarstvennyi biudzhet MNR na sluzhbe ekonomicheskogo i kultur'nogo stroitel'stva," *Finansy i Kredit,* no. 7 (1953).

Tsaplin, F. S. "Sel'skoe khoziaistvo," in I. Ia. Zlatkin (ed.), *MNR: Sbornik statei,* Akademiia Nauk SSSR, Institut vostokovedeniia. Moscow, 1952.

————. "Transport i sviaz'," in I. Ia. Zlatkin (ed.), *MNR: Sbornik statei,* Akademiia Nauk SSSR, Institut vostokovedeniia. Moscow, 1952.

Tsirniuk, A. P. "K predstoiashchemu sostavleniiu piatiletnego perspektivnego plana razvitiia Mongol'skoi narodnoi kooperatsii," *Khoziaistvo Mongolii,* no. 2(20) (1930).

Tugarinov, N. N. "Biudzhet MNR," *Novyi Vostok,* no. 15 (1926).

————. "Denezhnoe obrashchenie Mongolii," *Novyi Vostok,* no. 20–21 (1928).

Vargin, N. T. "Finansy," in I. Ia. Zlatkin (ed.), *MNR: Sbornik statei.* Moscow, 1952.

————. "Torgovlia," in I. Ia. Zlatkin (ed.), *MNR: Sbornik statei.* Moscow, 1952.

————. "Agrarnyi vopros i razvitie sel'skogo khoziaistvo MNR," in E. F. Kovalev (ed.), *Agrarnye preobrazovaniia v narodno-demokraticheskikh stranakh Azii.* Moscow, 1957.

Zhambolon, D. "Kak ne sleduet stavit' vopros o natsional'nom samoopredelenii Mongolii," *Revoliutsionnyi Vostok,* no. 3 (1928).

Zlatkin, I. Ia. "O roli Rossii v bor'be Mongolov za nezavistimosti' protiv man'chzhyrskikh zavoevatelei vo vtoroi polovine XVII, pervoi polovine XVIII v.," *Kratkie soobshcheniia instituta vostokovedeniia,* Akademiia Nauk SSSR, Institut vostokovedeniia, no. 6 (1952).

Zolotarev, L. "Denezhnaia reforma v Mongolii," *Novyi Vostok,* no. 13–14 (1926).

OTHER SOURCES

Books, Manuscripts, and Dissertations

Albano, Howard K. "An Analysis of the Crop Producing Potential of the MPR." Unpublished M.A. thesis, University of Washington, 1956.

Alioshin, Dimitri. *Asian Odyssey.* New York, 1940.

Allen, G. C., and Audrey G. Donnithorne. *Western Enterprise in Far Eastern Economic Development: China and Japan.* London, 1954.

Andrews, Roy Chapman. *Across Mongolian Plains.* New York, 1921.

————. *On the Trail of Ancient Man.* New York, 1926.

————. *The New Conquest of Central Asia.* New York, 1932.

Baranov, A. M. *Khalkha-Aimak Tsetsen Khana.* Harbin, 1919.

Beloff, Max. *The Foreign Policy of Soviet Russia.* Vol. I: 1929–1936. Vol. II: 1936–1941. London, 1947–1949.

————. *Soviet Policy in the Far East, 1944–1951.* London, 1953.

Bogolepov, M. I., and M. N. Sobolev. *Ocherki russko-mongol'skoi torgovli.* Vol. I. Tomsk, 1911.

Caroe, Olaf. *Soviet Empire: The Turks of Central Asia, and Stalinism.* London, 1953.

Carruthers, Douglas. *Unknown Mongolia.* London, 1913. 2 vols.

Conolly, Violet. *Soviet Economic Policy in the East: Turkey, Persia, Afghanistan, Mongolia and Tana Tuva, Sin Kiang.* London, 1933.

———. *Soviet Trade from the Pacific to the Levant: With an Economic Study of the Soviet Far Eastern Region.* London, 1935.

Cressey, George Babcock. *China's Geographic Foundations.* New York, 1934.

———. *Asia's Lands and Peoples.* 2d ed. New York, 1951.

———. *Land of the 500 Million: A Geography of China.* New York, 1955.

Dallin, David J. *Soviet Russia and the Far East.* New Haven, 1948.

———. *The Rise of Russia in Asia.* New Haven, 1949.

Davies, Raymond Arthur, and Andrew J. Steiger. *Soviet Asia: Democracy's First Line of Defense.* New York, 1942.

Degras, Jane (ed.). *Soviet Documents on Foreign Policy.* Royal Institute of International Affairs. London, 1951. 3 vols.

Eudin, Xenia Joukoff, and Robert C. North. *Soviet Russia and the East, 1920–1927: A Documentary Survey.* Stanford, 1957.

Fischer, Louis. *The Soviets in World Affairs.* New York, 1960.

Forbath, Ladislaus. *The New Mongolia: As Related by Joseph Geleta.* Trans. Lawrence Wolfe. London, 1936.

Friters, Gerard M. *Outer Mongolia and Its International Postition.* Ed. Eleanor Lattimore. Introduction by Owen Lattimore. London, 1951.

Gilmour, James. *Among the Mongols.* London, n.d.

Grumm-Grzhimailo, G. E. *Zapadnaia Mongoliia i Uriankhaiskii krai.* Vol. I. St. Petersburg, 1914. Vols. II–III. Leningrad, 1926–1930.

Harrison, Marguerite E. *Red Bear or Yellow Dragon.* London, 1924.

Haslund, Henning. *Tents in Mongolia.* New York, 1934.

———. *Mongolian Journey.* London, 1949.

Human Relations Area Files. *The Mongolian People's Republic.* New Haven, 1956. 3 vols.

Karamisheff, W. *Mongolia and Western China.* Tsientsin, 1925.

Kent, A. S. *Old Tartar Trails.* Shanghai, 1919.

Kervyn, Louis M. *Ourga: La Politique chinoise en Mongolie.* Peking, 1932.

Kolarz, Walter. *Russia and Her Colonies.* London, 1952.

———. *The Peoples of the Soviet Far East.* London, 1954.

Korostovetz, Iwan J. *Von Cinggis Khan zur Sowjetrepublik.* Berlin and Leipzig, 1926.

Kyokai, Zenrin. *Moko daikan.* Tokyo, 1938.

Larson, Frans August. *Larson, Duke of Mongolia.* Boston, 1930.

Lattimore, Owen. *Mongols of Manchuria.* New York, 1934.

———. *Manchuria: Cradle of Conflict.* Rev. ed. New York, 1935.

———. *Inner Asian Frontiers of China.* 2d ed. New York, 1951.

———. *Nationalism and Revolution in Mongolia.* New York, 1955.

———. *Nomads and Commissars: Mongolia Revisited.* New York, 1962.

Lévine, J. *La Mongolie: Historique, géographique, politique.* Paris, 1937.

Lobanov-Rostovsky, Prince. *Russia and Asia.* New York, 1933.

Lorimer, Frank. *Culture and Human Fertility.* Paris, 1954.

Ma Ho-t'ien. *Chinese Agent in Mongolia.* Trans. John de Francis. Baltimore, 1949.

Mandel, William. *The Soviet Far East and Central Asia.* New York, 1944.

Michaels, Franz H., and George E. Taylor. *The Far East in the Modern World.* New York, 1956.

Miller, Robert J. "The Socio-Political and Economic Aspect of the Monastery in Inner Mongolia." Unpublished Ph.D. dissertation, University of Washington, 1955.

———. *Monasteries and Culture Change in Inner Mongolia.* Wiesbaden, 1959.

Misshima, Yasuo, and Tomio Goto. *A Japanese View of Outer Mongolia.* Translated and condensed by A. J. Gradjdanzev. New York, 1942.

Montague, Ivor. *Land of Blue Sky.* London, 1956.

Moore, Harriet L. *Soviet Far Eastern Policy, 1931–1945.* Princeton, 1945.

Noskov, Konstantin. *Avantiura ili chernyi dlia russkikh bielykh v Mongolii.* Harbin, 1920.

———. *The Black Year.* Harbin, 1930.

Office of Strategic Services. *Outer Mongolia.* Study no. 86 (Feb. 23, 1943).

Ossendowski, Ferdynand. *Beasts, Men and Gods.* New York, 1922.

Pasvolsky, Leo. *Russia in the Far East.* New York, 1922.

Pavlovsky, Michel N. *Chinese-Russian Relations.* Trans. Ruth Krader. New York, 1949.

Perry-Ayscough, H. G. C., and R. B. Otter-Barry. *With the Russians in Mongolia.* London, 1914.

Pershin, D. P. "Baron Ungern, Urga and Altan Bulak: An Eyewitness' Account of the Troubled Times in Outer (Khalkha) Mongolia during the First Third of the Twentieth Century." Unpublished manuscript in the Library of the Hoover Institution, Stanford, California.

Phillips, G. D. R. *Dawn in Siberia.* London, 1942.

Pozdneev, A. *Mongoliia i Mongoli.* St. Petersburg, 1896–1898. 2 vols.

Riasanovsky, V. A. *Customary Law of the Mongol Tribes.* Harbin, 1929.

———. *Fundamental Principles of Mongol Law.* Tientsin, 1937.

Rupen, Robert A. "Outer Mongolian Nationalism, 1900–1919." Unpublished Ph.D. dissertation, University of Washington, 1954.

Smith, Robert. "Political, Economic and Trade Conditions in Outer Mongolia." Unpublished manuscript in Library of Hoover Institution, Stanford, California.

Strasser, Roland. *The Mongolian Horde.* London, 1930.

Strong, Anna Louise. *China's Millions.* New York, 1928. Books I and II.

Tang, Peter S. H. *Russia and Soviet Policy in Manchuria and Outer Mongolia.* Durham, 1959.

Thiel, Erich. *Die Mongolei.* Munich, 1958.

Tsybikov, G. Ts. "A Buddhist Pilgrim to the Holy Places of Tibet: Diaries Kept from 1899 to 1902." Unpublished translation by Robert Shaw. Human Relations Area Files. New Haven, 1952–53.

U.S. Department of Commerce. Bureau of Foreign and Domestic Commerce. *China: A Commercial and Industrial Handbook.* Trade Promotion Series, no. 38. Washington, 1926.

Vinacke, Harold M. *A History of the Far East in Modern Times.* 5th ed. New York, 1950.

Vreeland, Herbert Harold. *Mongol Community and Kinship Structure.* Human Relations Area Files. New Haven, 1954.

Whiting, Allen S. *Soviet Policies in China, 1917–1924.* New York, 1954.

Articles

Anon. "Biographies of Key Personalities," in *MPR. Human Relations Area Files*. New Haven, 1956. Vol. I.

———. "Sostoianie russkoi torgovli v severnoi Mongolii za 1910 g.," *Vestnik Azii*, no. 2 (1911).

Bacon, Elizabeth. "A Preliminary Attempt To Determine the Culture Areas of Asia," *Southwestern Journal of Anthropology*, II (1946).

———. "Types of Pastoral Nomadism in Central and Southwest Asia," *ibid.*, X (1954).

Ballis, William B. "The Political Evolution of a Soviet Satellite: The MPR," *Western Political Quarterly*, IX (1956).

Beardsley, Richard K. "Hypotheses on Inner Asia Pastoral Nomadism and Its Culture Area," *Supplement to American Antiquity*, XVIII, no. 3, pt. 2 (1953).

Binsteed, G. C. "Life in a Khalkha Steppe Lamasery," *Journal of the Royal Asiatic Society*, XXIII (1914).

———. "Mongolia," *China Year Book*, 1914, 1916, 1919.

Chesneaux, Jean. "Du Féodalisme pastoral à la planification socialiste," *Economique et Politique*, XX (1956).

Consten, Hermann. "Denominations of Monasteries in Outer and Inner Mongolia," *Collectanea Commissionis Synodalis* (Peking), XII (1939).

———. "The Secular Administration of Mongolian Monasteries and Their Shabinars," *ibid.*

Gur'ev, B. "Ekonomicheskoe polozhenie Mongolii," *Vestnik Azii*, no. 8 (1911).

———. "Russkaia torgovliia v Zapadnoi Mongolii," *ibid.*, no. 10 (1911).

Heissig, Walter. "Mongol Farming," *Contemporary Manchuria*, III (1939).

Holzman, F. D. "The Financial System of the MPR," in *MPR. Human Relations Area Files*. New Haven, 1956. Vol. III.

———. "Equity of the Livestock Tax of Outer Mongolia," *American Slavic and East European Review*, XV (1957).

———. "The Tax System of Outer Mongolia, 1911–1955," *Journal of Asian Studies*, XVI (1957).

———. "The Budget Expenditures of Outer Mongolia," *Finances Publiques*, XII (1957).

Ishida, Kiyoshi. "An Outline of Outer Mongolia," *Contemporary Manchuria*, III (1939).

Kool-Estivend, I. "O dvizhenii naseleniia v Mongolii," *Vestnik Azii*, no. 35–36 (1915).

Krader, Lawrence. "The Cultural and Historical Position of the Mongols," *Asia Minor*, III (1953).

———. "Buryat Religion and Society," *Southwestern Journal of Anthropology*, X (1954).

———. "Ecology of Central Asian Pastoralism," *ibid.*, XI (1955).

———. "Principles and Structures in the Organization of the Asiatic Steppe-Pastoralists," *ibid.*

———. "Feudalism and the Tatar Polity of the Middle Ages," *Comparative Studies in Society and History*, I (1958).

Kroeber, A. L. "Culture Groupings in Asia," *Southwestern Journal of Anthropology*, III (1947).

Krueger, John R., N. N. Poppe, and Martin Kilcoyne. "Education," in *MPR.* Human Relations Area Files. New Haven, 1956.

Lattimore, Eleanor. "Report on Outer Mongolia," *Far Eastern Survey,* XV (1946).

Lattimore, Owen. "Mongolia," *China Year Book,* 1933, 1934, 1935, 1936, 1937, 1949.

————. "Prince, Priest and Herdsman in Mongolia," *Pacific Affairs,* VIII (1935).

————. "The Geographical Factor in Mongol History," *Geographical Journal,* XCI (1938).

————. "Mongols of the Chinese Border," *Geographical Magazine,* VI (1938).

————. "The Outer Mongolian Horizon," *Foreign Affairs,* XXIV (1946).

Mandel, William. "Outer Mongolia's Five Year Plan," *Far Eastern Survey,* XVIII (1949).

Miller, Robert J. "Areas and Institutions in Eastern Asia," *Southwestern Journal of Anthropology,* IX (1953).

————. "Buddhist Monastic Finance and the Jisa Mechanism," *Comparative Studies in Society and History,* III (1961).

Murphy, George G. S. "Labor Force," in *MPR.* Human Relations Area Files. New Haven, 1956.

————. "Livestock-Breeding," in *ibid.*

————. "Industrial Potential," in *ibid.*

————. "Trade," in *ibid.*

————. "Transportation," in *ibid.*

————. "Recent Publications of the Mongolian Commission," *Far Eastern Survey,* XXV (1956).

————. "Planning in the MPR," *Journal of Asian Studies,* XVIII (1959).

————. "Buddhist Monastic Finance and the Jisa Mechanism: A Comment," *Comparative Studies in Society and History,* III (1961).

————. "On Satelliteship," *Journal of Economic History,* XXI (1961).

————. "The MPR: Dual Economy?" in *Trudy dvadtsat' piatogo mezhdunarodnogo kongressa vostokovedov.* Vol. V. Moscow, 1963.

Myres, Sir John L. "Nomadism," *Journal of the Royal Anthropological Institute,* LXXI (1941).

Naroll, Raoul S. "A Draft Map of Culture Areas in Asia," *Southwestern Journal of Anthropology,* VI (1950).

Ney, Elias. "Narrative of a Journey through Western Mongolia," *Journal of the Royal Geographical Society,* XLIII (1873).

Patai, Raphael. "Nomadism: Middle East and Central Asia," *Southwestern Journal of Anthropology,* VII (1951).

Phillips, G. D. R. "Bouryat-Mongolia," *Anglo-Soviet Journal* (1940).

Poppe, N. N. "MNR," *Vestnik institut po izucheniiu istorii i kul'tury SSSR,* no. 6(11) (1954).

Rupen, Robert A. "The Buryat Intelligentsia," *Far Eastern Quarterly,* XV (1956).

————. "Cyben Zamcaranociv Zamcarano," *Harvard Journal of Asiatic Studies,* XIX (1956).

————. "Mongolian Nationalism," *Royal Central Asian Journal,* XLV (1958).

————. "Inside Outer Mongolia," *Foreign Affairs,* XXXVIII (1959).

Stackelberg, G. A. von. "Mongolia and the XIIth Congress of the MNRP," *Bulletin of the Institute for the Study of the History and Culture of the USSR,* no. 2(4) (1955).

Svechikov, A. "Russkaia torgovlia v severo zapadnoi Mongolii po lichnym nabliudeniiam c 1905 po 1907," *Vestnik Azii,* no. 11–12 (1912).

Ul'rikh, S. F. "Tarabagany i tarabaganii promysel v Zabaikal' i Mongolii," *ibid.*

Wiens, Herold J. "Geographical Limitations of Food Production in the MPR," *Annals of the Association of American Geographers,* XLI (1951).

Woolf, Serge M. "Mongol Delegations in Western Europe, 1925–1929," *Royal Central Asian Journal,* XXXII (1945); XXXIII (1946).

Index

Geographic place-names do not appear in this index. As no glossary is included in the volume, the index shows on which page foreign terms are first explicitly or implicitly defined.

Mongol and Chinese names are dealt with as follows. Chinese style reverses the Western order: given name, then surname. Mongol names are often meant to be read as a unit—such as Sukhe Bator, meaning Red Hero—or to include ranks—such as Wang, Dorji, Khutukhtu, Khan—with the rank last. The rule followed in the text has been to treat Chinese names in Western style and to leave Mongol names as they generally appear in Western literature, that is, Urga Khutukhtu rather than the Khutukhtu of Urga. Such names have been entered in the index by the last name, even if it is a title.